Patrons of Enlightenment

Patrons of Enlightenment

The Free Economic Society in Eighteenth-Century Russia

Colum Leckey

UNIVERSITY OF DELAWARE PRESS
Newark

Published by University of Delaware Press
Co-published with The Rowman & Littlefield Publishing Group, Inc.
4501 Forbes Boulevard, Suite 200, Lanham, Maryland 20706
www.rowmanlittlefield.com

Estover Road, Plymouth PL6 7PY, United Kingdom

British Library Cataloguing in Publication Information Available

Library of Congress Cataloging-in-Publication Data
Leckey, Colum, 1963-
    Patrons of enlightenment : the Free Economic Society in eighteenth-century Russia /
Colum Leckey.
        p. cm.
    Includes bibliographical references.
    ISBN 978-1-61149-342-9 (cloth : alk. paper) — ISBN 978-1-61149-343-6 (electronic)
    1. Imperatorskoe vol'noe ekonomicheskoe obshchestvo (Russia) 2. Economics—
Russia—Societies, etc.—History—18th century. 3. Russia—Economic policy—18th
century. 4. Russia—Economic conditions—18th century. I. Title.
    HB113.A2L33 2011
    330.06'04721—dc22   2011014688

Printed in the United States of America

For Dolores,
and
for Tom, in memory

Contents

Acknowledgments

This book is a revision of a doctoral dissertation completed at the University of Pittsburgh in 1998. Over the years I have amassed many debts to various individuals and institutions in Russia, Europe, and the United States. In St. Petersburg, the excellent staffs at the Archive of the Russian Academy of Sciences, the Russian State Historical Archive, and the Russian National Library provided a friendly work environment as well as access to the many unpublished materials and rare books which serve as the foundation of this research. In Moscow, Maksim Antonshin of the Russian State Archive of Ancient Documents guided me to numerous materials which proved especially valuable to my work. Nikita Lomagin of the Russian Academy of Sciences and the late Oleg Ken of the European University of St. Petersburg served as my contacts to the archives and libraries of St. Petersburg. I am particularly indebted to Oleg for inviting me to his home and showering me with the hospitality and warmth for which the Russians are rightly famous. His sudden death in 2007 took away one of my most valued friends and critics—he is sorely missed.

Friends in Europe have also facilitated the completion of this book. I would like to thank Koen Stapelbroek of the Erasmus Institute in Rotterdam and Jani Marjanen at the University of Helsinki for organizing the seminar "Political Economy, Patriotism, and the Rise of Economic and Patriotic Societies in Europe, c. 1700–1850," which provided a unique and stimulating forum for me to share the results of my research with other scholars working on economic societies. In Great Britain, my colleagues in the Study Group on Eighteenth-Century Russia offered me their advice and hospitality at several meetings. The list of names is long—too long for this brief space—but here I must acknowledge Roger Bartlett, who kindly encouraged me to finish this project, and Isabel de Madariaga, whose foundational work on the age of Catherine II inspired me to specialize in eighteenth-century Russia long ago.

I am also grateful to the many colleagues in the U.S. who have heard installments of this research at academic conferences and the foundations whose financial support made this book possible. Generous grants from the Czechoslovak Nationality Room at the University of Pittsburgh, the United States Information Agency, and the Appalachian College Association enabled me to work in the libraries and archives of St. Petersburg and Moscow. The following people have read previous versions of separate chapters and offered their criticism: Lee Farrow, Marcus Levitt, Sue McCaffray, George Munro, Abby Schrader, Susan Smith-Peter, Steven Usitalo, and Ben Whisenhunt. Needless to say, I alone am responsible for whatever defects it may contain. I would also like to thank the teachers and advisors at the University of Pittsburgh who guided me in the formative stages of this research: Bill Chase, Bob Donnorummo, Hugh Kearney, the late Denison Rusinow, and especially Orysia Karapinka, who served as my dissertation director, mentor, friend, and most relentless critic. Closer to home, my wife Donna and children Roman and Maria stoically endured my many absences in Russia over the years as I worked to finish this project. A hearty thanks to them all.

Portions of this book have previously appeared in the following publications: "Provincial Readers and Agrarian Reform, 1760s–70s: The Case of Sloboda Ukraine," *Russian Review* 61 (2002): 535–59; "Patronage and Public Culture in the Russian Free Economic Society, 1765–96," *Slavic Review* 62 (2005), 355–79; and "Andrei Bolotov: Portrait of an Enlightened Seigneur," in *Russian and Soviet History: From the Time of Troubles to the Collapse of the Soviet Union*, eds. Steven Usitalo and Ben Whisenhunt (Lanham, MD: Rowman & Littlefield, 2008).

Introduction

The eighteenth century, widely regarded as the age of reason, was also an age of association. Across Europe and North America, public associations offered alternative communities beyond the official establishments of church and state. At the apex of this rising network stood the great scientific academies and salons catering to the intellectual, cultural, and social interests of the elite. Just as prestigious, though more secretive, were the Freemasons, who inspired a later generation of imitators to create their own republics of virtue during the American and French Revolutions. Most associations had more modest objectives. Many sought to alleviate the hardships of everyday urban life, while others promoted culture through museums, libraries, theaters, and learned societies. Still more tried to raise agricultural productivity, bringing profits to the elite while ameliorating the living conditions of rural commoners. Whatever their function, free associations all claimed to unite people of varied status, backgrounds, and ambitions and rouse them to serve the common good. By century's end, they had become the anchors of public culture in the West.

The following pages investigate the dynamics of associational culture in the Russian Empire of Catherine the Great. At the center of the story is an organization of nearly 600 men (and one woman), the Free Economic Society for the Promotion of Agriculture and Household Management, one of Russia's first institutions independent of the state and certainly the longest lasting of them all. Formed in 1765 by a handful of courtiers, civil servants, and academicians, the Society tested the waters of Russia's fledgling public sphere.[1] "Free" (*vol'noe*) signified its unique nongovernmental status, symbolized by the royal charter that guaranteed its autonomy and transformed its assembly hall on St. Petersburg's Nevskii Prospekt into a safe house for its members. "Economic" (*ekonomicheskoe*) stood for its range of expertise and interests, the parameters of which reflected the breadth and variety of the Russian Empire itself. "I see on the doors of this building the words 'Economic Society'! What does this mean?" the writer Jakob von Staehlin asked at his first appearance before the assembly in 1766:

> Estate management, agriculture, cereal cultures, soil improvement, the rich ex-
> traction of the land's treasures, the increase of profits, the enrichment of our in-
> habitants, the actual welfare of our citizenry, praiseworthy intentions, increased
> diligence, useful innovations, the search for easier methods, not to mention your
> and others' experiments and diligent endeavors—all this comprises your field
> of activities.[2]

Yet there was more to the Society than mere cows and plows. Staehlin also praised certain intangible virtues of "society" (*obshchestvo*)—diligence, curiosity, usefulness, and creativity. The audience to whom he directed his speech formed an exclusive club indeed. As cofounder Timothy von Kling-shtedt described them in the inaugural volume of the Society's journal: "Our Society is made up only of those people who have no intention for personal gain or a vainglorious exhibition of their talents, but who have only an incli-nation and desire to be useful to the fatherland."[3] For a country whose elites had hitherto only served God and tsar, this was unprecedented.

The Society also included in its full name the words "agriculture" (*zem-ledelie*) and "household management" (*domostroitel'stvo*). *Zemledelie* signi-fied its ambition for Russia to become the leading agricultural producer in Europe. Believing that the customs of its peasant farmers had condemned Russia's rural economy to perennial backwardness, the Society aimed to re-verse centuries of stagnation through a revolution from above comparable to the dramatic reforms of Peter the Great earlier in the century. Ironically, the term it used to describe this transformation—*domostroitel'stvo*—dredged up memories of the *Domostroi*, a notorious manual on household management dating back to the sixteenth century. The *Domostroi* presents a model of the patriarchal Christian household, starting with instructions on religious ritu-als and everyday conduct before outlining rules for marriage, childrearing, distilling, gardening, storing and preparing food, and supervising domestic help.[4] While painstakingly thorough in its directives for the elite household, the *Domostroi* had little to say about farming. Its silence here reflected the long-standing practice of the Muscovite boyar class to hand *zemledelie* over to peasants. It was this "old-fashioned way" (*po starine*) of estate manage-ment that the Society sought to abolish by concentrating power and respon-sibility in the hands of a new type of landowner, the *razumnyi domostroitel'*, or rational housekeeper.

Over the course of its long history, the Free Economic Society served as the model for Imperial Russia's nongovernmental culture. As Joseph Bradley has argued, its "links with government set a pattern for reciprocal and even mutually beneficial relations between Russia's voluntary associations and the state, a pattern that prevailed until the end of the nineteenth century."[5] When the autocracy forced the Society's doors to close in 1915, it could look back on 150 years of activity that mirrored the ebb and flow of Russian history since the reign of Peter the Great. In the eighteenth century, the Society functioned much like the academies of Renaissance Europe, establishing a "social space" framed by the personal status of its great patrons.[6] Emulating the economic societies of Western Europe, it steadily developed a public by establishing links between the Society's leadership in the capital and its supporters in the provinces and abroad. The Society strengthened these contacts through its flagship journal, *Trudy Vol'nago Ekonomicheskago Obshchestva* (*Transactions of the Free Economic Society*), and especially through the most signature ritual of eighteenth-century culture, the public essay competition. During the nineteenth century it extended its base of support from St. Petersburg into the countryside, loosening its dependence on officialdom and assuring for it a leading role in national public life during the era of the Great Reforms. By the eve of World War I the Society had evolved into a modern nongovernmental organization, staffed mainly by liberal professionals whose dedication to social justice and political freedom ultimately resulted in its suppression by the autocracy.[7]

There was no great secret to its remarkable longevity. The core argument of this book is that the Free Economic Society survived and prospered by adapting the culture of free associations to the politics of absolutism and the extreme social conservatism of Russia's educated public. As a nongovernmental association in an autocratic system, the Society skillfully replicated the power structures of Russia's service culture, anchoring its public in the traditional patron-client relationships that had sustained the country's elites for so long. Although parties on both ends were free to break the connection at any time, the organization existed primarily for the purpose of facilitating the exchange of goods and services.[8] At the highest level, it provided its most notable patrons with expert economic advice on agriculture, estate management, and animal husbandry—"popular enlightenment," as one historian has called it.[9] Although its efforts produced few, if any, tangible results for peasants, its promotion of rational and humanitarian management in the countryside lent substance to Catherine the Great's carefully crafted image as an enlightened ruler who worked for the betterment of all her subjects. In return, the Empress and her entourage gave the Society critical material and financial support, and, above all else, a halo of relevance before an unresponsive public that regarded agricultural improvement as a utopian dream. Sadly, farming in a barren land such as Russia offered few rewards. Far more useful was royal protection, and Catherine proved to be remarkably generous in providing it. The Society's relationship with the Empress enabled its leaders to extend their patronage system into the countryside. From the villages of Russia, a far-flung network of correspondents emerged to furnish their St. Petersburg colleagues with vital information in exchange for recognition before the public, an honor which carried great prestige value in such a rank-conscious society.

The patronage of Catherine and her court also gave the Society the space and freedom to transmit its message to the Russian public. Like its European counterparts, the Society vigorously promoted aristocratic agrarianism, defined by the philosopher James Montmarquet as "the celebration of a life thought especially worthy, and socially useful, for the nobility."[10] At first glance, the term suggests an affinity with the French physiocrats, the school of Enlightenment political economists who viewed agriculture as the basis of wealth and urged governments to promote it by lifting all restrictions on farming. In fact, the Society never developed policy recommendations as specific, substantive, or critical of the old regime as the physiocrats. It habitually avoided discussion of controversial legal issues like serfdom and land tenure. Drawing the line at politics, the Society instead tailored its version of aristocratic agrarianism to fit the private "housekeeping" circumstances of its many constituents: absentee landowners in possession of thousands of serfs; mid-level provincial squires personally managing their holdings; and even wealthy service nobles in cities employing large domestic staffs. In his recent study of agrarianism in eighteenth-century France, John Shovlin has demonstrated that "provincial nobles of modest means" particularly identified with the image of the rustic landowner because it reflected the values they wanted to see in themselves: independence and self-reliance, an aversion to urban luxury, and a paternalistic concern for their labor force. The Free Economic Society reworked this archetype for the Russian public. Removed from the distractions and corruptions of the city, the rational housekeeper could apply his talents to tasks of timeless significance—managing his household and improving his ancestral estate.[11]

For the eighteenth-century Russian nobility the Society's discourse also served a crucial ideological function. After the end of mandatory state service in 1762, nobles needed an explanation for their free and privileged status in a country where more than half of all subjects were private serfs—legally bound to their owners, scarcely protected under the law, and exploited to the extreme. The most famous episode in the Society's history—the peasant property competition of 1766–68—dealt directly with this controversial topic.

Many Russian scholars since the late nineteenth century have viewed the contest mainly as a cynical tactic for enhancing Catherine's prestige abroad as an enlightened reformer.[12] Western historians, for the most part, have a less jaundiced view, interpreting the essay competition as a tentative step in the direction of the reform of serfdom which the Empress was forced to abandon in light of the nobility's fierce opposition.[13] Although it made for spectacular political theater, it failed to produce legislation benefiting the Russian peasantry. Instead, the contest spurred the Society to solve the "peasant question" in a way that was consistent with the rationalist spirit of the age and digestible to a public averse to agrarian reform. It proposed transforming the nobility into a class of enlightened seigneurs who redefined the ideal of public service into an exemplary private life in the countryside. For a select few, this required preparing peasants and themselves for the inevitable abolition of serfdom in the future. For most, it meant updating the *Domostroi* to accommodate technical improvements in sowing, plowing, fertilizing, and animal husbandry. It was hardly a program for substantive agrarian reform. The Society's failure to confront serfdom comes as no surprise—comprised as it was of the leading members of Russia's landowning elite, it was unthinkable for them to act against their own interests. Like the founders of the United States, they passed the problem of forced labor on to future generations.

None of this is to say that the masses of Russian nobles refashioned themselves into agricultural improvers simply because the Free Economic Society said they should. Raised and trained to perform lifelong service to the state, few noblemen in Russia wanted to submit to the agrarian way of life. Modern agriculture required mastering the minutiae of estate management—everything from field rotation and animal husbandry to forest maintenance and small pox inoculation. Recasting noble servicemen into country squires would take decades, if not generations. Equally significant, the Society's agrarian ideals conflicted with the structural limitations imposed on Russian agriculture by the harsh natural environment, the peasantry's communal institutions, and the subsistence farming strategies embedded in Russia's economic customs. The pioneering works of Michel Confino and L. V. Milov have demonstrated how all these factors implanted a profoundly conservative cast of mind in peasants as well as nobles, the very people whom the Society hoped would spearhead the movement to transform Russia's notoriously infertile soil into another Garden of Eden.[14] Yet this was the lot of agricultural improvers everywhere: whoever tries to take on millions of peasants is bound to lose. In the end, the Society's perseverance in the face of these obstacles distinguished it from its European counterparts and made it the prototype for the hundreds of free associations in nineteenth-century Russia that followed its example.

*****

Beyond exploring the development of associational life in eighteenth-century Russia, this book also considers the Free Economic Society's place in the broader culture of the Enlightenment. Few subjects have caused as much scholarly dissension as the "Russian Enlightenment." For many historians, the Enlightenment was an episode confined exclusively to the educated classes of Western Europe and British North America. According to one view, its leading advocates formed an exclusive fraternity, the philosophes, whose works still constitute the canonical works of eighteenth-century thought and whose tumultuous lives made them huge celebrities in their day. In Peter Gay's seminal history of the movement, it was men like Voltaire, Hume, Diderot, Beccaria, and Jefferson who imparted the Enlightenment with its core values: the revival of civic virtue as it was practiced in classical antiquity; the defense of civil liberties, personal freedom, and religious toleration; the abolition of torture and capital punishment; and the suppression of slavery and forced labor.[15] More recently, the historian John Robertson has equated the Enlightenment with a movement of ideas which rejected the theological worldview and aimed to improve "human society and the physical and moral well-being of individuals in this world."[16] Since these ideas anticipated so much in modern liberalism, it is hard not to see the Enlightenment as prelude to the great revolutionary upheavals of the late eighteenth and early nineteenth centuries.

In more recent decades, alternative interpretations of the Enlightenment have appeared that emphasize its march across social class, gender, culture, and nationality. For these historians, the philosophes were just the most visible members of a transnational civil society that also included salon-goers, Freemasons, clandestine booksellers, pastors, physicians, casual readers, scientists, agricultural improvers, and so on. Few of these people had ever seen, let alone met, a philosophe. Inevitably, expanding the Enlightenment's cast of characters from a handful of intellectuals to a large and anonymous public dilutes its liberal programmatic qualities. According to this view, it is more accurate to speak of a multiplicity of enlightenments, loosely held together by the conviction that reason should be applied to human affairs.[17]

Whichever definition of the Enlightenment one uses, it is debatable if Russia experienced either one of them. Ever since the first descriptions of Eastern Europe appeared in the West in the sixteenth century, Europeans tended to link Russia with "slavery" and "despotism." The writings of these ethnographers, as one historian has labeled them, gave rise to a discourse of Russian otherness that carried over into the Enlightenment and persists to this day.[18] Their perceptions had some basis in fact. As late as the 1680s Russia was still the personal patrimony of the Muscovite tsar, anointed by God, sanctified by the Orthodox Church, and seen by his people as the "little father." His realm lacked the institutions of secular intellectual life that European elites had taken for granted since the Renaissance. When Peter the Great ascended the throne as sole ruler in 1696, there were only two centers of higher education, the Kiev and Moscow Academies, both grounded in a Latinist neo-scholastic curriculum and designed to produce church leaders. There was one printing press in the lands of old Muscovy, established in the 1550s under Ivan the Terrible. By 1700, it had published a mere 500 titles, nearly all of a religious stamp. The small number of schools, academies, and books denoted a deeper cultural divide separating Muscovy from Europe. It was not simply that the Russians were ignorant of Copernicus—they still had not heard of Ptolemy.[19] To be sure, growing numbers of Western Europeans had resided in the so-called "German quarter" of Moscow since the early seventeenth century, but most of them were merchants and mercenaries, not bearers of culture and learning. In any case, governmental restrictions on fraternizing with foreign nationals limited their impact mainly to the military, administrative, and economic spheres. After 1650 there was also a growing number of humanistic clergy who participated in Europe's revival of classical antiquity, amassing impressive libraries of Greek and Latin authors. All of these men came from Ukraine, annexed by Muscovy between 1654 and 1667 from the Polish Commonwealth. By contrast, only a handful of native Russians proved receptive to these trends; not surprisingly, they all had close ties to the Romanov court.[20]

The reforms of Peter the Great in the first quarter of the eighteenth century attempted to reverse Russia's exclusion from Europe within the span of a single generation. The consequences, while by no means revolutionary, were certainly controversial. Although his immediate predecessors had adapted innovations from Europe in a piecemeal way, they never dreamed, as Peter did, of secularizing and westernizing Muscovite culture. "Locating Russia in Europe," writes James Cracraft, "was the salient feature, it bears repeating, of the entire Petrine project."[21] As he laid the foundations for Russia's modern state—including a standing army, modern navy, centralized administration, and mercantilist economy—Peter also sought to infuse his nobles with the semblance of European education and manners. At first his cultural reforms focused on westernizing the outward appearance of his nobles. Soon after, he required them to attain some education, either by studying abroad or enrolling in one of Russia's new technical institutes. Schooling inevitably stimulated literacy rates—for the elite at any rate. Four new state-run presses were founded under his watch as government newspapers, technical manuals, and textbooks flooded the nonexistent book market. One of the few secular books to meet popular demand was the *Honorable Mirror of Youth*, "a comparative best seller" which went through six printings between 1717 and 1767. Essentially an etiquette primer inspired by Renaissance models, it offered lessons in Western manners, everything from fluency in foreign languages to the proper use of silverware.[22] The rising demand for the *Mirror* is understandable. Forced to relocate to St. Petersburg, nobles had to endure an endless round of balls, assemblies, celebrations, and firework displays, all hallmarks of everyday life in Peter's window on the West.

Along with establishing Russia's military dominance in Eastern Europe, one of Peter's most cherished goals was to create a highly regulated society founded on rational principles of governance. At the heart of his domestic reforms lay the idea of the "well-ordered police state," a vision of society in which individuals belonged to legally incorporated and hierarchically arranged social estates (*soslovie*), each with clearly defined duties and obligations. Developed in the seventeenth and eighteenth centuries by the German cameralist school, the well-ordered police state held the ruler to be the sole agent of the state's welfare, espousing activist royal power which governed with the general welfare in mind.[23] Emblematic of this trend was the General Regulation, arguably the most far-reaching decree of the Petrine era. Issued in 1720, it provided a blueprint for the new system of government and specified in minute detail the norms and procedures expected of Peter's service nobility, a "regulation of regulations" in other words.[24] One especially revealing passage underscores the intrusive embrace of Peter's ambitions: "Upon arrival at the Senate, there should be no useless work or babbling, but speak . . . about nothing but the matter at hand. Likewise, whoever starts to speak, another is not to interrupt, but let him finish and then another speak, as befits honest people, and not like old women haggling at market." Beyond micromanaging the behavior of the tsar's servicemen, the General Regulation, as the Russian historian Evgenii Anisimov has argued, applied "military principles into the sphere of civilian life and state administration."[25] In practice, regulating such a large and fluid society proved to be far beyond the state's capability. Even in the westernized capital of St. Petersburg, undoubtedly the most policed city in the Empire, the system of legal estates failed to keep pace with all the amorphous social groups that bubbled up from its real life.[26] Unfazed, the government unleashed a flood of regulatory measures anyway. Before too long, hundreds of formal and informal rules were in place to order everyday life, affixing the outward signs of social status to one's rank in the service hierarchy.

By the second half of the eighteenth century it had become the custom for Russians and Europeans to assess the country's progress from Muscovite "barbarism" to civilization. Despite being latecomers to Europe, educated Russians liked to think that they belonged in some way to the age of reason. Their native word for enlightenment, *prosveshchenie*, came to signify the most outstanding qualities of a humanist: erudition, virtuous conduct, and the ability to apply reason to human affairs. They used it in a variety of contexts. In *Orenburg Topography* (1762), for instance, the geographer, civil servant, and future Society member Peter Ivanovich Rychkov used *prosveshchenie* as an ornament of the Russian Empire's triumphant absorption of the Central Asian frontier. As he claimed in its preface, the vast Kirghiz steppe, inhabited from time immemorial by Turkic tribes, was "bereft of scholarship and learning." "Dear God," he exclaimed, "if only the local rulers and [native] peoples with all their powers had been enlightened with a complete knowledge of all that lives inside and outside this expansive province, [knowledge] so necessary and useful for state interests."[27] It was precisely this thirst for encyclopedic understanding that distinguished the Russians from the "unenlightened" and justified their exploitation of a province whose native peoples were too lazy, uncivilized, and unimaginative to develop on their own. Describing the Free Economic Society's goals three years later, Klingshtedt similarly linked *prosveshchenie* with a civilizing mission, but recast it to fit the hierarchical social relations of the Russian village. "With sciences and experiments," he proclaimed, "the enlightened man has far more ability to make useful observations than he who everyday engages only in agricultural work with his own hands. And for this reason we may comfort ourselves with the hope that many of our members will be able to do useful work, despite the fact that not a single one can work a plow himself."[28] Here Klingshtedt equated enlightenment with the privileges and expectations of Russia's noble estate. Exempt from the daily grind of manual labor, "the enlightened man" viewed everything from his lofty summit just as the general did the battlefield or the ruler his country. And in his *Historical Dictionary of Russian Writers*, published in 1772, the journalist Nikolai Novikov chose to situate *prosveshchenie* in the broad sweep of Russian history. Tellingly, not a single writer from the Kievan or Muscovite periods was celebrated as "enlightened" (*prosveshchennyi*); Novikov reserved that label exclusively for people from his own century. They were a diverse lot: Orthodox priests like the Moscow Archbishop Ambrosius, brutally killed in the plague riots of 1771 ("a lover of science and friend of all enlightened people"); the poet Kantemir ("a man of sharp and enlightened reason who still remained a Christian"); and Maria Khrapovitskaia, wife of Catherine II's future secretary Alexander Khraprovitskii ("a good and enlightened mind").[29] Here then were the makers of European civilization in Russia—men and women who were good with a pen, Christian but not superstitious, European but not slavishly so, and destined to win fame and honor in this life.

European writers were less unanimous. Voltaire's views typified Peter's admirers: he likened pre-Petrine Russia to a *tabula rasa* on which the tsar-reformer and his successors built an exemplary kingdom of enlightenment that might avoid all the mistakes of Europe. Writing in the *Encyclopédie*, Louis de Jaucourt similarly praised Peter's reforms for taming the wild eastern kingdom but feared that Russia might "[relapse] into barbarism" if it did not do more to advance the arts and sciences.[30] Other writers proved to be less munificent, insisting that the Russians had blindly copied the ways of Europe without trying to cultivate their own traditions. Rousseau's famous broadside against Peter in *The Social Contract* epitomizes this view:

> The Russians have never been effectively governed because the attempt to govern them was made too early. Peter the Great had the talent of a copyist; he had no true genius, which is creative and makes everything from nothing. Some of the things he did were sound; most were misguided. He saw that his people was uncivilized, but did not see that it was unready for government: he sought to civilize his subjects when he ought to have drilled them. He tried to turn them into Germans or Englishmen instead of making them Russians. He urged his subjects to become what they were not and so prevented them from becoming what they might have been.[31]

In 1795, more than three decades after the publication of *The Social Contract*, an English visitor to St. Petersburg closed the book on Peter's experiment once and for all. The Russians, he sadly reported, were "born to slavery." "In whatsoever country we seek for original genius," he went on, "we must go to Russia for the talent of imitator. This is the acme of Russian intellect; the principle of all Russian attainments . . . [Neither] the drivellings of Voltaire nor all the hired deceptions of French philosophers and *savans* will change it."[32]

Yet downgrading the Enlightenment in Russia to blind imitation of European models drastically distorts the motivations of Russia's rulers and their Western admirers. As Martin Malia once stated, eighteenth-century writers regarded the Russian Empire less as an Asiatic menace than a shapeless mound of humanity in desperate need of development.[33] In *The Spirit of the Laws* (1748), to cite just one example, Montesquieu praised the "government of Moscow" for endeavoring "to emerge from despotism, which it finds even more of a burden than does its people." Although Montesquieu censured Peter's coercive methods, he did believe that westernization had introduced the Russians to laws for the first time in their history. Much work remained to be done—the vast majority of the population languished in servitude while property rights for even the nobility were nebulous to say the least. But all of this could be reversed, he claimed, through the gradual reform of manners and mores which would enable Russia to take its place alongside other European nations as a true monarchy: "Means exist for preventing crimes, the establishment of penalties by law; means exist for changing manners, the power of example."[34]

Catherine's approach to governance reflected these assumptions. Like Peter before her, she equated *prosveshchenie* with reform from above intended to integrate Russia into Europe. Her system has carried a number of labels: enlightened despotism, enlightened absolutism, and, most recently, legal monarchy. Whatever modern historians have chosen to call it, they largely agree that it was no mere slogan, but an attempt to systematize and codify the well-ordered police state introduced to Russia by Peter the Great.[35] The Russian historian Alexander Kamenskii even speaks of a "reform program" which Catherine hoped would lead to the creation of an independent nobility, a third estate, and an educated public.[36] To be sure, the absence of what Montesquieu called "intermediary powers" ensured that the state and its service elite would assume the leading role in the reform process. As a result, *prosveshchenie* under Catherine became virtually synonymous with the state-sponsored westernization of traditional Muscovite culture. By the end of the century, it had become the monopoly of the nobility and hastened its transformation into a "ruling class," as one historian has called them.[37] Whereas the Enlightenment in Western Europe encouraged the emancipation of the educated elite from the state, *prosveshchenie* in Russia led to the opposite result—the fusion of noble culture with the government.[38]

Did Russia's *prosveshchenie* correspond to any of the national Enlightenments of Europe? For historians who regard the Enlightenment as a coherent movement directed by a small group of philosophes, the answer is negative. To paraphrase one scholar: since the Russians "rejected" the core Latin curriculum that had distinguished European education since the Renaissance, there was no Russian Enlightenment. Most Russians displayed a profound hostility to the inquisitive and skeptical spirit of the age and remained doggedly religious, anti-intellectual, and xenophobic.[39] As for those who see the Enlightenment as the secularizing movement of Europe's rising middle classes, the answer is the same. Exceedingly small, interchangeable with the privileged service culture, and isolated from the larger society, Russia's educated public under Catherine had little in common with Europe's "bourgeois pubic sphere," whose independence and achievements, as Jürgen Habermas once argued, derived from the strength of the market economy and the middle classes who profited from it.[40] Public culture in Russia was simply too primitive compared to Western Europe. Whatever impact it may have had was muted by low levels of education and literacy, wide-ranging overlap between the public and officialdom, and the educated nobility's preoccupation with defining and securing its corporate status in relation to other social groups. Soviet scholarship, it is true, once tried to argue that the Petrine reforms produced an Enlightenment movement led by the so-called "*raznochintsy* intelligentsia," an assortment of writers who supposedly articulated the "class interests" of peasants and commoners.[41] Few historians outside the Soviet Union were convinced by this far-fetched argument.[42] Recent scholarship has demonstrated that the "*raznochintsy* intellectuals" were neither rebels nor even critics, just professional courtiers at the bottom rung of a cultural patronage system that began at court and transmitted the government's version of *prosveshchenie* across the Empire.[43]

Nonetheless, the Westernizing reforms of the eighteenth century did spur the development of a modest network of new congregational spaces for the Russian elite—Masonic lodges, private clubs, cultural organizations, theaters, and learned societies.[44] In the relaxed atmosphere of the time, its members were free to engage in what two historians have recently described as a "wide-spread public dialogue" and "a conversation about Russian society."[45] Needless to say, the exchange was conciliatory and avoided direct confrontation with the established authorities. Eighteenth-century Russia produced no great social theories, no oppositional movement, no political ideologies, no real philosophes. As Elise Wirtschafter has stressed, its leading thinkers instead "focused on how to lead an enlightened, morally purposeful, and spiritually uplifting life and on how to foster enlightenment through education, sociability, and public discussion."[46] Although members of the public endorsed Enlightenment notions of progress, their identification with the state ensured the "[subordination of] their belief in progress and human freedom to the assumed rightness of the God-given natural order."[47] Russian civic culture in the late eighteenth century presented a rare moment when educated society and government were in fundamental agreement on policies and principles, blissfully unaware of the parting of ways impending in the nineteenth century.

The history of the Free Economic Society in the eighteenth century mirrors all the contradictions of the Enlightenment in Russia. Created and protected by the Romanov court, it endeavored to accustom the rising public to enlightened norms of sociability (both in its assembly hall and in print) and to prove Montesquieu's claim that a true monarchy could enlighten its people through "the power of example." Most of the time it lived up to its promises: by the end of the century it offered *the* model of autonomous self-governance for subsequent public organizations in Russia. Moreover, in its publications it vigorously propagated the same moral and nonpolitical solution to the country's problems endorsed by the other representatives of Russia's Enlightenment. Yet the Society also sought to introduce Petrine principles of order and rationality to Russian agriculture, using its noble members and affiliates to bridge the gap between town and country. All too often it equated enlightening the countryside with policing it through the same kind of decrees and regulations to which the General Regulation had subjected the service nobility. Many of these ordinances were well intended—new tools, crops, fertilizers, and medical treatments, etc. Yet in the absence of meaningful land reform and personal freedom for the peasantry, they had little impact. By turning enlightenment into a badge of honor for the nobility, the Free Economic Society constructed a justification for serfdom that helped prolonged its life well into the nineteenth century.

NOTES

1. Arguably the first nongovernmental association in Russia was the Society for Historical Research, founded by the Archangel merchants Vasilii Krestinin and Alexander Fomin in 1759. It lasted until 1768. Fomin later joined the Free Economic Society as a corresponding member. See Susan Smith-Peter, "How to Write a Region: Local and Regional Historiography," *Kritika* 5 (2004): 529.

2. "Rech' statskogo sovetnika Shtelina pri vstuplenii ego v VEO," *Trudy Vol'nago Ekonomicheskago Obshchestva* (hereafter *Trudy*) 4 (1766): 188.

3. "Preduvedomlenie," *Trudy* 1 (1765): no pagination.

4. *The Domostroi: Rules for Russian Households in the Time of Ivan the Terrible*, edited and translated by Carolyn Johnston Pouncy (Ithaca, NY: Cornell University Press, 1994).

5. Joseph Bradley, "Subjects into Citizens: Societies, Civil Society, and Autocracy in Tsarist Russia," *American Historical Review* 107 (October 2002): 1110.

6. Richard Stites, *Serfdom, Society, and the Arts in Imperial Russia: The Pleasure and the Power* (New Haven: Yale University Press, 2005), 6.

7. On the Society's history in the nineteenth and early twentieth centuries, see Joan Klobe Pratt, "The Russian Free Economic Society, 1765–1915" (PhD diss., University of Missouri, 1983), 56–301.

8. On patronage and politics in eighteenth-century Russia, see Geoffrey Hosking, "Patronage and the Russian State," *Slavonic and East European Review* 78 (2000): 301.

9. Roger Bartlett, "German Popular Enlightenment in the Russian Empire: Peter Ernst Wilde and Catherine II," *Slavonic and East European Review* 84 (2006): 257–59.

10. James Montmarquet, *The Idea of Agrarianism: From Hunter-Gatherer to Agrarian Radical in Western Culture* (Moscow, ID: University of Idaho Press, 1989), 25.

11. Ibid., 32–34; John Shovlin, *The Political Economy of Virtue: Luxury, Patriotism, and the Origins of the French Revolution* (Ithaca, NY: Cornell University Press, 2006), 8, 73–76.

12. V. I. Semevskii, *Krest'ianskii vopros v Rossii v XVIII i pervoi polovine XIX veka*, volume 1 (St. Petersburg: Tipografiia tovarishchestva 'obshchestvennaia pol'za', 1888), 45–94; M. T. Beliavskii, "Frantsuzskie prosvetiteli i konkurs o sobstvennosti krepostnykh krest'ian v Rossii," *Vestnik Moskovskogo universiteta* series 9, 6 (1960): 26–51; idem, *Krest'ianskii vopros v Rossii nakanune vosstaniia E.I. Pugacheva* (Moscow: Izdatel'stvo Moskovskogo universiteta, 1965), 281–304.

13. See, for instance, Roger Bartlett, "The Free Economic Society: The Foundation Years and the Prize Competition of 1766 on Peasant Property," in *Russland zur Zeit Katharinas II: Absolutismus—Aufklärung—Pragmatismus*, ed. Eckhard Hübner, Jan Kusber, and Peter Nitsche (Cologne: Bohlau, 1998), 181–214; Isabel de Madariaga, *Russia in the Age of Catherine the Great* (New Haven, CT: Yale University Press, 1981), 134–36; Robert Jones, *The Emancipation of the Russian Nobility* (Princeton, NJ: Princeton University Press, 1973), 137–39; Paul Dukes, *Catherine the Great and the Russian Nobility* (Cambridge: Cambridge University Press, 1967), 91–105.

14. Michel Confino, *Domaines et seigneurs en Russie vers la fin du XVIII siècle* (Paris: Institut d'études slaves d'Université de Paris, 1963); idem, *Systèmes agraires et progrès agricole: L'assolement triennial en Russie aux XVIIIe-XIXe siècles* (Paris: Mouton, 1971); L.V. Milov, *Velikorusskii pakhar i osobennosti rossiiskogo istoricheskogo protsessa*, second edition (Moscow: Nauka, 2006).

15. Peter Gay, *The Enlightenment: An Interpretation. The Rise of Modern Paganism* (New York: Norton, 1967), 18–19.

16. John Robertson, *The Case for the Enlightenment: Scotland and Naples,1680–1760* (Cambridge: Cambridge University Press, 2005), 41.

17. See Thomas Munck, *The Enlightenment: A Comparative Social History, 1721–1794* (London: Hodder Arnold, 2000); Ulrich Im Hof, *The Enlightenment* (Oxford: Oxford University Press, 1994); and James Van Horn Melton, *The Rise of the Public in Enlightenment Europe* (Cambridge: Cambridge University Press, 2001).

18. Marshall T. Poe, *"A People Born to Slavery": Russia in Early Modern European Ethnography, 1476–1748* (Ithaca, NY: Cornell University Press, 2000), 202.

19. James Cracraft, *The Petrine Revolution in Russian Culture* (Cambridge, MA: Harvard University Press, 2004), 195, 259.

20. Max J. Okenfuss, *The Rise and Fall of Latin Humanism in Early Modern Russia: Pagan Authors, Ukrainians, and the Resiliency of Muscovy* (Leiden: Brill, 1995), 70.

21. Cracraft, 185.

22. Lindsey Hughes, *Russia in the Age of Peter the Great* (New Haven: Yale University Press, 1998), 289–90; Cracraft, 228–34; Pavel Miliukov, *Ocherki po istorii russkoi kul'tury*, volume three (Paris: Sovremennyia zapiski, 1930), 244–46; and Marc Raeff, "The Enlightenment in Russia and Russian Thought in the Enlightenment," in *Political Ideas and Institutions in Imperial Russia* (Boulder, CO: Westview, 1994), 293, 297–98.

23. Cracraft, 161–71; Marc Raeff, *The Well-Ordered Police State: Social and Institutional Change through Law in the Germanies and Russia, 1600–1800* (New Haven: Yale University Press, 1984), 237–44; Leonard Krieger, *An Essay on the Theory of Enlightened Despotism* (Chicago: University of Chicago Press, 1975), 61.

24. Hughes, 109–10.

25. Evgenii Anisimov, *The Reforms of Peter the Great: Progress through Coercion in Russia*, translated by John T. Alexander (Armonk, NY: M.E. Sharpe, 1993), 150, 155.

26. George E. Munro, *The Most Intentional City: St. Petersburg in the Reign of Catherine the Great* (Madison, NJ: Fairleigh Dickinson University Press, 2008), 57–59.

27. P.I. Rychkov, *Topograficheskiia Orenburgskaia, to est': obstoiatel'noe opisanie orenburgskoi gubernii*, volume two (St. Petersburg: Imp. Akademii Nauk, 1762), 4, 7.

28. "Preduvedomlenie," no pagination.

29. N. Novikov, *Opyt istoricheskago slovaria o rossiiskikh pisateliakh. Iz raznykh pechatnykh i rukopisnykh knig, soobshchennykh izvestii, i slovesnykh predanii* (St. Petersburg, 1772), 11–12, 88–90, 233.

30. Larry Wolff, *Inventing Eastern Europe: The Map of Civilization on the Mind of the Enlightenment* (Stanford: Stanford University Press, 1994), 190, 203.

31. Jean-Jacques Rousseau, *The Social Contract*, translated by Maurice Cranston (Harmondsworth: Penguin, 1968), 90.

32. Quoted in Anthony Cross, *By the Banks of the Neva: Chapters from the Lives and Careers of the British in Eighteenth-Century Russia* (Cambridge: Cambridge University Press, 1997), 388–90.

33. Martin Malia, *Russia under Western Eyes: From the Bronze Horseman to the Lenin Mausoleum* (Cambridge, MA: Harvard University Press, 1999), 71.

34. Montesquieu, *Selected Political Writings*, edited and translated by Melvin Richter (Indianapolis, IN: Hackett, 1990), 153, 202, 212–13.

35. N. Druzhinin, "Prosveshchennyi absoliutism v Rossii," in *Absoliutizm v Rossii* (Moscow: Nauka, 1964), 437–39; Paul Dukes, "The Russian Enlightenment," in *The Enlightenment in National Context*, ed. R. Porter and M. Teich (Cambridge: Cambridge University Press, 1981), 182–84; Isabel de Madariaga, "Catherine the Great" in *Enlightened Absolutism*, ed. H. M. Scott (Ann Arbor, MI: University of Michigan Press, 1990), 292–94; Oleg Omel'chenko, *"Zakonnaia monarkhiia" Yekateriny II: Prosveshchennyi absoliutizm v Rossii* (Moscow: O.A. Omel'chenko, 1993), 70, 72–73, 81; Cynthia Hyla Whittaker, *Russian Monarchy: Eighteenth-Century Rulers and Writers in Political Dialogue* (DeKalb, IL: Northern Illinois University Press, 2003), 103.

36. A. B. Kamenskii, *Ot Petra I do Pavla I : Reformy v Rossii XVIII veka* (Moscow: RGGU, 1999), 344–47.

37. John LeDonne, *Absolutism and Ruling Class: The Formation of the Russian Political Order, 1700–1825* (New York: Oxford University Press, 1991), 10–15.

38. V. Zhivov, *Language and Culture in Eighteenth–Century Russia*, translated by Marcus Levitt (Boston: Academic Studies Press, 2009), 350–53. See also A. V. Gordon, "Rossiiskoe prosveshchenie: znachenie natsional'nykh arkhetipov vlasti," in *Evropeiskoe prosveshchenie i tsivilizatsiia Rossii*, ed. A. Ia. Karp and S. A. Mezin (Moscow: Nauka, 2004), 117–18.

39. Okenfuss, 234.

40. Jürgen Habermas, *The Structural Transformation of the Bourgeois Public Sphere*, translated by T. Burger and F. Lawrence (Cambridge, MA: MIT Press, 1989), 14–26.

41. See, for instance, M. T. Beliavskii, *Lomonosov i osnovanie Moskovskogo universiteta* (Moscow: Izdaetl'stvo Moskovskogo universiteta, 1955); and M. M. Shtrange, *Demokraticheskaia intelligentsia Rossii v XVIII veke* (Moscow: Nauka, 1965).

42. For a critical overview of Soviet historiography of the "Russian Enlightenment," see David Griffiths, "In Search of Enlightenment: Recent Soviet Interpretations of

Eighteenth-Century Russian Intellectual History," *Canadian-American Slavic Studies* 16 (1982): 317–56.

43. Okenfuss, 178–80.

44. Marc Raeff, "Transfiguration and Modernization: The Paradoxes of Social Disciplining, Pedagogical Leadership, and the Enlightenment in 18th Century Russia," in *Political Ideas and Institutions in Imperial Russia*, 334–47. See also Douglas Smith, *Working the Rough Stone: Freemasonry and Society in Eighteenth-Century Russia* (DeKalb, IL: Northern Illinois University Press, 1999), 56–59.

45. Whittaker, 3; Elise Kimerling Wirtschafter, *The Play of Ideas in Russian Enlightenment Theater* (DeKalb, IL: Northern Illinois University Press, 2003), 174.

46. Elise Kimerling Wirtschafter, *Russia's Age of Serfdom, 1649–1861* (Malden, MA. Blackwell, 2008), 163. See also Whittaker, *Russian Monarchy*, 7; Smith, *Rough Stone*, 42–48; Walter Gleason, *Moral Idealists, Bureaucracy, and Catherine the Great* (New Brunswick, NJ: Rutgers University Press, 1981), 104–5; Nicholas Riasanovsky, *A Parting of Ways: Government and the Educated Public in Russia, 1801–1825* (Oxford: Oxford University Press, 1976), 23.

47. Wirtschafter, *Russian Enlightenment Theater*, 175.

Chapter One

Foundations and Façades

Economic societies made their first appearance in the British Isles. In 1723, a small group of landed aristocrats, country gentry, and professors assembled in Edinburgh to form "The Honorable Society of Improvers." Responding to the downturn in the Scottish economy caused by the 1707 union with England, the Society wanted Scotland's agriculture and linen manufacturing to compete better with its neighbor to the south. Quickly growing to more than 300 members, it built an extensive network of affiliates across the country, offering a successful organizational model for subsequent economic associations. Certainly its most famous descendants were the Dublin Society for Promoting Husbandry and Other Useful Arts and the London Society for the Encouragement of Arts, Manufacturers and Commerce, established in 1731 and 1754 respectively. Like its Scottish counterpart, the Dublin Society struggled against the harsh restrictions imposed on Ireland's economy by England. Barred from trading and developing its native industries, the great landowners who joined it focused instead on perfecting agricultural techniques. Within decades of the Society's founding, Ireland was exporting wheat to England and feeding its peasants with potatoes, the most revolutionary crop of the eighteenth century. The Dublin Society also promoted a distinctive culture of agrarian innovation and emulation through "plowing matches," popular festivities which soon took on a life of their own and allowed farmers to show off their dexterity behind a plow.[1] The London Society drew much inspiration from its precursor in Dublin. Its lax admission requirements and large volunteer membership opened it to a broad cross section of people and ensured that it responded to the demands of the public. Its many essay competitions and tasks elicited an enormous response. Within a few decades, the London Society boasted hundreds of supporters who employed it as an information exchange for economic and agricultural improvements.[2]

Intensifying national rivalries after 1750 triggered the remarkable proliferation of economic societies across Europe and the Americas. The Seven Years' War in particular motivated governments everywhere to use them for strengthening their respective economies. Before the war had ended in 1763, France boasted nine provincial economic societies as well as a central one in Paris. The Spanish monarchy quickly followed suit, establishing almost 100 such organizations in Spain and its American colonies by the end of the century. Central Europe, Scandinavia, Italy, and the Low Countries also witnessed an enormous burst of activity, as hundreds of societies surfaced in the Netherlands, Denmark, Sweden (including Finland), Switzerland, Austria, and the German states between 1755 and 1774. Before the end of the century, they had spread to North America as well. Like their counterparts in the British Isles, European economic societies had to adapt to local conditions. In France, they were soon dragged into the ceaseless power struggles between the provincial estates and the authorities in Paris. In the Netherlands, economic societies sponsored lively public debates on reversing the country's gradual economic decline at the hands of Britain. In the German principalities, local patriotic associations worked closely with monarchs and scientific academies to promote technical education in agriculture and manufacturing, while in Austria noble agricultural associations became virtual arms of Maria Theresa's government.[3]

These variations notwithstanding, continental economic societies shared three important features in common. First, as with the Academies of Sciences,[4] royal patronage validated their activities, if not their existence. Even in England, whose associational life was the oldest and most vibrant in all of Europe, monarchical endorsement provided a magic touch. Although the London Society was funded entirely by the voluntary donations of its membership, it still sought a royal charter. Not until the 1830s did it manage to get it, long after its founder William Shipley went to his grave.[5] Second, all had as their chief objective the reversal of what they called the "decay of agriculture." They typically began by collecting economic data through detailed surveys, publishing the results in their journals and promoting correctives to what they decried as backward agricultural practices. Their remedies were narrowly technical—more efficient field rotation, new grasses and forage crops, greater attention to animal husbandry. Unlike the Dublin and Edinburgh Societies, which quickly became political outlets for landed elites, they usually suppressed discussion of the extreme political, social, and economic inequalities of the age. Comprised of cautious men from the privileged classes with vested interests in the existing social order, they knew that political and legal questions were off-limits.[6] Finally, in their daily practices they harbored decidedly low expectations of their members. Entrance requirements were kept to a minimum—usually personal connections and promises to promote the general welfare. Few attended meetings on a regular basis; fewer still engaged in agricultural experiments or wrote articles for publication. The unwillingness of the leaders to enforce the statutes reinforced these tendencies. For this reason, economic societies came under fire from various quarters for degenerating into social clubs. Summarizing the views of his opponents, the founder of the Basque Economic Society in Spain wrote that "[some] painted this respectable body as being dedicated only to shallow diversion; others estimated it as directed to a search for shallow applause; others saw it as a school of idleness, and even of libertinism." In the German states, critics similarly compared the economic societies to schools of etiquette and flattery.[7] These negative perceptions reflected the shallowness of the "agromania" that swept Europe's educated classes after 1750, famously ridiculed by Voltaire in his *Dictionnaire philosophique*: "Useful books were written about farming: everyone read them except the farmers."[8] Significantly, neither the Dublin nor the Edinburgh Society published journals on a regular basis—they were too busy profiting from the new agriculture to pause and write about it.

The Russian Free Economic Society merged with these international trends. Writing in the first volume of the *Trudy*, Timothy von Klingshtedt praised the Society's predecessors in England, France, and the German states for treating agriculture as "the foundation of all useful economic knowledge." Following their example, the Society began by circulating an economic survey in order to "find out in detail the domestic situation of our provinces, to discover their deficiencies, and to find useful ways of correcting those deficiencies."[9] It also struggled against the same ignorance, apathy, and inertia that its European cousins encountered. In moments of despair, the satisfaction of belonging to the international public offered recompense for so much hard work that seemed to lead nowhere. In 1775, at the end of a disappointing campaign to circulate the *Trudy* in the provinces, Klingshtedt suggested that the Society begin distributing its publications to fellow economic societies in Europe—precisely where they were needed the least. "Although it would not further the domestic welfare of the state," he reasoned, "it would serve to spread the glory of our great monarch."[10]

Despite the many similarities it exhibited with its European counterparts, the Free Economic Society still operated in a larger cultural environment quite unaccustomed to free associations. Aside from official government institutions, there were no native Russian precedents for it to follow. The Medical College, founded in 1763, offered one possible prototype. As one historian has written, it was "a civilian-oriented, patronage-dispensing bureaucracy," administered by a civil servant experienced in natural science and medicine. It displayed some openness to the public and encouraged medical personnel to submit their own projects. Some of these men were later admitted as honorary members of the college.[11] There was also the Academy of Sciences, whose mission, activities, and personnel frequently overlapped with the Free Economic Society over the years. Yet the Academy was still a state institution governed under the General Regulation. Its 1747 charter allotted extensive powers to its president who was appointed by the monarch and had the authority to determine salaries, frame research agendas, and evaluate the work of the Academy's staff.[12]

Given the dominance of the state in Russian culture, it comes as no surprise that the earliest blueprints for the Free Economic Society adhered closely to official models. The first project, attributed to Catherine herself, recommended an "agricultural class" within the Academy of Sciences.[13] A second plan was advanced by the academician Mikhail Vasil'evich Lomonosov, who in 1761 had urged the government to establish medical agencies, welfare services, and resettlement programs for foreign colonists. He also underscored the need for more Russian books on practical topics like midwifery, medicine, and "measures to correct the morals of the people."[14] Writing in response to Catherine's proposal, he now requested a government college separate from the Academy.[15] Its mission was to promote agricultural improvement through farming experiments, the translation and dissemination of foreign literature, the publication of original works, and essay competitions. Lomonosov's project made no room for grand seigneurs and high-ranking service nobles, not even at the administrative level. Directing his college was a president, "highly knowledgeable in the natural sciences," below who sat a board of advisors, all scientific experts falling between the fifth and seventh grades in the Table of Ranks. Beneath them was yet another layer of college assessors specializing in chemistry, mechanics, geology, forestry, and other scientific fields. Lomonosov also included a select group of gentry who would form a network of correspondents spanning the Empire. The mission of Lomonosov's proposed college closely resembles that of the Free Economic Society, and there is some foundation to the claims of certain Soviet historians that he deserves credit as its spiritual founder.[16]

In the end, the Empress rejected Lomonosov's plan in favor of a free association. The idea came from Catherine's close advisor, Novgorod governor Jakob Sievers, who had attended meetings of the London Society in the 1750s and was impressed by the spirit of cooperation it fostered between political and intellectual elites. Writing in 1764, he suggested starting with a group of "three or four members" all handpicked by the Empress. Their task would be to produce a "complete course of agriculture" based on foreign literature. Ever the optimist, he anticipated that the club would expand to include various "enthusiasts" as well as "correspondents in the provinces who would send their observations to the society, as has been the case for several years in numerous places."[17] Unlike Lomonosov, Sievers assigned no role to the state. Instead, he expected that the same patriotic impulses at work in the London Society would motivate Russians to gravitate voluntarily toward useful service.

True to Sievers's vision, the 15 cofounders of the Free Economic Society ranged from fabulously wealthy aristocrats and civil servants to academicians and literati.[18] None had any experience as agricultural managers. Six were landed nobles, mostly middle-aged, well educated and well versed in Western European languages and culture. Bearing strong ties to the court at one time or another, all had risen to the pinnacle of the service ladder by the time of the Society's establishment in June 1765. Two in particular—Roman Larionovich Vorontsov and Ivan Grigor'evich Chernyshev—came from two of the most powerful families in the empire. The other four included Grigorii Grigor'evich Orlov, the Guards officer who had helped organize Catherine's seizure of power and then served as her favorite until 1772; Adam Vasil'evich Olsuf'ev, the Empress's personal secretary and the Society's first President; Ivan Ivanovich Cherkasov, former Cambridge student, first President of the Medical College, and one of Catherine's closest confidantes; and Wil'helm von Pol'man, a German baron from the Baltic province of Estland. Another five cofounders, all of German or Scandinavian origin, represented a range of scientific disciplines: Dr. Christian Pecken, member of the Medical College and author of the popular *Household Medical Book*; Johann Leman, chemist and academician; Johann Falk, director of the botanical gardens at the Academy of Sciences and former student of the Swedish botanist Linnaeus; Johann Model, apothecary and academician; and Heinrich Ekleben, court gardener and horticulturalist. Completing the slate were four civil servants: Timothy von Klingshtedt, a prominent member of the Commerce Commission and the Society's chief spokesman in its formative years; Grigorii Nikolaevich Teplov, Catherine's main troubleshooter throughout the 1760s and Klingshtedt's colleague on the Commerce Commission; Ivan Andreevich Taubert, Chancellor of the Academy of Sciences and Catherine's court librarian; and Andrei Andreevich Nartov, poet, writer, translator of Herodotus, and son of A. K. Nartov, Peter the Great's personal mechanic and inventor. At 28, he was the youngest of the charter members.

It is remarkable that so much ambition gathered under one roof did not tear the Society asunder from the beginning. In his influential study of politics at Catherine's court, David Ransel has argued that power structures in eighteenth-century Russia revolved around "familial and personal patronage networks" whose leaders strived to advance the interests of their own "patronage hierarchy." And in fact, Roman Vorontsov and Grigorii Orlov, the first two names on the official list of cofounders, represented two of the leading rival factions at court.[19] Orlov was so preoccupied with his official duties, however, that he rarely showed up for meetings, giving Vorontsov ample opportunity to pursue his own agenda in the assembly. Fragmentary anecdotal evidence paints an unflattering picture of Vorontsov. According to his daughter Princess Ekaterina Romanovna Dashkova, he "paid scant attention to his children, and was delighted when my uncle, in grateful memory of my late mother as much as out of friendship for him, assumed the responsibility for my upbringing." He even required his sons to refer to themselves as "your most humble slaves" when corresponding with him. Later, as governor-general of Vladimir province, Vorontsov's reputation for bribery earned him the nickname "Roman of the Big Pocket" as well as dishonorable mention in Prince Mikhail Mikhailovich Shcherbatov's *On the Corruption of Morals in Russia*, the most famous exposé of scandal and corruption under Catherine the Great.[20]

Whatever the failings in his personal life, Vorontsov was well known as one of the major spokesmen for noble interests in the 1750s and 1760s. As a member of Empress Elizabeth's Legislative Commission in the 1750s, he had lobbied for transforming the highest echelons of the nobility into a closed corporation, free of state service and entitled to numerous privileges unthinkable under previous rulers. Central to his vision was an economic program granting nobles the rights to trade in agricultural products, to own and operate rural factories, and to distill and sell alcohol. For provincial gentry, he recommended establishing elected assemblies for the discussion and dissemination of agricultural innovations.[21] Now as a charter member of the Free Economic Society he urged Russian nobles to take the initiative in improving the rural economy, promoting stable villages teeming with strong peasant families. He especially wished for peasants and nobles to perform their "natural callings"—farming and animal husbandry for the former and all-purpose leadership for the latter. He reassured skeptical readers that enlightened nobles would treat their peasants as good fathers did their children. In the hopes that he might spread an enlightened example across Russia, he promised a gold medal to the person who first established a system of peasant grain reserves.[22]

Vorontsov found support in the Society's assembly hall from Klingshtedt. In a series of articles published in 1765 and 1766, the latter argued in favor of a national economic policy that harmonized closely with Vorontsov's defense of the nobility's right to maximize profits from their land. A strong advocate of increasing the nobility's commercial prerogatives, Klingshtedt believed that Russia was destined to become the "breadbasket for a great part of Europe." Although he praised England, Holland, and France for the profitability of their industries, he also contended that their small size and high population density left them no choice but to concentrate on their manufacturing. Neither of these restrictions applied to Russia. "Such a state, which possesses boundless expanses of fertile land and a sufficient amount of inhabitants," he proclaimed, "may enrich itself more reliably through the production of raw materials and an extension of agriculture than through the most productive factories."[23] Klingshtedt downplayed the many impediments to productive agriculture in Russia: poorly developed roads and waterways, communal farming practices, serfdom, and a hostile natural environment. Instead, borrowing the rhetoric of the French physiocrats, he urged Russians to apply themselves to the branches of the economy anchored in traditional agriculture. Grain remained the foundation, but he also predicted a bright future for hemp, flax, and distilling, at least "so long as Russia's happy inhabitants wish to work hard in tapping into the profits of the fertile Russian soil."[24] Like Vorontsov, Klingshtedt used public competitions as a mechanism for spurring nobles and merchants "to engage in such activities voluntarily."[25] And like so many other Russian policymakers of the time, he advocated learning from Europeans such as the "English *pomeshchiki*" (gentry) whose improvements in cereals, land use, artificial grasses, and fibers had begun to revolutionize farming.[26]

If Vorontsov hoped to turn the Society into an instrument of his own political faction, two factors conspired against him. First, his fellow members displayed little interest in political matters—their orientation was overwhelmingly practical. Shorn of specific political demands, Vorontsov's program became a harmless checklist of prescriptions for strengthening Russia's agricultural basis and catering to the material needs of its peasantry more efficiently. In fact, most of the *Trudy*'s original contributors were scientists who focused on economic issues like forestry, distilling, housing, medicine, and granaries. Appalled by the terrible living conditions of Russian peasants yet hesitant to tackle the systemic causes of the problem, they settled for treating the symptoms—hardly the stuff of controversy.[27]

A second factor limiting the influence of Vorontsov (or any other member) was the Society's loose and egalitarian structure. Its original statute, first read by Ivan Taubert on 15 June 1765, placed virtually all power in the hands of the rank-and-file membership of the assembly. Within its walls, members governed themselves under the tutelage of a weak president elected every four months by secret ballot. Prizing "usefulness" and "patriotism" over rank and seniority, members of different social status chatted with each other as equals, sat wherever they pleased, and were allowed to get coffee or tea during presentations. Candidates for admittance, rather than being appointed by the president, were accepted or rejected by a majority vote after their nomination by three active members. In its regular work, the Society collectively judged the experiments, essays, and projects submitted to it, showing that a member by virtue of his enlightenment was qualified to determine what was "most becoming to the constitution of the state."[28] In other words, Society membership entailed a personal transformation that Harold Mah, describing the eighteenth-century public in Western Europe, has called a "phantasmic reshaping of social identity."[29] Evidence of this appeared at its very first meetings. When the assembly presented Vorontsov the post of president, he politely declined, citing his poor knowledge of foreign languages. Grigorii Orlov, the assembly's second choice, likewise turned down the offer. The top two candidates having canceled each other out, the position went to Adam Olsuf'ev, a survivor of court intrigues for more than four decades.[30]

Secure in its self-governance, the Society steadily branched out to include new members from a wide variety of backgrounds and occupations (Table 1.1). To be sure, servicemen between the fifth and eighth ranks remained its primary recruits. It also continued to attract large numbers of grand seigneurs and nobles from the top four grades of the civil and military service (the *Generalitet*). Well into the 1790s, aristocrats, courtiers, royal favorites, and high-ranking service nobles appeared on the Society's membership lists. A few of these men even distinguished themselves as gentlemen farmers.[31] Yet it is the influx of foreigners, clergy, merchants, and people of low or undetermined rank that stands out. By the end of Catherine's reign, more than 100 foreigners had been admitted as regular and honorary members, including representatives of economic societies from Zurich, Leipzig, Bern, Heidelberg, and London. Prominent names included the British Lord Admiral Rodney; the French Minister of Finance Jacques Necker; the renowned English agricultural improver Arthur Young; and J. K. Hirzel, Swiss author of the international best seller *The Economy of*

Table 1.1. Free Economic Society Membership, 1765–96

Member type	1765–72	1773–80	1781–88	1789–96
Ranks 1–4	31 (35.6 %)	19 (20.0 %)	8 (11.6 %)	52 (15.5 %)
Ranks 5–8	43 (49.4 %)	37 (38.9 %)	39 (56.5 %)	110 (32.8 %)
Ranks 9–14	3 (3.4 %)	3 (3.2 %)	3 (4.3 %)	22 (6.6 %)
Clergy/Merchant	3 (3.4 %)	2 (2.1 %)	1 (1.4 %)	33 (9.9 %)
Foreign	5 (5.7 %)	22 (23.2 %)	6 (8.7 %)	77 (23.0 %)
Undetermined	2 (2.3 %)	12 (12.6 %)	12 (17.4 %)	41 (12.0 %)
Total	87 (100 %)	95 (100 %)	69 (100 %)	335 (100 %)

Sources: *Trudy Vol'nago Ekonomicheskago Obshchestva* (St. Petersburg, 1765–75), 1–30; *Prodolzhenie Trudov Vol'nago Ekonomicheskago Obshchestva* (St. Petersburg, 1779–94), 1–19; *Novoe Prodolzhenie Trudov Vol'nago Ekonomicheskago Obshchestva* (St. Petersburg, 1795–97), 1–2. (Percentage figures do not add up to 100 % due to rounding.)

a Philosophical Peasant. Just as notable were a host of other names from outside the nobility: enlightened clergymen like Archbishop Platon and Johann Eisen; Heinrich Fick and Iogan Loretz of the Volga German colony at Sarept; the Finnish physician Dr. Gustav Orraeus, the first recipient of a medical degree in Russia; the Archangel merchant Alexander Ivanovich Fomin, who in 1759 cofounded Russia's first public organization, the Society for Historical Research; and Ivan Mikhailovich Komov, a protégé of Arthur Young who preached the gospel of agricultural innovation to Russian peasants. In 1783 the Society even crossed the gender line when it inducted Ekaterina Dashkova, daughter of Roman Vorontsov, President of the Academy of Sciences, patron of the arts, friend to Catherine, and the only woman to join before 1800.

Self-governance also liberated the Society from the maddening rules and constraints of the General Regulation. At first, many members interpreted their freedom as license to do—or not do—anything they pleased. As early as September 1765 the assembly had to issue a formal reprimand to Ivan Chernyshev for his failure to appear at any of the meetings.[32] Chernyshev's chronic absenteeism in the Society's first months clearly underscored the need for stronger presidential leadership. This did not materialize until 1788 with the election of Count Fedor Angal't to the position. Until then, the only officers permitted to serve indefinitely at their posts were the Russian and foreign secretaries, whose duties included keeping detailed minutes of assembly meetings, maintaining correspondence with its Russian and international membership, announcing to the public its essay competitions, and informing members of regular and extraordinary meetings. It fell to Russian Secretary Andrei Nartov, who held the position for most of Catherine's reign, to bring some semblance of order to the chaos. For much of the eighteenth century, the assembly typically gathered once a week for two hours, recessing only for the Christmas holiday and during the summer as members retreated to their country estates or the royal residence at Tsarskoe Selo.[33] At first they met at Roman Vorontsov's palace on Vasilevskii Island—yet another indication that he aspired to fashion himself into the Society's grand patron.[34] Once the assembly settled into its permanent quarters on Nevskii Prospekt across from the Admiralty, however, more routine behavior set in. Normally, members sat at a round table as their colleagues delivered reports of economic experiments, after which the assembly discussed the presentations, took a vote on their usefulness, and considered publishing the pieces in the *Trudy*. By the mid-1780s the assembly had also begun to hear regular reports on the condition of the Society's finances, *Trudy* sales and distribution, as well as news from the network of provincial and foreign correspondents. If there was little or no business to conduct, as was often the case in the Society's first decade,

the president adjourned the meeting early.[35] All official business and correspondence was recorded by Nartov and preserved in the Society's archives.

Like the economic societies of Europe, the Free Economic Society tried to
submerge the many social distinctions of its membership beneath an ideological façade of equality before the public. It encountered considerable difficulties putting this equality into practice. As Mah writes, "[people] have always
belonged to groups . . . [and] when people present themselves publicly there
are always group identities at work behind those presentations."[36] At his first
appearance before the assembly, Zakhar Grigor'evich Chernyshev, hero of
the Seven Years' War, invoked the image of Cincinnatus, the legendary military dictator of the ancient Roman Republic who worked his fields in times
of peace. For Chernyshev, the example of Cincinnatus demonstrated that the
"military calling, which seems to have nothing in common with farming, considers agriculture to be its foundation and bedrock. How could we support an
enormous military, which is so necessary and essential to the defense of the
state, if the farmer did not apply himself to his work?"[37] Chernyshev's praise
for the hierarchical division of labor between farmers and soldiers suggests
that he had no intention of returning to the farm any time soon or checking his
warrior status at the assembly's door. Other high-ranking officials stressed
the practical difficulties in juggling service in the capital with agriculture and
estate management. In an article from 1769, Vorontsov urged landowners to
retire from service for several years and relocate to the countryside to conduct farming experiments.[38] Four years later the assembly heard from Stepan
Fedorovich Ushakov, another military official and former Governor of St.
Petersburg, who "dared" to act on Vorontsov's advice. Taking temporary
leave from service in 1771–72, he returned to his Novgorod estate where he
instituted a new practice for seed preparation that produced a bumper rye
harvest. Ushakov attributed his success to his desire for praise from the Free
Economic Society and its protector, Catherine II.[39] For these men, public
service was inseparable from their identities and accomplishments as war
heroes, administrators, and courtiers. Rather than assimilating the values of
equality proclaimed in the Society's statute, membership in the organization
validated and reinforced their preexisting status.[40]

The rhetoric of the Society's academicians and civil servants similarly
acknowledged the hierarchical structure of the Russian public, although for
these members it was their scientific proclivities and foreign origins that
constituted the chief obstacles to forging a common identity with the likes
of Chernyshev, Vorontsov, and Ushakov. The biologist Model spoke for this
group when he frankly admitted to being a "mere lover of economics, and
not a practitioner."[41] Nor did it bode well that academicians had never fully
trusted their court-appointed presidents and chancellors, whose acrimoni-

ous relations with them often brought the Academy's work to a halt.[42] The prestigious physicist Fedor Epinus, for example, still carried some personal resentment from his fights with the recently deceased Lomonosov and the latter's supporters at court. In his first speech to the assembly in 1766, Epinus dismissed those "vainglorious men" whose ignorance led them to mistake pseudoscientific claptrap for true knowledge. Progress depended on "real science," Epinus reminded his colleagues, and only the "skillful artist" who studied nature first and then applied his knowledge could serve the world in a useful and rational manner.[43] Others were more optimistic. They understood that the organization's effectiveness required cooperation between themselves and the wealthy and powerful landowners who formed the greater part of its membership. Speaking in May 1769, the Swedish naturalist Erik Laksman posed the following question to the assembly: "To whom does primacy belong—to him who has more knowledge of the natural order than [knowledge of] how to use it, or to him who, not knowing nature itself, thinks about putting [knowledge] to use?" Laksman found his answer in the noble landowner thoroughly versed in modern science: "If the gentry, who typically choose the country life after growing weary of military service, have already in their childhood years grown accustomed to the study of natural history, then they could greatly promote the improvement of estate management [*domostroitel'stvo*] and gain for themselves true pleasure."[44]

These tussles never threatened to unravel the handiwork of the 15 charter members, at least so long as they enjoyed the personal protection of the ruler. Standing above the fray, Catherine II infused the Society with a sense of enlightened public service that transcended all its divisions. The mortar binding the Russian public together was the personal charisma of royal authority.

*****

From the time of its founding the Society cultivated a personal relationship with Catherine, whose patronage over the course of her reign both facilitated and obstructed the Society's efforts to forge a public culture independent of the court and state institutions. An exchange of letters from the first volume of the *Trudy* expresses the complexities of their relationship.[45] While acknowledging its dependence on the monarch for validation and critical material support, the Society also requested and received from Catherine her personal protection (*pokrovitel'stvo*). Often understood as patronage in the narrow financial sense of the word, pokrovitel'stvo more broadly signified the monarch's conscious decision to permit the Society to govern and constitute itself under her watchful eye. For Catherine, protecting and nurturing the new association entailed surrendering some of her own power to a portion of the educated public. Individual Society members in the capital and the provinces were likewise required to subordinate their personal interests to the general welfare, thus forming a pyramid of public service. In this respect, the Society helped to concretize the "ruling myth" of enlightenment, which, according to V. M. Zhivov, credited the monarch with "establishing common justice and creating harmony for the world" while concealing the autocratic character of Russian governance.[46] Thus, despite the Society's claims to represent an educated public whose independence and enlightenment made it a worthy partner of the Crown, the mere fact of Catherine's protection forced its members into a dance of power brokering that worked to preserve and reinforce the social distinctions and privileges emanating from the court.

Each volume of the *Trudy* offered a vivid reminder of the hierarchies that encased the Russian public and structured so much of its autonomous activity. Gracing the cover was Catherine's personal coat of arms, featuring bees swarming around their hive set against a pastoral background, an image consistent with motifs of the eighteenth-century paradise myth, particularly the monarch's unique power to transform Russia's infertile soil into another Garden of Eden.[47] Instead of farmers laboring in the fields, the cover depicted rays of light extending to the horizon, thus linking the Society's practical achievements in agriculture not to the hard work of human hands but ultimately to Catherine's good blessing. The response of the young Andrei Timofeevich Bolotov to the first volume of the *Trudy* confirms the catalytic effect of this image and of Catherine's protection: "Seeing from this booklet that now we too had established such a [society], and moreover that it was distinguished to have been taken under the special protection of the Empress herself, I nearly jumped for joy, reading it with enormous greed from front to back."[48] While recognizing her personal connections to the Society, the *Trudy*'s cover likewise stressed the deific qualities separating the Empress from the Russian public. As Richard Wortman has argued, most educated Russians liked to think that they enjoyed an individual relationship with Catherine, even though contemporary panegyrics depicted her as Minerva enthroned, inaccessible on her Olympian summit.[49]

All of the Society's famous public dialogues on serfdom and the agrarian economy similarly bore the imprint of Catherine's enlightened reformism. As sovereign, Catherine approached agricultural matters from a broad juridical perspective, providing a conceptual framework inspired by Montesquieu's idea of fundamental laws and leaving the details to be worked out by the Society. In her view, each social estate—peasants included—should possess duties, privileges, and callings specific to that social order, spelled out in law and enforced by the state.[50] In the chapter on serfdom from the *Great Instruction*, the Empress advocated certain laws in order "to alleviate the Situation of Subjects, as much as sound Reason will permit," particularly "a

Law . . . which gives some *private* Property to a Slave." Lest we misinterpret Catherine here, it should be stressed that this was simply an unconventional means to a very conservative end. In practically the same breath she explicitly reaffirmed her support for the traditional estate structure. Her main idea pivoted on making farming an attractive calling to peasants through laws that "[tend] least to separate the Peasant from his House and Family."[51] No Society member could disagree with this—not only did they understand that enlightenment was synonymous with the circulation of Catherine's example, but they shared her preference for a rationally ordered society, so long as their leading roles in it were assured.

None of this is meant to imply that Catherine dictated the Society's program—only that their shared assumptions regarding Russia's agrarian foundations helped structure the debates that transpired within the assembly in the 1760s and 1770s. In fact, Catherine typically maintained a safe distance between herself and the assembly, acting like an exemplary intercessor that neither meddled in the Society's affairs nor forgot that it ever existed.[52] Of the sixteen projects she initiated between 1765 and her death in 1796, most were simple requests for the assembly to review books and articles on various technical subjects that had come across her desk. At other times, she used the assembly as a board of advisors, such as in 1789 when it investigated the environmental impact of slash-and-burn farming in the St. Petersburg region.[53] The Society cheerfully responded to her requests, even if they were especially time-consuming. Like many eighteenth-century women, Catherine nursed a penchant for beekeeping, and for five years in the 1770s she had the assembly provide logistical support for two seminarians studying apiculture in Germany under Pastor Schirach, one of Europe's most eminent authorities on the subject and an honorary Society member.[54] Later in the decade the Empress enlisted the assembly's services for another major project, this time a translation into Russian of John Mills's *New System of Practical Husbandry* (1767) and Arthur Young's *Six Months' Tour through the North of England* (1770). It fell to the assembly to hire translators and edit their work, an assignment that took almost six years to complete.[55]

The assembly countered Catherine's sporadic attentions in a variety of ways that acknowledged her offstage presence while tightening the bonds of dependence linking the Society to the court. Unlike Catherine, whose singular position as ruler and protector allowed her to interact with the Society whenever and however she pleased, the Society had to submit to a set of procedures incumbent upon clients of insecure status. Foremost among them was regularly sending Catherine the bill for publication of the *Trudy*, payment for which came directly out of her own pocketbook. Reserving the first copy of each volume for the Empress,[56] the assembly typically used one of their highest-ranking members to courier the new book to the Winter Palace or Tsarskoe Selo. The Society also began holding anniversary celebrations in 1770 that opened with the reading of Catherine's protection letter of October 1765. By the 1790s, anniversary meetings and the publication of each new volume of the *Trudy* became occasions for demonstrating the tentacular range of the Empire's most visible public association. Nearly 50 members appeared for the celebrations in 1792 and 1793, as courtiers, titled nobles, generals, and governors sat shoulder-to-shoulder with assessors, merchants, school-teachers, Academy adjuncts, and gentry of low rank and unknown pedigree. Distribution lists for complimentary copies of the *Trudy* in 1793 similarly underscore the plenitude that unfolded with Catherine's protection: included among the recipients were the Empress and the royal family, the Society's inner circle, and an assortment of aristocrats, intellectuals, civil servants, clergy, and provincial landowners.[57]

A discernible pattern of patron-client etiquette thus evolved over the course of Catherine's reign that stabilized her relationship with the Society and regulated the flow of power and influence from the top down. Even the most mundane practices that, on the surface, seem to highlight the breadth, inclusiveness, and diversity of the Russian public served as embellishments for a traditional social and cultural order that glorified those closest to Catherine and the court. When readers opened the *Trudy*, the first thing they saw was a register of newly admitted members displayed in order of rank, title, and prestige. In volume one, for instance, the list of charter members awarded Roman Vorontsov and Grigorii Orlov first and second place respectively, while the court gardener Heinrich Ekleben lagged behind in fourteenth. The custom of ranking members, who, in theory, had no rank in Russia's public, grew more pronounced with the passage of time. By the 1790s, it was normal for the *Trudy* to present new members with their full panoply of honors, titles, and positions, a practice which tended to reinforce the status distinctions between those with access to the Empress and the others clustered in the middle and bottom of the list. Rather than discourage the inflation of honors so pervasive toward the end of Catherine's reign, the Society promoted it. To be sure, all names appeared together under one category of "members," signifying a certain equality bestowed by the educated public upon its participants. But it was an equality made possible only by the monarch's personal protection, a fact which the Society's regular members, experienced courtiers all of them, had internalized and integrated into their everyday public practices.

*****

While striving to emulate European associations, the Free Economic Society also evolved out of a nexus of social, economic, and political circumstances specific to Russia in the eighteenth century. Like so much else in the history of this period, the Society is best understood through its relationship to Russia's noble estate and the millions of serfs whose labor underwrote the country's public culture. Beyond providing the vast majority of its membership, the nobility formed the audience for its publications and served as the target for so much of its criticism. And although the Society aimed primarily to improve agricultural productivity, its unique status as a free and self-governing public association infused its work with a cultural significance that transcended bottom-line concerns like grain prices and output-seed ratios. Its broader purpose was to enlighten Russia's serf-owning class in an era of noble freedom.

That said, few people in the eighteenth century could agree on exactly just what it meant to be a member of the Russian nobility, for the country's elite possessed little internal solidarity or esprit de corps. Rooted in the princes, boyars, and military service class, or *pomeshchiki*, of the Muscovite period, in 1764 Russia's nobility consisted of nearly 55,000 males from a mix of social, economic, and ethnic backgrounds.[58] In the absence of corporate institutions like assemblies and courts that might have lent some legal precision to their ambiguous status, Russia's nobles were united primarily by the experience of personal service to the ruler. As a result of Peter the Great's reforms, which consolidated pre-existing noble groupings into a single legal category that later came to be called *dvorianstvo*, state service became the dominant element in the life of the Russian nobility. Regardless of distinctions in wealth and lineage, all noble males were required to perform mandatory state service from their teenage years into the infirmities of old age, serving wherever and however the state needed them.[59] For those blessed with wealth, connections, and talent, the system offered numerous rewards through promotion in the Table of Ranks and the patronage of powerful families. These men formed what one historian has called "the ruling elite of Russian politics."[60] Numbering approximately 8,000 at the opening of Catherine's reign, together they owned about 80 percent of Russia's serf population and monopolized the highest positions in the state. At the apex stood the great seigneurs whose serfs numbered in the thousands (in some instances tens of thousands) and whose power extended deep into the court, military, and bureaucracy. Immediately beneath them were thousands of modest nobles, owners of about 100 to 500 serfs who held respectable mid-level positions in the Table of Ranks and who, by virtue of their education, rank, wealth, and numbers, comprised the greater part of Russia's educated public. Conscious of their leading roles in the Russian state, they identified so avidly with its service ethic and Westernizing culture because they benefited so much from it.[61] Their power and good fortune contrasted starkly with the masses of petty nobles who served

in the lowest rungs of the military and civilian administration and who possessed few, if any, serfs. Many were landless and dependent on their meager
government salaries to support themselves and their families. Theirs was a
dicey material existence, different from the lives of their peasants only in the
knowledge that they served the monarch, and, as members of the nobility,
were entitled in theory to some privileges: land ownership, serf ownership,
and exemption from the dreaded poll tax. Few of these men subscribed to the
Westernizing policies of the Russian state; even fewer shared the elite's service orientation. What they did value was the authority and self-respect that
came with owning land and serfs.[62]

Although nobles saw themselves as seigneurs accountable for the wellbeing of their estates, lifelong state service made it difficult for them to exercise
as much control over their demesnes as they would have liked. For the great
magnates, whose holdings were often scattered across the Empire, it was
virtually impossible. Compelled into state service for life, yet responsible for
their landed and human property, the nobility lacked the means and resolve to
develop personal ties to their estates. Cultivating strong local and provincial
identities was equally difficult under these conditions.[63] A testament composed in 1733 by Vasilii Nikitich Tatishchev, one of Russia's first modern
historians, exemplifies this emerging absentee mentality and underscores the
Russian nobleman's dilemma. Writing to his son, Tatishchev stressed that
everything worthy of note in his life derived from his relationship to the state
and sovereign. Military and civil service filled him with direction, zeal, and
ambition, teaching him the universal values of discipline and order while
breeding in him a hearty contempt for the "domestic manners and willfulness" of private life, which, without a serviceman at the helm, invariably
disintegrated into idleness and disorder.[64]

Given the nobility's dependence on state service for income, status, and
identity, it followed that in managing their property nobles tended to apply to
their country estates the same organizational models they had absorbed in service.[65] Consider, for instance, four sets of instructions for estate management
dating from 1724 to 1764, all written by high-ranking and wealthy members
of the service elite: Artemii Petrovich Volynskii, Peter Aleksandrovich Rumiantsev, Peter Borisovich Sheremetev, and the same Vasilii Tatishchev,
whose testament we have just examined. For all their natural talents and intelligence, none of the authors displayed the calculating foresight of agricultural
entrepreneurs, let alone much interest in the technical details of farming or
agriculture as a way of life. Aiming to eliminate what they perceived as law-
lessness and disorder, they instead emphasized extracting as much as possible
from their labor force. Only the most trustworthy serfs were permitted access
to local markets, while the others remained bound to the estate, cut off from

the "idleness and drunkenness" of the marketplace. Tatishchev expressly forbade his peasants from selling anything or working outside the village "since from this peasants will fall into poverty, give away all their belongings, and through this enrich other villages." In order to ensure the execution of their orders, all four authors threatened "severe punishments" for even the mildest insubordination, Rumiantsev devoting an entire chapter to the matter.[66] An instruction from 1755 written by Captain T. P. Tekut'ev demonstrates that petty nobles shared the same attitudes. Stationed in St. Petersburg and earning only 360 rubles a year, Tekut'ev lavished great attention on his 160 serfs as well as the details of farming and animal husbandry.[67] Because his salary was so meager, his livelihood depended on perfecting the mechanisms of revenue extraction. Tekut'ev viewed peasants less as thinking individuals than an elemental force of nature that had to be harnessed and made productive against their will. Nor did commercial farming interest him. His goal was rather a self-sufficient natural economy, symbolized by traditional crops earmarked for his personal consumption: rye, barley, oats, wheat, and peas. And although he himself was rarely on his estate, Tekut'ev still insisted on the need for a "rational and conscientious" lord, without whom peasants would slip into irreligion, drunkenness, and thievery.[68]

Not everything in their instructions came from the patriarchal household of the *Domostroi*. Edgar Melton has written that eighteenth-century Russian nobles possessed great faith in Petrine administrative principles, above all "the belief that laws, properly formulated and carried out, could regulate and direct human behavior toward desired social and economic ends."[69] In managing serfs, they employed essentially the same logic that Peter the Great had used to justify his own treatment of the nobility. If the chief sin of the Muscovite nobleman was excessive ancestral pride, then the dominant behavioral flaws of Russian peasants were idleness and drunkenness. Uprooting these customs necessitated stern measures—reprimands, incarceration, the knout, and Siberian exile.[70] Tatishchev, it is true, believed that peasants could learn to excel at agriculture just as the Muscovite boyar had learned to serve the Emperor with zeal and competence. In a chapter entitled "Morals of the life of the good peasant and craftsman," he argued that peasant vices were the product of custom and could be supplanted by a program of moral instruction (*nravouchenie*). In practice, moral instruction required parents to set examples of diligence and sobriety for their children and to educate them in cleanliness, a healthy diet, the rudiments of farming and animal husbandry, and even basic literacy. Such an upbringing, he reasoned, would accustom the peasant to hard work, teach him to "know and fear God's law," and enable him "to call himself a true man and to distinguish himself from cattle."[71] Tatishchev's attention to moral instruction was exceptional and probably ineffective. It remained more common for nobles to stay within the traditional bounds of noblesse oblige, taking measures to prevent fires, establish grain reserves, and provide for the elderly, orphaned, and disabled.[72] The privilege of serf-ownership came with the duty of providing safeguards against destitution, although the prospect of actually improving the material conditions of life for peasants seemed dim indeed.

Acknowledging the negative repercussions of noble absenteeism on the domestic economy, the government decreased the length of noble service to twenty-five years in 1731, followed five years later by a law exempting youngest sons from service in order to manage family properties. On February 18, 1762, Peter III ended mandatory noble service once and for all, a fateful decision which over the long stretch of time allowed nobles to establish a much greater presence in the countryside than ever before. Immediate responses to emancipation varied considerably. The Russian historian I.V. Faizova has suggested that many petty nobles regarded it as a chance to retire from service and assert control over their properties which had fallen into total chaos in their absence. In a formal request for release from the military, one junior officer and owner of 97 souls complained that "[my] villages in [my] absence have been ruined due to neglect and due to the injuries and oppression of [my] neighbors and kinsmen." Still another petty noble stated that "my villages from the beginning of my uninterrupted service in the army, and then through my uninterrupted posting in Kazan, have fallen into extreme ruin without my supervision; moreover, several pomeshchiki have seized my serfs and land, tying me up in endless court proceedings."[73] Such testimonies call to mind the earlier lamentations of Tatishchev, who, after a lifetime of service, likewise perceived his estate as an alien culture when he returned to it in later years: "Upon release from service," he advised his son, "it is necessary to inspect your village, to return all things that do not belong there, to demand amicably the return of things that are yours, and, if possible, to turn down the requests of greedy petitioners; stay away from those accursed greedy informers, spiritually depraved swindlers and thieves."[74]

For wealthy nobles, the end of mandatory service promised a brighter and more profitable future. As several scholars have written, Peter III's emancipation decree reflected the "rising economic aspirations" of Russia's ruling class.[75] In his preface to the *Trudy*, Klingshtedt boldly and programmatically pronounced the eighteenth century to be "the economic century."[76] At a time when Russian nobles were still reveling in their newly won personal freedom, these words invoked images of a pastoral cornucopia available to anyone willing to join the Society's efforts. And in fact, governmental legislation and long-term economic trends indicate that some Russian nobles—at least those with enough land and serfs—had begun to see themselves as private seigneurs as well as public servants. With the dismantling of the Empire's domestic tariffs in 1754, the elimination of the state's monopoly on alcohol production in the 1750s, and the opening of new ports in the Baltic and Black Seas under Catherine, Russia's grand seigneurs certainly had many new economic opportunities on which to capitalize. Rising prices on the domestic and international markets boosted Russia's grain exports to record levels by the 1790s and spurred a new wave of settlement in the fertile black-earth lands of New Russia, Ukraine, and the southeastern regions.[77] Soviet historians rightly saw these developments as signs of an emerging market economy designed to benefit the wealthiest members of the imperial elite, many of whom used their freedom to "enrich" themselves.[78] All this crowned the Society's work with the fuzzy aura of profitability, at least in the short run.

Public opinion in the 1750s and early 1760s further aroused the nobility's nostalgia for their ancestral demesnes. Numerous articles published in *Monthly Compositions*, Russia's first popular periodical, expressed in literary form the same cravings for patrimonial authority that Tatishchev and Tekut'ev had shown in their instructions. Whereas real-life instructions reveal hand-wringing frustration over the mismanagement of property and labor, *Monthly Compositions* emphasized the numerous benefits to the individual and society of a rational, virtuous, and paternalistic seigneur at home on his estate. The most prominent theme was the cult of antiquity, complete with quotations from Cato, Cicero, Virgil, and Pliny, all of whom regularly sought refuge in the country from fast-paced city life. For Russian nobles accustomed only to military barracks or administrative offices, the pastoral writings of the ancients offered an alternative lifestyle: gardening, hunting, fishing, quiet reading and writing, and meditative walks through the forest. As Iurii Lotman has written, the second half of the century witnessed the proliferation of new roles and façades for the Russian nobility, including that of the "nobleman in the village," and this presents a particularly transparent example of this phenomenon.[79] Although little more than posturing, the new pastoral ideal denoted a certain discontent with the artificiality, acquisitiveness, and materialism of Russia's urban service culture.[80]

At a more profound level, the ideal village life imagined in the literary discourse of the time promised the nobleman some power and independence. Service might have reduced him to a cog in an impersonal bureaucratic machine, but on his estate he had the freedom to create his own machine that reflected what he valued most: economic self-sufficiency, family pride, and patriarchy. The food in his village was plain and simple, but at least it came from his own land and by the labor of his peasants. He also knew his role in the larger social hierarchy, serving his sovereign with the same loyalty and deference that his peasants displayed for him. In his daily life he set an example of frugality and self-reliance. And although his wife was no great beauty, she certainly knew her proper place as head of the domestic sphere, not interfering in her husband's work and reversing the trend since Peter the Great for noblewomen to manage estates in the absence of their husbands.[81]

With the advantage of hindsight, historians have long regarded the emancipation of the Russian nobility as the beginning of a split between nobles whose allegiance lay with state service and nobles whose identities were rooted in their landed estates.[82] While the manifesto of February 1762 did not mention the need for a greater noble presence in the countryside, its buoyant rhetoric certainly implied a more flexible definition of noble service. In establishing the principle of noble freedom, it contained the seeds of a new type of public man whose unique legal status reflected his personal independence and a moral-ethical duty to live a "useful" life. To quote one of its better known passages: "Manners have been improved, knowledge has replaced illiteracy . . . civil and political concerns have attracted many intelligent people; in a word, noble thoughts have penetrated the hearts of all true Russian patriots . . . "[83] The emancipation legislation also underscored the nobility's obligation to continue serving the state while including numerous restrictions on its newly acquired freedoms.[84] As Zakhar Chernyshev put it on numerous occasions, the end of mandatory service had inspired him to fulfill his obligations more "zealously" than ever before—a turn of phrase that later surfaced quite frequently in the discourse of the Free Economy Society.[85] And in fact, the manifesto had only a modest impact on career patterns for the minority of nobles at the top of the hierarchy. Not only did they remain in service, but they tended to look upon retired nobles in the countryside as shirkers and spongers who should be pressured back into service.[86] They were especially concerned over the fate of tens of thousands of rank-and-file nobles who had spent their careers in provincial garrisons with no hope of promotion or monetary reward. Ironically, the immediate reason for ending the service requirement was to purge these men from the state apparatus, strained as it was to the breaking point by Russia's involvement in the Seven Years' War and swollen with an excess of petty officers whom the government could no longer pay.[87] According to Faizova, the vast majority of petitioners seeking release from service between 1762 and 1771 came from these strata of middling and petty nobles—men like Tekut'ev who represented nearly half of the Russian officer corps. From a sample of 4,366 petitions studied by Faizova for this ten-year period, 69.2 percent cited the manifesto as their main reason for retiring.[88] Poorly paid and badly educated, these men associated state service with barracks life, battle scars, and boredom. Seeking escape from the dead-end of state service, many hoped to live off their tiny estates in their retirement.

What function were these free men supposed to perform now that their services were no longer needed? As we have already seen, in his first speech before the Free Economic Society Zakhar Cherynshev praised the ancient Romans for their ability to balance soldiering with farming. The periodicals of the 1760s echoed his sentiments. One story translated from the German and published shortly after the nobility's emancipation offered a cautionary tale for retired nobles seeking to restore their patriarchal authority in the countryside. Its protagonist, Mr. Hans, belongs to an impoverished branch of an old aristocratic lineage. After serving in the military for several years, he resigns and returns to his tiny estate where he races his coach, carouses with friends, steals from his neighbors, and brutalizes his peasants. Upon the death of his father eight years later, he fires the estate manager and replaces him with a young sycophant who establishes a new regime marked by cease-less work and cruel punishment. Mr. Hans's life takes a dramatic turn for the better when he becomes infatuated with a local girl whose humility and good looks make her the ideal candidate for a wife. Unlike the peasant girls he had conquered previously, however, this one declares that "she loves virtue, good morals, and a peaceful, orderly life; her chief enjoyments consisted of the management and care of domestic tasks and in reading useful books."[89] In drawing a visible line between permissible and unacceptable behavior, Mr. Hans's future wife inspires his eventual rebirth as an exemplary country gentleman: "His only pleasure came in reading useful books, in experiencing nature, and in the company of rational and virtuous individuals. Nothing was as pleasing to him as the country life, and everyday he found a new theater of endless enjoyment, courtesy of the wise creator."[90]

One of the missing ingredients in Mr. Hans's neo-stoic country life, was real work. This was a typical omission for the periodicals of the 1750s and 1760s—not only *Monthly Compositions*, but other popular journals printed primarily moralistic fare without much practical advice.[91] The *Trudy* of the Free Economic Society would later fill that gap, but in the early 1760s few writers thought that hands-on estate management was a suitable task for the liberated nobility. The Empress agreed. Catherine herself opposed Peter III's emancipation decree because she believed that state service was the appro-priate noble calling. If they wanted to spend more time on their estates, she reasoned, they had better improve the lot of their serfs first.[92] She resisted confirming the manifesto until much later in her reign just for this reason. Her advisors had other ideas. The Commission on the Freedom of the Nobility, formed at Catherine's request in 1763 to study the legal ramifications of the emancipation, suggested broadening the definition of noble service to include agriculture and estate management, just as the manifesto had implied. It also recommended strengthening and protecting noble landholdings, arguing that if nobles were to succeed in farming, it stood to reason that they should be fully secure in their property rights.[93] These ideas denoted significant shifts in elite opinion. As Carol Leonard has argued, a "milieu and culture" within Russia's ruling class had been forming since the 1750s that favored a greater noble presence in the countryside and increased attention by the state to the rural economy.[94] Moreover, as several studies of the Legislative Commission of 1767–68 have stressed, these sentiments had begun to trickle down to middle and petty nobles who evidently lived in constant fear of losing control over their land and serfs.[95]

The Commission on the Freedom of the Nobility also deliberated on the broader meaning of noble freedom. In its final report, written by Grigorii Teplov, the Commission urged the monarch to guarantee the nobility a full slate of liberties: to travel abroad and serve foreign governments; exemption from corporal punishment; and protection from arbitrary treatment by courts, officials, and police.[96] Although the report made no specific reference to freedom of assembly, its focus on noble liberties was compatible with the rising spirit of association which had been spreading across Europe since the 1750s in the form of economic societies. All told, the Free Economic Society's appearance in 1765 reflected the "spirit and the fashion of the time," to quote Roger Bartlett.[97] In the absence of mandatory service, a voluntary association dedicated to the general welfare appealed to the so-called "gentry liberals," who ardently defended their new freedoms, and the Empress, whose misgivings about the nobility's emancipation were no secret. How the Society tried to put these ideals into practice—in St. Petersburg, in the provinces, and in the minds of its members—presented another problem altogether.

NOTES

1. Brian Bonneyman, "Agrarian Patriotism and the 'Landed Interest': The Honourable the Society of Improvers and the Culture of Improvement in Eighteenth-Century Scotland," and James Livesay, "A Kingdom of Cosmopolitan Improvers: The Dublin Society, 1731–1798," papers delivered at "Political Economy, Patriotism, and the Rise of Economic and Patriotic Societies in Europe, c. 1700–1850," International Conference in Helsinki, Finland, May 2009.

2. Peter Clark, *British Clubs and Societies, 1580–1800: The Origins of an Associational World* (Oxford: Oxford University Press, 2000), 85–86.

3. Emile Justin, *Les Sociétés Royales d'Agriculture au XVIII siècle (1757–1793)* (Saint-Lo: 15 Rue de la Marne, 1935), 36–39, 42–43, 75; Shovlin, 85–87; R. J. Shafer, *The Economic Societies in the Spanish World (1763–1821)* (Syracuse, NY: Syracuse University Press, 1958), 28, 48–49, 54; Jerome Blum, *The End of the Old Order in Rural Europe* (Princeton, NJ: Princeton University Press, 1978), 288–89; idem,

Noble Landowners and Agriculture in Austria, 1815–1848 (Baltimore, MD: Johns Hopkins University Press, 1948), 132–44; Henry Lowood, *Patriotism, Profit, and the Promotion of Science in the German Enlightenment: The Economic and Scientific Societies, 1760–1815* (New York: Garland, 1991), 25–30.

4. Roger Hahn, *The Anatomy of a Scientific Institution: The Paris Academy of Sciences, 1666–1803* (Berkeley: University of California Press, 1971), 8–9, 46–47; James McClellan, *Science Reorganized: Scientific Societies in the Eighteenth Century* (New York: Columbia University Press, 1985), 24–26.

5. D. G. C. Allan, "The Society of Arts and Government, 1754–1800: Public Encouragement of Arts, Manufacturers and Commerce in Eighteenth-Century England," *Eighteenth-Century Studies* 7 (Summer 1974): 439, 442, 451–52.

6. Justin, 39–41; Shafer, 34–5; Blum, *End of the Old Order*, 290; Lowood, 41, 135–38, 150–64.

7. Shafer, 29; Lowood, 42.

8. Quoted in Blum, *End of the Old Order*, 248.

9. "Preduvedomlenie,": no pagination.

10. Rossiiskii gosudarstvennyi istoricheskii arkhiv (hereafter RGIA), fond 91, opis' 1, delo 394, list 5.

11. *Polnoe sobranie zakonov Russkoi Imperii s 1649 goda* (hereafter *PSZ*) (St. Petersburg: Tipografiia 2 otdeleniia sobstvennoi E.I.V. kantseliarii, 1830), sobranie 1, volume 16, 416, 417, 418; John Alexander, *Bubonic Plague in Early Modern Russia: Public Health and Urban Disaster* (Baltimore, MD: Johns Hopkins University Press, 1980), 42.

12. *PSZ*, sobranie 1, volume 12, 731–33.

13. Catherine had an extraordinary commission formed to devise a plan for the "agricultural class." The commission included, among others, four future members of the Free Economic Society and Mikhail Lomonosov. See document 254 in *Materialy dlia biografii Lomonosova*, ed. P. S. Bilarski (St. Petersburg: Akademiia nauk, 1865), 616. The four commission members who later joined the Society were Johann Leman, Fedor Epinus, Gerhard Müller, and Ivan Taubert.

14. M. V. Lomonosov, "O sokhranenii i razmnozhenii rossiiskogo naroda," in *Dlia pol'zy obshchestva* (Moscow: Sovetskaia Rossiia, 1990), 158–60, 165–67, 169–70.

15. See "Mnenie o uchrezhdenii gosudarstvennoi kollegii (sel'skago) domostroistva," in *Lomonosov kak pisatel': Sbornik materialov dlia razsmotreniia avtorskoi deiatel'nosti Lomonosova*, ed. Anton Budilovich (St. Petersburg: Akademii nauk, 1871), 313–14.

16. N. K. Karataev, *Ocherki po istorii ekonomicheskikh nauk v Rossii XVIII veka* (Moscow: Nauka, 1960), 41–2; V. V. Oreshkin, *Vol'noe ekonomicheskoe obshchestvo v Rossii, 1765–1917* (Moscow: Nauka, 1963), 15, 18.

17. James Arthur Prescott, "The Russian Free Economic Society: Foundation Years," *Agricultural History* 51 (1977): 505–6.

18. On the cofounders, see A. I. Khodnev, *Istoriia imperatorskago vol'nago ekonomicheskago obshchestva c 1765 do 1865 goda* (St. Petersburg, 1865), 4–13.

19. David Ransel, *The Politics of Catherinean Russia: The Panin Party* (New Haven, CT: Yale University Press, 1975), 1, 40–41, 103–4, 112.

20. V. V. Ogarkov, *Vorontsovy, ikh zhizn' i obshchestvennaia deiatel'nost'* (St. Petersburg: Tipografiia "obshchestvennaia pol'za", 1892), 33–34; *The Memoirs of Princess Dashkova: Russia in the Time of Catherine the Great*, translated by Kiril Fitzlyon and with an introduction by Jehanne M. Gheith (Durham, NC: Duke University Press, 1995), 32; M. M. Shcherbatov, *On the Corruption of Morals in Russia*, edited and translated by A. Lentin (Cambridge: Cambridge University Press, 1969), 249. Recent research has shown that the Senate posthumously cleared Vorontsov of all the charges brought against him as governor. See V. N. Alekseev, "Graf R.I. Vorontsov," *Voprosy istorii* 4 (2009): 148.

21. N. L. Rubinshtein, "Ulozhennaia komissiia 1754–1766 gg. i ee proekt novago ulozheniia 'o sostoianii poddanykh voobshche'," *Istoricheskie zapiski* 38 (1951): 232–37; Robert Jones, *The Emancipation of the Russian Nobility, 1762–1785* (Princeton, NJ: Princeton University Press, 1973), 93, 111, 117; Carol Leonard, *Reform and Regicide: The Reign of Peter III of Russia* (Bloomington, IN: Indiana University Press, 1993), 53.

22. R. Vorontsov, "O sposobakh k ispravleniiu sel'skago domostroitel'stva," *Trudy* 5 (1767): 1–12; idem, "O zavedenii zapasnago khleba," *Trudy* 2 (1766): 3–4, 7, 9–10.

23. T. von Klingshtedt, "Reshenie voprosa: kotoroi iz zemnykh nashikh produktov bol'she sootvetstvuet obshchei pol'ze i rasprostraneniiu nashei kommertsii, pochemu i razmnozhenie onago dolzhenstvuet byt' vsemi vozmozhnymi sposabimi pooshchriaet'?" *Trudy* 1 (1765): 160–61, 168–69; idem, "O pol'ze proizkhodiashchei ot umnozheniia l'na v Rossii, i o sredstvakh k tomu sluzhashchikh," *Trudy* 3 (1766): 133–34. See also Wallace L. Daniel's discussion of Klingshtedt's work in the Commerce Commission in *Grigorii Teplov: A Statesman at the Court of Catherine the Great* (Newtonville, MA: Oriental Research Partners, 1991), 86–87; and S. M. Troitskii, "Obsuzhdenie voprosa o krest'ianskoi torgovle v komissii o kommertsii v seredine 60-kh godov XVIII v.," in *Rossiia v XVIII veke* (Moscow: Nauka, 1982), 210–14.

24. "O pol'ze proizkhodiashchei ot umnozheniia l'na v Rossii," 132; "Predstavleni VEO ot sochlena onago, Vitse-Prezidenta-fon Klingshteta," *Trudy* 2 (1766), 268; Daniel, *Grigorii Teplov*, 88.

25. "Reshenie voprosa," 179–80; "Predstavleni VEO ot sochlena onago, Vitse-Prezidenta-fon Klingshtedt," 274–76.

26. Klingshtedt, "O privedenii v lutshee sostoianie senokosov, o raznykh rodakh trav upotrebiaemykh v drugikh gosudarstvakh k seianiiu lugov, o potrebnom zemledelii dlia vozrashcheniia semian, i o upotreblenii onykh trav," *Trudy* 3 (1766): 55–56; "O pol'ze proizkhodiashchei ot umnozheniia l'na v Rossii," 137–38.

27. See, for instance, C. Pecken, "O stroenii zhilykh pokoev dlia prostago naroda," *Trudy* 1 (1765): 106–7; Ekleben, "O sibirskom gorokhovom dereve, i o velikoi ego pol'ze," *Trudy* 1 (1765): 67–68.

28. "Ustav Vol'nago Ekonomicheskago Obshchestva," *Trudy* 1 (1765): no pagination.

29. Harold Mah, "Phantasies of the Public Sphere: Rethinking the Habermas of Historians," *Journal of Modern History* 72 (2000): 164.

30. Khodnev, 6–7.

31. Membership rolls after 1788 included past and future war heroes such as Aleksei Grigor'evich Orlov-Chesmenskii, Mikhail Larionovich Kutuzov, Alexander Nikolaev-

ich Samoilov, Aleksei Naumovich Seniavin, and Peter Isaevich Arshenevskii; representatives of the Rumiantsev, Durnovo, Passek, and Iusupov families; outstanding domestic administrators like Alexander Andreevich Bekleshev and Nikolai Petrovich Arkharov, and Catherine's last favorite, Platon Alexandrovich Zubov. In 1792, the assembly began corresponding with Nikita Afonas'evich Beketov, the former governor of Astrakhan', who for two decades had devoted his time to improving his estate in Saratov guberniia. Although a notable member of the Generalitet whose long career included service at Empress Elizabeth's court, significant military action in the Seven Years' War, and a productive tenure as Astrakhan' governor, from the assembly's point of view Beketov was primarily a "true estate manager (*domostroitel'*)" in the same class as the Society's most industrious and knowledgeable provincial correspondents. See RGIA, f. 91, op. 1, d. 42, ll. 170–74. As part of his service to the Society, Beketov joined 20 other provincial correspondents in a study on the uses of *trostnikovoi*, a fibrous plant native to many parts of Russia. Correspondents on this project included two other high-ranking aristocrats (Orlov-Chesmenskii among them); a handful of mid-level retired landowners, such as Vasilii Alekseevich Levshin and Andrei Bolotov; several Volga German colonists; two merchants; and a number of economic directors. See "Izvestiia Vol'nago Ekonomicheskago Obshchestva s 13 Dekabria 1791 po 8 Dekabria 1792 goda," *Prodolzhenie Trudov Vol'nago Ekonomicheskago Obshchestva* 18 (1793): 377, 397–98.

32. RGIA, f. 91, op. 1, d. 1, l. 13–13ob.

33. "Ustav Vol'nago Ekonomicheskago Obshchestva," *Trudy* 1 (1765): no pagination.

34. RGIA, f. 91, op. 1, d. 1, l. 9.

35. See the undated, unsigned note addressing these procedural issues in RGIA, f. 91, op. 1, d. 394, l. 17. Given the note's references to the four-month presidential term, it was probably written in the 1760s.

36. Mah, 168.

37. "Rech', govorennaia v sobranii Ego Siatel'stvom Grafom Zakharom Grigor'evichem Chernyshevym," *Trudy* 1 (1765): 184.

38. "Priglashenie sel'skikh domostroitelei k chineniiu nekotorykh opytov kasaiushchikhsia do khlebopashestva," *Trudy* 13 (1769): 2–3, 6. Although the article appears anonymously, the minutes for the meeting of 2 December 1769 indicate that the assembly approved of Vorontsov's instructions "for bringing cereal cultures to greater perfection and agreed to publish them in part 13 of the *Trudy*. See RGIA, f. 91, op. 1, d. 6, l. 42.

39. Stepan Ushakov, "Delo sovershenno ispytannoe v plodorodii ozimago khleba," *Trudy* 23 (1773): 1–11.

40. E. Marasinova, *Psikhologiia elity rossiiskogo dvorianstva poslednei treti XVIII veka (po materialam perepiski)* (Moscow: ROSSPEN, 1999), 66–67, 71.

41. Model, "Fizicheskiia i khimicheskiia razsuzhdeniia o natural'nom udobrenii semian, i o umnozhenii chrez to khleborodiia," *Trudy* 2 (1766): 75.

42. Alexander Vucinich, *Science in Russian Culture: A History to 1860* (Stanford, CA: Stanford University Press, 1963), 85–87, 141–43.

43. "Perevod rechi chitannoi kollezhskim sovetnikom G. Epinusom pri vstuplenii ego v Vol'noe Ekonomicheskoe Obshchestvo," *Trudy* 4 (1766): 198–99. On Epinus's rivalry

with Lomonosov, see R. W. Home, "Science as a Career in Eighteenth-Century Russia: The Case of F.U.T. Aepinus," *Slavonic and East European Review* 51 (1973): 81–88.

44. "Rech', govorennaia g. pastorom Laksmanom v sobranii Vol'nago Ekonomicheskago Obshchestva," *Trudy* 11 (1769): 77, 84–85.

45. *Trudy* 1 (1765): no pagination.

46. V. M. Zhivov, "Gosudarstvennyi mif v epokhu prosveshchenniia i ego razrushenie v Rossii kontsa XVIII veka," in *Iz istorii russkoi kul'tury*, vol. 4 (XVII-nachalo XIX veka), ed. A. D. Koshelev (Moscow: Shkola Iazyki russkoi kul'tury, 1996), 668.

47. Stephen Baehr, *The Paradise Myth in Eighteenth-Century Russia: Utopian Patterns in Early Secular Russian Literature and Culture* (Stanford, CA: Stanford University Press, 1991), 65–67, 78–79.

48. Andrei Timofeevich Bolotov, *Zapiski Andreia Timofeevicha Bolotova, 1737–1796*, volume 1 (Tula: Priokskoe knizhnoe izdatel'stvo, 1988), 436–37.

49. Richard Wortman, *Scenarios of Power: Myth and Ceremony in Russian Monarchy*, volume 1 (Princeton, NJ: Princeton University Press, 1995), 144–45.

50. A. Kamenskii, "Znachenie reform Ekateriny II v russkoi istorii," in *A Window on Russia*, ed., Maria Di Salvo and Lindsey Hughes (Rome: La Fenice, 1996), 60. See also Oleg Omel'chenko, 52, 70.

51. "The Grand Instruction to the Commissioners Appointed to Frame a New Code of Laws for the Russian Empire: Composed by Her Imperial Majesty Catherine II," in *Documents of Catherine the Great: The Correspondence with Voltaire and the Instruction of 1767, in the English Text of 1768*, ed. W. F. Reddaway and translated by M. Tatischeff (Cambridge: Cambridge University Press, 1931), 256–58.

52. W. R. Augustine has mistakenly asserted that Catherine not only founded the Free Economic Society, but came up with all its contest questions and the money for its prizes. See "Notes toward a Portrait of the Eighteenth-Century Russian Nobility," *Canadian Slavic Studies* 4 (1970): 390.

53. RGIA, f. 91, op. 1, d. 32, ll. 116ob–117.

54. On women's interests in bees and Pastor Schirach's contributions to apiculture, see Lowood, 77–78, 176–77. Catherine was impressed enough with Schirach's published work to provide full support for the apiculture students. See RGIA, f. 91, op. 1, d. 15. ll. 22–3; d. 17, l. 3ob; d. 18, l. 18.

55. RGIA, f. 91, op. 1, d. 15, ll. 22–3; d. 17, l. 3ob; d. 18, l. 18. The manuscripts evidently were never published.

56. This was one of the Society's earliest decisions. See RGIA, f. 91, op. 1, d. 1, l. 27.

57. RGIA, f. 91, op. 1, d. 44, ll. 113–14, 289–90.

58. For demographic data on eighteenth-century Russia, see Madariaga, *Russia in the Age of Catherine the Great*, 80–81.

59. A. Romanovich-Slavatinsky, *Dvorianstvo v Rossii ot nachala XVIII veka do otmena krepostnago prava* (St. Petersburg: Tipografiia Ministerstva vnutrennykh del, 1870), 43; Marc Raeff, *Origins of the Russian Intelligentsia: The Eighteenth-Century Nobility* (New York: Harcourt Brace, 1966), 42–45.

60. LeDonne, *Absolutism and Ruling Class*.

61. Jones, *Emancipation*, 14–15; Romanovich-Slavatinsky, 67. On social and economic divisions among the nobility, see Jerome Blum, *Lord and Peasant in Russia*

from the Ninth to the Nineteenth Century (Princeton, NJ: Princeton University Press, 1961), 367, 370.

62. John LeDonne, *Ruling Russia: Politics and Administration in the Age of Absolutism* (Princeton, NJ: Princeton University Press, 1984), 5; Augustine, 385, 388–90; Blum, *Lord and Peasant*, 375–76; Jones, *Emancipation*, 88–89.

63. Peter Kolchin, *Unfree Labor: American Slavery and Russian Serfdom* (Cambridge, MA: Harvard University Press, 1987), 58, 64–65.

64. V. N. Tatishchev, *Dukhovnaia* (St. Petersburg, 1773), 30.

65. Raeff, *The Well-Ordered Police State*, 198–200; idem, *Origins*, 77–79; and V. A. Aleksandrov, *Sel'skaia obshchina v Rossii (XVII-nachalo XIX v.)* (Moscow: Nauka, 1976), 50, 111.

66. "Uchrezhdenie Gr. P. A. Rumiantsev," *Universitetskaia izvestiia* (Kiev), 43 (December 1903): 2–3; A. I. Volynskii, "Instruktsiia dvoretskomu Ivanu Nemchinovu o upravlenii domu i dereven'," *Moskvitianin*, 1–4 (1854): 11; "Instruktsiia prikashchiku Muromskoi votchiny sela Kacharova, dannaia grafom Petrom Borisovichem Sheremetovym," *Universitetskaia izvestiia* (Kiev), 45 (August 1905): 102; V. N. Tatishchev, "Kratkiia ekonomicheskiia do derevni sleduiushchiia zapiski," *Vremennik Imperatorskago Moskovskago Obshchestva istorii drevnostei rossiskikh*, 1–2 (1852): 24.

67. *Dvorianskoe gnezdo serediny XVIII veka: Timofei Tekut'ev i ego Instruktsiia o domashnikh poriadkakh*, ed., E. B. Smilianskaia (Moscow: Akademiia nauka, 1998), 9.

68. Ibid., 37, 41–43.

69. Edgar Melton, "Enlightened Seigniorialism and Its Dilemmas in Serf Russia, 1750–1830," *Journal of Modern History* 62 (1990): 691–92.

70. Sheremetev, 101; Rumiantsev, 7, 22; ibid., *Universitetskaia izvestiia* (Kiev), 44 (June 1904): 41, 48; Volynskii, 14, 26, 28.

71. Tatishchev, "Kratkiia ekonomicheskiia," 27–28.

72. Volynskii, 19–20, 24–25; Tatishchev, "Kratkiia ekonomicheskiia," 19–20, 21, 30; Rumiantsev, 8, 12, 22, 45–46; Sheremetev, 101.

73. I. V. Faizova, *"Manifest o vol'nosti" i sluzhba dvorianstva v XVIII stoletii* (Moscow: Akademiia nauk, 1999), 120, 122–23.

74. Tatishchev, *Dukhovnaia*, 48.

75. Leonard, 40; Confino, *Domaines et seigneurs*, 24–26.

76. "Preduvedomlenie," no pagination.

77. Boris Mironov, "Vliianie revoliutsii tsen v Rossii XVIII veka na ee ekonomicheskoe i sotsial'no-politicheskoe razvitie," *Istoriia SSSR* 1 (1991): 88–89, 97–98.

78. N. L. Rubinshtein, *Sel'skoe khoziaistvo Rossii vo vtoroi polovine XVIII v.* (Moscow: Gosudarstvennoe izdatel'stvo politicheskoi literatury, 1957), 62, 66, 70; P. I. Liashchenko, *Istoriia narodnogo khoziaistva SSSR*, volume 1 (Moscow: Gosudarstvennoe izdatel'stvo politicheskoi literatury, 1947), 441–47; K. N. Shchepetov, *Krepostnoe pravo v votchinakh Sheremetevykh* (1708–1885) (Moscow: Izdatel'stvo dvortsa muzeia, 1947), 44–45.

79. "O bezporuchnosti i priiatnosti derevenskiia zhizni," *Ezhemesiachniia sochineniia* (July 1757), 69, 72; "Pis'mo o oprazhnenii v derevenskom zhitii," *Ezhemesiachniia sochineniia* (November 1757), 411–13, 416, 420, 426; I. Lotman, "The Poetics of Everyday Behavior in Eighteenth-Century Russian Culture," in *The*

44 Chapter One

Semiotics of Russian Cultural History, ed. Alexander D. Nakhimovsky and Alice Stone Nakhimovsky (Ithaca, NY: Cornell University Press, 1985), 74–75. See also Thomas Newlin, *The Voice in the Garden: Andrei Bolotov and the Anxieties of Russian Pastoral* (Evanston, IL: Northwestern University Press, 2001), 28–89.

80. "Dvorianin v derevne," *Ezhemesiachniia sochineniia* (December 1757), 532–33; "O bezporuchnosti," 66, 72–73, 75.

81. "Dvorianin v derevne," 537; "Vseobshchiia o khoziaistve nemetskom pravila," *Ezhemesiachniia sochineniia* (January 1760), 84–85, 87–88; "Uveshchanie umirai-ushchago otsa k synu," *Ezhemesiachniia sochineniia* (April 1756), 316–17, 321–22. See also Michelle Lamarche Marrese, *A Woman's Kingdom: Noblewomen and the Control of Property in Russia, 1700–1861* (Ithaca, NY: Cornell University Press, 2002), 182.

82. Romanovich-Slavatinskii, 119, 135; Raeff, *Origins*, 104–15; LeDonne, *Absolutism and Ruling Class*, 25; I. Lotman, *Besedy o russkoi kul'ture: byt' i traditsii russkogo dvorianstva* (St. Petersburg: Iskusstvo-SPB, 1994), 41–42; Priscilla Roosevelt, *Life on the Russian Country Estate: A Social and Cultural History* (New Haven, CT: Yale University Press, 1995), 125, 138, 148.

83. *PSZ*, sobranie 1, volume 15, 912.

84. Ibid., 915.

85. Marasinova, *Psikhologiia elity rossiiskogo dvorianstvo*, 63.

86. Ibid., 65–66; Faizova, 107–11.

87. Jones, *Emancipation*, 33–34.

88. Faizova, 107–8, 110–11, 113, 115–17.

89. "Zhizn' sel'skago dvorianina Gospodina Gantsa," *Sobranie lushchikh sochinenii* 4 (1762), 224.

90. Ibid., 228.

91. J. L. Black, *G.-F. Müller and the Imperial Russian Academy* (Kingston: McGill-Queen's University Press, 1986), 124–25; Gleason, 38–44, 60–69.

92. S. M. Troitskii, "Kommissia o vol'nosti dvorianstva 1763 g. (K voprosu o bor'be dvorianstva s absoliutizmom za svoi soslovnye prava)," in *Rossiia v XVIII veke* (Moscow: Nauka, 1982), 144–45, 188; Madariaga, *Russia in the Age of Catherine the Great*, 83; Jones, *Emancipation*, 96–97.

93. Troitskii, "Kommissia o vol'nosti dvorianstva," 178–80, 186; Lee Farrow, *Between Crown and Clan: The Struggle to Define Noble Property Rights in Imperial Russia* (Newark: University of Delaware Press, 2004), 99.

94. Leonard, 27–28; Omel'chenko, 205–11.

95. Jones, *Emancipation*, 6-7; Augustine, 385–88.

96. Troitskii, "Kommissia o vol'nosti dvorianstva," 180–85.

97. Roger Bartlett, "The Free Economic Society," 188.

Chapter Two

"The Decay of Agriculture"

Historians often assume that the Free Economic Society arrived with a ready-made program in hand for the modernization of Russian agriculture. In his recent study of agrarian innovators in the eighteenth and nineteenth century, Sergei Kozlov introduces the Society as a group of "progressive" lords dedicated to publicizing new tools and crops like the English plow and the potato as well as innovative methods for sowing, fertilizing, seed preparation, and artificial grass cultivation—in other words, the interlocking components of the so-called "agricultural revolution."[1] The reality was far more complex. To begin, the concept of an agricultural revolution is problematic—it appears more clearly in hindsight to historians than it did to its practitioners of the eighteenth century. Agricultural innovation—then as now—was a moving target whose whole constituted much more than the sum of its individual parts. It offered no tool kit, no comprehensive manual, no production quotas, only an experimental spirit and a commitment to farming as a way of life. We should not give the Society's founders credit for something they never did. As it turned out, the Society in its first decades disseminated new farming techniques only sporadically and unsystematically, not because its members lacked the vision or desire to apply them, but simply because they knew too little about agriculture to make such recommendations.

In an effort to learn more about farming in Russia, the Society disseminated topographical surveys to the public. The primary tools of choice for agricultural improvers everywhere, these surveys sprang from the Enlightenment impulse to describe society and nature in a way that was comprehensible, systematic, and accessible. Surveys also allowed respondents to view their world critically. "Agronomists described the old agricultural routines in order to attack them," as Marc Bloch once put it.[2] In Russia, the Imperial Senate and Cadet Corps circulated the first surveys in the 1750s and early

45

1760s, using chancellery scribes to supply the information. Novgorod governor Jakob Sievers conducted a similar investigation of his province in 1764
that was so exhaustive that it detailed all the species of fish swimming in its
rivers and lakes.[3] Following the same trend, the Free Economic Society appended its own sixty-five-item questionnaire the next year to the inaugural
volume of the *Trudy*. Compiled by Klingshtedt, it invited readers across the
Empire to engage in a publicized exchange over farming, animal husbandry,
and labor and life in the countryside.[4] Over the course of the following decade, the *Trudy* published 17 full responses representing the main regions of
European Russia: six from the black earth and non-black-earth zones of the
historic heartland; six from the southern steppe and grasslands; and five from
the enormous forests of the north and northwest.

The survey had its biases. Consider, for instance, question 28: "Has agriculture in certain areas decayed or improved, and if so for what reason?"
Klingshtedt's choice of words is interesting. Beginning in the 1750s, noble
agrarians in Western Europe had used the slogan "decay of agriculture"
to condemn a number of trends—some real, others perceived: the rising
consumption of luxury items and the consequent loss of rustic virtue; the
part-time migration of the farming population to the cities for better-paying
manufacturing jobs; and the decline of agricultural productivity resulting
from the use of outmoded farming techniques inherited from the Middle
Ages.[5] To the masses of Russian nobles who still drew their idea of household management from the *Domostroi*, the answer to the question was almost
too easy—the more arable sown, the greater the improvement. By the same
logic, the inverse also held true—the less arable sown, the greater the decay.
As for the peasants who did the work, they probably would have said that the
question made no sense because agriculture in Russia had always been bad. It
had the shortest growing season west of the Urals, the coldest climate in the
hemisphere, and the most infertile soil in all of Europe. Under such harsh environmental conditions, the sole measure of success or failure was what L.V.
Milov has called the "expediency criterion": anything that minimized risk and
reduced drudgery was good agriculture.[6] Klingshtedt did not explain what he
meant by "decay of agriculture," but in his preface to the questionnaire he
stated that Russian peasants needed to be "won over" to rational agriculture
"no matter how low an opinion we have of them."[7] While acknowledging the
difficulties of working in Russia's northerly climate, he took it for granted
that they were bad farmers. Agricultural progress—whatever form it took—
would have to be applied from above by enlightened lords performing the
duties expected of Russia's leading estate.

But to return to the loaded question posed above—"Has agriculture decayed
or improved?" Nobody really knew for sure. Consider the six answers from

the central black earth and non-black-earth regions, the historic core of the Muscovite state and in 1762 home to more than nine million people, practically half the population of European Russia. Nearly 75 percent of Russia's seignio-rial peasants, or private serfs, resided in these provinces at the beginning of Catherine's reign.[8] It was also the geographical stronghold of Russia's landed nobility, rich and poor alike. Peasants here performed a mix of obligations for their lords. Where conditions favored farming, nobles often placed peasants on *barshchina,* or labor dues, which typically entailed three days of agricultural work per week on the lord's demesne. Elsewhere, particularly in the non-black-earth districts, peasants often paid a quit-rent called *obrok,* which usu-ally required them to supplement farming with wage labor off the estate.[9] No other part of the empire was so homogenously Russian in ethnicity, Orthodox in religion, and agrarian in lifestyle than the Moscow hinterland. According to one correspondent from the historic town of Pereslavl-Zalesskii, located to the northeast of the old capital, "[farming] today is found in the same condition as in ancient times, and there is no decrease in grain." Other writers from the cit-ies of Vladimir, Kaluga, and Riazan believed that agriculture had actually im-proved due to forest clearance and extension of arable land.[10] Moreover, when describing peasant morals, these same correspondents intoned only positive virtues: diligence, self-sufficiency, responsibility, and a strong family orienta-tion. And although the combination of high rents and land scarcity compelled many plowmen to work outside their villages in transport, carpentry, and weav-ing, peasants still considered farming to be their primary occupation.[11] None of these reports suggest agricultural decline or even the perception of it. There was one naysayer, Andrei Bolotov, a correspondent from the central black-earth province of Tula, who reported a decline in cereal production, mainly as a result of soil exhaustion. He also judged peasants more harshly than the others—"tactless, capricious, envious, and vengeful," to use his own words. Even so, he grudgingly acknowledged that peasants in his district worked ex-traordinarily hard under difficult conditions and that there were "a few diligent men who raise good, strong families, who are on the same [economic] level as their lords, and who prepare themselves for lean times. These peasants are as well off or even better off than some nobles, the latter who have reached such destitution that there is little to distinguish them from peasants." He even had a few words of praise for some of his fellow nobles who had begun to experi-ment: "[Farming] and estate management have generally improved day by day and especially in the homes of pomeshchiki, undoubtedly due to the fact that many of them, having taught themselves sciences and seen foreign places, have established new ways as much as possible."[12]

Contradictory as these responses may be, they do convey values and in-securities common to many pre-modern agrarian societies. Russians equated improvements in farming with sown fields, bumper harvests of staple crops, and the opening of virgin land for cultivation. The opposite also held true: aside from an empty field, the only thing more symptomatic of agricultural decline was an exhausted one. Given the devastatingly high frequency of crop failures in eighteenth-century Russia, their pragmatism is understandable.[13] At the same time, most correspondents from the central regions admitted that the reigning methods of cereal and animal husbandry had begun to overreach their limits. Take the three-field system of crop rotation, the technological foundation of early modern Russia, if not most of northern Europe. At the time of its introduction to Russia between 1500 and 1700, it represented a dramatic improvement over its long-fallow predecessors.[14] According to all the questionnaires, peasants throughout the central black earth and non-black-earth regions relied on it because it was so well suited to farming conditions there.[15] In early autumn, one third of arable land was sown with rye, Russia's chief staple crop, renowned for its versatility and toughness. This winter field, as it was customarily called, usually received the lion's share of fertilizer—if farmers had enough manure—and was harvested the following summer. The second portion of arable was reserved for spring crops—mainly oats, barley, buckwheat, peas, flax, and hemp—planted in May or June and harvested three to four months later. What rye was to humans, oats were to horses—a hearty grain well suited to mediocre land and minimal plowing. Barley was the peasant's safety net. Doggedly resistant to frost, drought, and the north wind, it substituted for rye in case the latter failed.[16] Completing the system was the third field, which peasants left fallow in preparation for next year's rye crop and which doubled as additional grazing land for livestock.

For all its advantages, the three-field rotation compelled peasants to cope with the consequences of its extended use. By the time the Society circulated its survey in 1765, the system had absorbed virtually all the available land in the central regions. Six of the seven correspondents reported overpopulation in their respective districts, while four of them linked peasant poverty directly to land hunger, insufficient cattle holdings, or a combination of both.[17] It triggered other imbalances as well. Jerome Blum has noted that wherever in Europe the three-field system was used animal husbandry invariably fell into decline.[18] Russia presented no exception. Correspondents observed that most seigniorial peasants in the central regions owned no more than two or three draught animals plus a few sheep, cows, and pigs. Such tiny herds barely met the subsistence needs of households, and in lean times could spell devastation.[19] To compound the problem, the brief growing season coupled with freezing temperatures diminished the amount of grazing land. In Moscow and Tver provinces, peasants possessed miniscule portions of pasture, resulting in the drastic reduction of the manure they needed to fertilize the rye fields.[20]

Consequently, grain production in the heartland remained mediocre at best and ruinous at worst. According to the Society's own surveys, rye harvests typically produced an average of three to five kernels for every seed sown, lower than any other country in Europe. Records from the great estates of the region indicate that the actual returns were even poorer.[21] Mikhail Shcherbatov, for instance, attempted to increase cereal production on his Yaroslavl estates in the late 1750s. Using the traditional methods of crop rotation, he received only three seeds for each one sown. That was in the good years. Undaunted, he decided to switch his peasants to obrok—exactly the opposite of what he believed was best for his peasants and society in general. But at least it paid off. After 10 years, he had laid the foundations for a profitable textile enterprise, which, by the time of his death in 1790, was one of the most successful in Russia.[22]

The Soviet economic historian P. I. Liashchenko once argued that Russia at the beginning of Catherine's reign stood on the brink of an "agricultural crisis" triggered by the use of primitive farming tools, soil depletion, the short growing season, and epidemics of cattle plague.[23] Alarmist as this interpretation may be, a number of other regional studies of the rural economy corroborate the picture of a steady decline in grain production in the central regions. In an analysis of the Senate's economic questionnaire, Boris Mironov determined that crop failure occurred on average once every seven years. Cattle plague struck with similar frequency. Moreover, in 33 districts of the central region, respondents to the Senate survey complained of constant land hunger, an observation echoed by the Society's provincial writers.[24]

Still, the balance sheet for the central regions indicated that the three-field system met the subsistence needs of the population. Russian peasants might have been poor and exploited, but at least they were hard-working farmers. And although traditional tillage practices certainly diminished the soil's fertility, respondents were encouraged to see all available arable land under cultivation. Moreover, turning to agriculture in the outlying areas to the north, south, and east, we find that public opinion regarded the central regions as the model for an orderly rural economy. In St. Petersburg, Novgorod, and Vologda, for instance, correspondents noisily lamented the decay of agriculture even though their northern provinces were much more thinly populated and the environment ill-suited to farming.[25] In some regions, the dense network of lakes and rivers submerged as much as 50 percent of arable land under water, while arctic winds, autumn rains, and spring frosts often brought devastating crop failures. No small wonder that Jakob Sievers once likened the wasteland of Olonets in Novgorod province to a "monster." So extreme was the climate that Tekut'ev assumed a work season of only 100 days in his instruction for his estate in the same province.[26] To function profitably under these conditions, the three-field system demanded an extraordinarily intensive labor regime. According to Fedot Udolov, manager of government estates in St. Petersburg province, its maintenance required heavy doses of manure, four separate plowings, extensive drainage systems, and constant removal of debris from the fields—all done by hand no less.[27] Although one writer noted that a few lords hired wage labor to perform such backbreaking work, these men were the exception.[28] In the long run, these northerly provinces were destined to become dependencies on grain imports from Ukraine and southern Russia. As settlement and cultivation of the south intensified after 1750, the trend in the north was to place peasants on obrok and to supplement arable farming with so-called "secondary pursuits," usually wage labor in the booming capital of St. Petersburg.[29] It made little sense for northern farmers to agonize over turning bad land into a Garden of Eden.

For the Society's northern correspondents, therein lay the problem. Writing from the swamps of Olonets, Erik Laksman said agriculture was slumping because peasants preferred working in St. Petersburg as carpenters and stone masons to the drudgery of farming. Wage labor also paid considerably more. Having grown accustomed to city life, they regarded "arable farming as work suitable only for old women and children." Other writers likewise emphasized a noticeable decline in cereal cultures due to the combination of infertile soil and rising opportunities for nonagricultural work elsewhere. Aleksei V. Oleshev of Vologda argued that obrok peasants "set a bad example for others who [in time] will likewise wish to abandon agriculture; those left to farm the land will do so half-heartedly and without any good intentions." Baron Frederick von Wol'f from Ingermanland concurred. Obrok triggered a kind of amnesia in peasants, he maintained, making them lose their "taste" for farming or "forget about it altogether."[30] Still another cause of agricultural decline was the peasantry's neglect of the three-field system, which in many areas had to compete with long-fallow and slash-and-burn techniques. Under one method called *podstoi*, old trees were stripped of their bark, dried of their natural juices, and then burned to create a mixture of ash and topsoil. Although capable of producing bumper harvests for two or three years,[31] *podstoi* rapidly depleted the soil of its nutrients and hastened the indiscriminate destruction of Russia's forestland. "[Peasants] go through the old forests," Laksman wrote, "and with their axes mark a spot on an arbitrary number of the biggest trees so that nobody else can take it. Sometimes it happens that the peasant, although having started the job, is unable to finish it, so that the trees dry out and rot without [being put to] any use."[32] Aleksei Aleksandrovich Zasetskii, a *pomeshchik* from Vologda, further noted that many of the local plowmen still employed a primitive two-field rotation, while his neighbor Oleshev bemoaned the three-field system's precarious status and blamed its lapse on the peasantry's "negligence and idleness."[33]

None of the correspondents acknowledged that the peasant's preference for better paying nonagricultural work was entirely rational. Nor did they seem to understand that long-fallow methods, as David Moon has written, "were appropriate in circumstances where there was an abundance of land and a shortage of labor."[34] Instead, they urged managers on government lands and private lords on their own estates to reassert control over their labor force. Laksman recommended forcing *barshchina* on peasants in order to establish orderly agriculture, which for him was synonymous with the three-field system. Oleshev and Zasetskii were less extreme. They hoped for landowners to manage their holdings personally, dispensing bits of practical and philosophical wisdom intended to inspire "every farmer [to] respect his own and the general welfare without severity and cruel punishment."[35]

Like their northern counterparts, correspondents from the black-earth zone also discerned a causal relationship between labor shortages and the "decay of agriculture." As the Orenburg geographer Peter Rychkov wrote: "Owing to its great quantity of the very best farming land, Orenburg province could be counted amongst the most productive places in the entire Russian Empire, if only there were more diligent farmers in it."[36] Historically the frontier where Turkic nomads, Ukrainian Cossacks, and Russian military personnel jostled with each other for supremacy, its rich soil and fertile grasslands had begun to attract Russian settlers in search of more land, abundant harvests, and bigger herds. They were also attracted by a freedom of movement and large landholdings practically unheard of in the heartland. The Soviet historian N. L. Rubenshtein calculated that the average allotment for black-earth peasants after 1750 measured five-six *desiatiny*, as opposed to two-three *desiatiny* in the center.[37] Agricultural productivity also tended to be higher. According to the surveys, the output-seed ratio for winter grain was four times higher than in the center, while spring grains sometimes delivered truly fantastic harvests.[38] Cattle holdings were even more impressive. The correspondent from Sumy in Sloboda Ukraine reported that "lords raise a great deal of cattle," while peasants of the same district typically owned five to ten oxen, three to five horses, and comparable numbers of smaller animals. Moving eastward to Orenburg, where Kirghiz and Bashkir tribes vastly outnumbered Russians, the conditions for animal husbandry were so propitious that Russian peasants owned at least two to three horses, and in some instance as many as twenty.[39]

Yet whenever settlers brought with them their agrarian way of life, serfdom was quick to follow.[40] The surveys vividly captured this process. In Sloboda Ukraine, a province whose native peasants were enserfed only in 1763, one writer from Ostrogozhsk argued that serfdom had actually improved agricultural performance because peasants now had no choice but to cultivate the allotments assigned to them. Another correspondent from the same province reproved peasants for their love of freedom, which supposedly made them bad and lazy farmers.[41] Russification also proceeded in more subtle ways. Throughout Sloboda Ukraine the Society's correspondents observed symptoms of a mature agricultural economy imported from the Russian heartland: the widespread use of the three-field system; the replication of its cereal hierarchy with rye as the chief crop; and the marginalization of nonagricultural work.[42] Two districts even reported equilibrium between farmers and land, a clear indication of the region's assimilation into Russia and a portent of the Empire's further expansion to the south.[43]

Nevertheless, hardly any of the writers from the southern regions observed improvements in farming. Rychkov of Orenburg said it was actually in "decline," an odd claim given that agriculture had barely gotten started in his frontier province.[44] There was a lesson here: while virgin land may promise abundance, outcomes never match the high expectations that inspire its settlement. Indeed, for the Society's correspondents, the natural wealth of the black-earth zone invited its inhabitants to squander it. Rather than devise methods of animal husbandry appropriate to the steppe, peasants used the same techniques developed in the forests of central Russia: in spring and summer they grazed cattle on land abandoned "to nature," while in winter they stabled their livestock in ramshackle barns. Even more disturbing, peasants refused to clean up after their animals. When the mess got out of control, they either dumped it into the street or built a new stable.[45] Correspondents were equally critical of the peasantry's land use practices. Around the Volga town of Saratov, Russian peasants employed field-grass husbandry, a long-fallow method predating the two-field system in which land was cleared of trees and brush, sown for several years, and then left for as long as a decade before being turned over again.[46] Like slash-and-burn in the north, field grass husbandry was a natural adjustment to an abundance of land and scarcity of farmers to work it. While wasteful and primitive from the standpoint of the Society's correspondents, it met the expediency criterion of peasants and required less work than the three-field system. In a similar vein, correspondents from Sloboda Ukraine reproached the peasantry's preference for rye over wheat, even though the latter crop demanded intensive tillage with an English-style plow and was susceptible to weeds. Rychkov alone understood that wheat offered peasants no incentive: "Under these circumstances, is it not difficult to see why we may not increase our wheat harvest without a loss to other crops, and without increasing [the number] of farmers, even though we have suitable land for it in every spot?"[47]

All this carping contained a cruel irony. While writers from the peripheries bemoaned the "decay of agriculture" in their respective provinces, correspondents from the center depicted a stable rural economy rooted in serfdom and the three-field system. Their descriptions of annual peasant work schedules are especially revealing in this regard. Because the three-field rotation framed nearly every aspect of production in the central regions, agricultural labor had to conform to its rhythms and routines. From April through September, peasant life consisted of a long sequence of interlocking and overlapping jobs—"ceaseless work" to quote one writer. Their proper execution demanded strict discipline and exact timing: plowing, fertilizing, sowing, haycutting, harvesting, and threshing.[48] And while the routine slowed down in the winter months, it never stopped altogether as peasants made repairs to tools and houses, cut firewood, grinded grain, weaved sandals, and worked outside the village. Meanwhile in the north, the agricultural regime demanded even closer supervision. In Ingermanland, Baron von Wol'f placed all farming tasks on a timetable so inflexible that, in his mind at least, only serfdom guaranteed their completion:

April 1–April 20: clear fields of debris.
April 20–early May: burn brushwood; plowing and harrowing.
May: sow spring crops (barley, peas, oats, wheat, hemp, flax).
May–June: clear, fertilize, and drain fallow field.
June–July: hay-cutting.
July 20: plow fallow field.
July 25–August 27: sow fallow field with rye.
August: harvest rye; begin harvesting peas and flax.
August 25–September 30: harvest remaining spring crops.
October: carting, threshing, clear debris.[49]

Correspondents from the black-earth region shared Wol'f's sentiments. Rychkov and his counterparts from Sloboda Ukraine sadly reported that most peasants had no work routine of any kind. While peasants in the center spent the winter months engaged in wage labor and secondary pursuits, their counterparts in the south chose to wander around in idleness and drunkenness.[50] The black-earth region needed the institutions of control and the systems of production that had transformed the inhabitants of the heartland into productive farmers.

It is significant that the survey did not include a single question on peasant collective institutions, the village commune in particular. Indeed, the Society showed relatively little interest in what Slavophiles, Populists, and peasant sociologists of the early Soviet period later regarded as the true foundation of Russian civilization. The Society expected the institutions and customs of the Russian peasantry to bend and eventually break under the pressure of improved economic practices. Especially in the central black-earth and non-black-earth regions, whose resources were scarce and population most dense, peasants depended on the commune (*obshchina, mir*) to achieve collective survival. In most cases, the commune consisted of all the households (*dvor*) in a village, while each household in turn included smaller labor teams (*tiaglo*), typically comprised of an able-bodied married couple, and, on some estates, a draught animal.[51] The labor teams, household, and commune converged in a single mechanism of production that adapted to shifting conditions. Flexibility was its chief virtue. On any given estate, the communal assembly assigned strips of land of varying size and fertility to labor teams in individual households. Large households blessed with multiple labor teams typically cultivated a commensurately large number of strips, while smaller ones were allotted modest ones or perhaps none at all. In extreme circumstances, the commune had the power to dissolve dilapidated households and disperse their members amidst other families of the village. These were exceptional cases, however, and the majority of peasant households in the central regions contained two or three labor teams.[52] It was these middle peasants who paid most of the rent and taxes and shouldered the responsibilities in the village. In the absence of provincial government at the district level, middle peasants performed a variety of other services: law enforcement, estate management, tax collection, land surveying, and conscription of soldiers. The commune wielded considerable power in the day-to-day administration of the estate, and lords only rarely interfered in agricultural production and land redistribution.

In adjusting to exploitation from above and material scarcity from below, the commune perpetuated a remarkable welfare system based on the life cycle of the peasant household.[53] Yet communal practices also clashed with the spirit of innovation that the Free Economic Society wished to promote. In a classic study of peasant mentalities, the anthropologist George M. Foster once argued that constant scarcity at the village level produces a "cognitive orientation" founded on the premise that "all of the desired things in life such as land, wealth, friendship, and love... *exist in finite quantity and are always in short supply.*" As a result of this "limited good" mentality, peasants tend to view modern economic virtues like thrift, innovation, and investment as unnecessary and irrational burdens because wealth, like land, "can be divided up and passed around in various ways, but, within the framework of the villagers' traditional world, it does not grow." Like agricultural producers in most subsistence economies, Russian peasants reacted to material scarcity through "maximum cooperation" institutionalized in the commune.[54] To the improvers in the Society, however, peasant collective practices symbolized the stubborn persistence of custom. In describing the allocation of strips in his village, Bolotov observed that nowhere did the peasant "[have] all his own land enclosed around his own house, or at least close to it, but everywhere it is generally scattered across all the fields which belong to the village." Bolotov saw two contrary forces at work: on one side the household, the nucleus of a potential family farm, and on the other the commune, which he branded as the "greatest obstacle" to agricultural progress.[55] In his view, the intermingling of strips made it virtually impossible for the peasant to use the land "according to his wishes." Everywhere the peasant looked, he beheld a bewildering mishmash of strips belonging simultaneously to everybody and nobody:

> [The] peasant cannot walk one step from his house without being cramped on two sides by other houses, on the third side by a river, brook, or hill, and on the fourth by a house belonging to another landowner. Owing to this he not only has no place where he can set up a garden, orchard, or something else that is useful to his household economy, but he does not even have enough space for a vegetable garden which is so essential for his sustenance... [he remains] silent over the land belonging to foreign households which surround his own, and [says nothing] about the cattle and poultry overrunning his own land which he is powerless to stop.[56]

The economic orientation of the peasantry also percolated up to the land-owning class. In the interests of expediency, nobles and peasants found themselves "prisoners of the same system," to use Michel Confino's words. Even the large estates of the wealthiest absentee aristocrats were managed like the dwarf holdings of the petty nobility, for virtually all land throughout the central regions was under the direct administration of peasant communes, divided into strips scattered far and wide across different estates, and redistributed with the cyclical formation and disintegration of peasant households. Given that inheritance practices required nobles to divide their own property equally among all their heirs, even the largest and most sprawling manors tended to fragment quickly and blend into neighboring estates.[57] None of this boded well for the improvers and modernizers in the Free Economic Society.

Yet for the vast majority of peasants and provincial nobles, there was no decay of agriculture. The Society's questionnaire presented evidence of Russian agriculture's slow and steady expansion. Emanating from the Muscovite heartland, Russia's agrarian systems had spread northward through the vast forests while colonizing the black soil of the southern steppe as far east as the Central Asian frontier. By the mid-eighteenth century in the central region, extensive long-fallow practices such as slash-and-burn had yielded almost

completely to the cyclical, and unspectacular regularities of the three-field
system. The stability of the three-field system made peasant culture and
economy seem so timeless to correspondents from the heartland. Moreover,
the availability of fertile black soil in the southern expanses of the empire
and opportunities for supplementary wage labor in St. Petersburg offset the
temporary imbalances caused by Russia's growing population. As Arcadius
Kahan once wrote, "there was no scarcity of land in general or even within
particular regions. Land scarcity could occur on a particular estate and persist
only under conditions of immobility of resources, an untenable assumption."[58] Meanwhile, peripheral areas to the north, south, and east continued
to employ a diverse array of farming strategies adapted to the specificities of
their natural environments and the needs of their inhabitants. Correspondents
from these parts tended to be more critical of local peasant practices than
their counterparts from the center where serfdom and the three-field system
were entrenched.

Analyzing the survey data in 1771, Klingshtedt discerned the deterioration
of Russia's traditional agrarian regime the further one moved from the central
regions. Why, he asked, did peasants in the most fertile areas of the empire
seem to be the least productive? He concluded that the root cause of Russia's
woeful agricultural performance was the peasantry's subsistence mentality, not
the servile labor regime or the harsh extremities of its climate. Russian peasants
were no lazier than European ones, just a lot more primitive: "The history of
European countries demonstrates that in their youthful days, nations (*narody*)
tend to produce only for subsistence... It is well known that the less corrected
the morals of a nation, the less it is aware of the comforts of life because of its
own wildness, and, not extending its wants any further, prefers idleness alone
to all other pastimes."[59] Klingshtedt noted the most visible symptoms of the
peasantry's fatalism: bland and boring diets; simple fur coats; bast sandals;
dingy taverns. Who could blame peasants for living in squalor and passing
the same low expectations on to the next generation? To break the cycle of
poverty, he recommended implanting peasant communities with a taste for the
"luxuries" that Erik Laksman had condemned as ruinous to agriculture. The
time had come for Russia to advance to the next stage of societal development
by "applying all our efforts to the general prosperity... [As] soon as a demand
[for luxury] is transformed into a necessity through the force of custom, then we
can undoubtedly expect that every peasant will attempt to improve and increase
animal husbandry and to satisfy his demands through his own labor, and thus,
hoping to work only to satisfy his own desires, will further the general welfare,
while satisfying his most essential needs through arable farming."[60]

Klingshtedt assured his readers that accustoming peasants to certain "luxuries" did not entail granting them personal freedom and property rights. The

surveys from Sloboda Ukraine demonstrated that "giving freedom to people who do not know how to use it does them far more harm than good, and that freedom alone cannot prevent idleness nor prevent the poverty that results from it." Nor did he cave in to the widely held assumption that peasants feigned poverty in order to prevent landowners from stealing their surplus. While he admitted that a few "simpleminded lords" might tyrannize their peasants in that way, such conduct was obviously out of step with the "gentle morals and ideas" of this "enlightened century."[61] Klingshtedt took the middle ground between these two extremes. Surveys from the central regions generally depicted lords as fair, reasonable, and reluctant to abuse their power over their serfs. The same data presented peasants as responsible and hard-working subjects despite their servile legal status and adherence to custom. Furthermore, the reforms of Peter the Great and his successors offered proof that new "tastes" could indeed be implanted in a people from above. "Human nature is the same regardless of morals, status, inclinations, and geographical location," Klingshtedt reminded his readers. If Westernization worked for the nobility, then similar results could be achieved for the peasantry, provided it was done slowly and without disrupting Russia's social hierarchies.[62]

Many people disagreed with Klingshtedt. Some could not trust nobles to implement meaningful improvements without being forced to do it by the state. Others wondered why serfs should work harder at anything, let alone agriculture on such barren soil. And then there were those who had trouble imagining treating their peasants like anything other than cattle. But in the 1760s and early 1770s, when Catherine's reform program was still a novelty, the idea of the enlightened seigneur who voluntarily limited his power while leading his "natural inferiors" to the next stage of civilization resonated with portions of the educated public. It would guide the Free Economic Society as it hesitantly opened the first public debate on the peasant question in Russia.

NOTES

1. S. Kozlov, *Agrarnye traditsii i novatsii v doreformennoi Rossii (tsentral'no-nechernozemnye gubernii)* (Moscow: ROSSPEN, 2002): 138–39.

2. Marc Bloch, *French Rural History: An Essay on Its Basic Characteristics*, translated by Janet Sondheimer (Berkeley: University of California Press, 1966), xxvi.

3. On the Senate and Cadet Corps surveys, see Michael Confino, "Les enquêtes économiques de la 'Société libre d'économie de Saint-Pétersbourg' (1765–1820)," *Revue Historique* 227 (1962): 156–58; on Sievers, see Robert E. Jones, *Provincial Development in Russia: Catherine II and Jacob Sievers* (New Brunswick, NJ: Rutgers University Press, 1984), 52.

4. "Ekonomicheskie voprosy kasaiushchiesia do zemledeliia po raznosti provint-sii," *Trudy* 1 (1765): 190–203 (pagination incorrect in original).

5. Shovlin, 53.

6. Milov, *Velikorusskii pakhar'*, 33.

7. Klingshtedt, "Opisanie nadobnosti v poluchenii luchshago svedeniia o zem-ledelii i o vnutrennem derevenskom khoziaistve, kak onyia nyne v raznykh provint-siiakh i nekotorye voprosy kasaiushchiesia do sei materii," *Trudy* 1 (1765): 186–87.

8. David Moon, *The Russian Peasantry: The World the Peasants Made* (London: Longman, 1999), 104; V.M. Kabuzan, *Narodonaselenie Rossii v XVIII-pervoi po-lovine XIX v. (po materialam revizii)* (Moscow: Nauka, 1963), 159–63.

9. Moon, 70–71.

10. "Otvety Pereslavl'skoi provintsii Rezanskago," *Trudy* 7 (1767): 62; "Eko-nomicheskie otvety Pereslavl'skoi provintsii Zalesskago," *Trudy* 7 (1767): 96; "Otvety na ekonomicheskie voprosy po Galitskoi provintsii," *Trudy* 10 (1768): 86; "Otvety po Kaluzhskoi provintsii na zadannye ekonomicheskie voprosy," *Trudy* 11 (1769): 101; "Otvety kasaiushchiesia do zemledeliia na ekonomicheskie voprosy, o uezde goroda Volodimira," *Trudy* 12 (1769): 105.

11. *Trudy* 7 (1767): 75, 81–82, 105, 109–10; *Trudy* 10 (1768): 93, 96; *Trudy* 11 (1769): 114, 119–20; *Trudy* 12 (1769): 112, 115.

12. A. Bolotov, "Opisanie svoistva i dobroty zemel' Kashirskago uezda i prochikh do sego uezda kasaiushchikhsia obstoiatel'stve, otvetami na predlozhennye voprosy," *Trudy* 2 (1766): 184, 210–11, 216–19; see also V. Priklanskii, "Otvety na zadannye ot Vol'nago Ekonomicheskago Obshchestva, kasaiushchiesia do zemledeliia i vnutren-niago derevenskago khoziaistva po Kashinskomu uezdu," *Trudy* 26 (1774): 45–46, 89.

13. Arcadius Kahan, *The Plow, the Hammer, and the Knout: An Economic His-tory of Eighteenth-Century Russia* (Chicago: University of Chicago Press, 1985), 13; Milov, *Velikorusskii pakhar'*, 14–15, 157.

14. Michel Confino, *Systèmes agraires et progrès agricole: L'assolement triennial en Russia aux XVIIIe-XIXe siècles* (Paris: Mouton, 1971), 33–7; Moon, 127.

15. *Trudy* 2 (1766): 155–7; *Trudy* 7 (1767): 56, 89–90; *Trudy* 10 (1768): 83; *Trudy* 11 (1769): 93; *Trudy* 12 (1769): 101; *Trudy* 26 (1774): 22.

16. On rye, oats, and barley, see Milov, *Velikorusskii pakhar'*, 35–37.

17. *Trudy* 2 (1766): 180–81, 197, 208–10; *Trudy* 7 (1767): 60–61, 94, 105; *Trudy* 10 (1768): 85, 95; *Trudy* 11 (1769): 99, 113, 118; *Trudy* 12 (1769): 104, 112, 114. See also Milov, *Velikorusskii pakhar'*, 55.

18. Blum, *End of the Old Order*, 147–50.

19. *Trudy* 2 (1766): 146–7; *Trudy* 7 (1767): 53, 85; *Trudy* 11 (1769): 89; *Trudy* 12 (1769): 99; *Trudy* 26 (1774): 11–12; see also Milov, *Velikorusskii pakhar'*, 212.

20. Milov, *Velikorusskii pakhar'*, 195–98.

21. *Trudy* 2 (1766): 129–34; *Trudy* 7 (1767): 51, 83–84; *Trudy* 10 (1768): 79–80; Trudy 11 (1769): 86; *Trudy* 12 (1769): 97; *Trudy* 26 (1774): 5. See also the data for output/seed ratios in Milov, *Velikorusskii pakhar'*, 159, 164–65; Kahan, 50; and Blum, *Lord and Peasant in Russia*, 330.

22. Wallace Daniel, "Conflict between Economic Vision and Economic Reality: The Case of M. M. Shcherbatov," *Slavonic and East European Review* 67 (1989): 52–63.

23. P. I. Liashchenko, "Krepostnoe sel'skoe khoziaistvo Rossii v XVIII veke," *Istoricheskie zapiski* 15 (1945): 120–21.

24. B. N. Mironov, "Sel'skoe khoziaistvo Rossii v 60-kh godakh XVIII veka (po dannym senatskoi ankety 1767 goda)," in *Materialy po istorii sel'skogo khoziaistva SSSR*, sbornik 4 (Moscow: Nauka, 1980), 224–28, 233. See also E. A. Nersesova, "Ekonomicheskoe sostoianie Kostromskoi provintsii Moskovskoi gubernii po khoziaistvennym anketam 1760-kh godov," *Istoricheskie zapiski* 40 (1952): 161, 173; B. D. Grekov, "Opyt obsledovaniia khoziaistvennykh anket XVIII veka," in *Izbrannye trudy*, 3 (Moscow: Nauka, 1960), 279–80; L.V. Milov, "O proizvoditel'nosti truda v zemledelii Rossii v seredine XVIII v. (po materialam monastyrskoi barshchiny), *Istoricheskie zapiski* 85 (1970): 229–31, 243–45, 256–68, 264.

25. On the low population density in Olonets, Vologda, and Esel, see E. Laksman, "Ekonomicheskie otvety kasaiushchiesia do khlebopashestva v lezhashchikh okolo reki Sviri i Iushnoi chasti Olontsa mestakh," *Trudy* 13 (1769): 37; I. Gronov, "Poluchennye iz Ezel'skoi provintsii otvety na zadannye ot V-ago E-ago O-va voprosy, kasaiushchiesia do khlebopashestva i sel'skago domostroitel'stva," *Trudy* 13 (1769): 90; A. Zasetskii, "Otvety na ekonomicheskie voprosy, kasaiushchiesia do zemledeliia v Vologodskom uezde," *Trudy* 23 (1773): 268.

26. Quoted in Jones, *Provincial Development in Russia*, 78. See also *Trudy* 13 (1769): 8; "Prodolzhenie otvetov gospodina Barona Vul'fa na zadannye v pervoi chasti ekonomicheskie voprosy," *Trudy* 3 (1766): 124–30; A. Oleshev, "O neurozhae rzhi," *Trudy* 5 (1767): 132–34; and Smilianskaia, 71–75.

27. F. Udolov, "Sobranie ekonomicheskikh pravil," *Trudy* 15 (1770): 91–94, 98–99, 101–2.

28. *Trudy* 3 (1766): 120.

29. V. M. Kabuzan, *Izmeneniia v razmeshchenii naseleniia Rossii v XVIII-pervoi polovine XIX v.* (Moscow: Nauka, 1971), 22–28. See also Kahan, 49; and Moon, 56, 71.

30. *Trudy* 13 (1769): 25–26; A. Oleshev, "Opisanie godovoi krest'ianskoi raboty," *Trudy* 2 (1766): 111–12; Wol'f, "Prodolzhenie otvetov gospodina Barona fon Vul'fa na zadannye v pervoi chasti ekonomicheskie voprosy," *Trudy* 10 (1768): 66. See also *Trudy* 13 (1769): 99.

31. *Trudy* 1 (1765): 93; *Trudy* 13 (1769): 14.

32. *Trudy* 13 (1769): 20; Milov, *Velikorusskii pakhar'*, 46–52.

33. *Trudy* 23 (1773): 237; *Trudy* 2 (1766): 109.

34. Moon, 128.

35. *Trudy* 13 (1769): 28; *Trudy* 23 (1773): 249; "Druzheskie sovety blagorodnym sel'skim zhiteliam, v dvukh otdelenniakh sostoiashche: iz onykh pervoe o Dobrodetelei i Porokakh, vtoroe o Zemledelii i Domostroitel'stvo," *Trudy* 6 (1767): 3.

36. P. I. Rychkov, "Otvety na ekonomicheskie voprosy, kasaiushchiesiia do zemledelii, po raznosti provintsii kratko i po vozmozhnosti iz"iasnenye v razsuzhdenii Orenburgskoi gubernii," *Trudy* 7 (1767): 115.

37. Rubinshtein, *Sel'skoe khoziaistvo Rossii*, 218, 228, 232. One *desiatin* equals 2.7 acres.

38. "Prodolzhenie otvetov, na predlozhenye v pervoi chasti trudov V-ago E-ago O-va voprosy, o nyneshnem sostoianii v raznykh guberniiakh i provintsiiakh zemledeliia i

domostroitel'stva, po Slobodskoi Ukrainskoi provintsii," *Trudy* 8 (1768): 76; "Toishe Slobodskoi gubernii po Iziumskoi provintsii," *Trudy* 8 (1768): 101–2; "Po Akhtyrskoi provintsii," *Trudy* 8 (1768): 134; "Po Ostrogozhskoi provintsii," *Trudy* 8 (1768): 160–61. Rychkov claimed that the seed/output ratio for millet in Orenburg often soared to 1:70. See *Trudy* 7 (1767): 116.

39. *Trudy* 7 (1767): 135–6; *Trudy* 8 (1768): 78, 103–4, 189.

40. Willard Sunderland, *Taming the Wild Field: Colonization and Empire on the Russian Steppe* (Ithaca, NY: Cornell University Press, 2004), 61. See also Bolotov's observations on resettlement from Tula to the Belgorod region in *Trudy* 2 (1766): 197.

41. *Trudy* 8 (1768): 112, 129, 170–71.

42. Ibid., 80–82, 95–96, 105–6, 107–9, 125, 138, 141–43, 148, 154, 164, 181, 191, 192–3, 200.

43. Ibid., 84, 95, 197, 213.

44. *Trudy* 7 (1767): 155; *Trudy* 8 (1768): 86, 114, 148, 200.

45. *Trudy* 7 (1767): 135–36; *Trudy* 8 (1768): 78–79, 105, 137, 146, 163, 190, 196.

46. "Primechaniia na lezhashchiia okolo Saratova mesta, v razsuzhdenii sel'skago domostroitel'stva," *Trudy* 7 (1767): 31–32.

47. *Trudy* 7 (1767): 123.

48. Ibid., 105; Moon, 123–26.

49. *Trudy* 3 (1766): 122–28.

50. *Trudy* 7 (1767): 185; *Trudy* 8 (1768): 96, 125, 183.

51. Moon, 119, 200–201.

52. Aleksandrov, 191–203.

53. On the peasant household under serfdom, see Peter Czap Jr., "The Perennial Multiple Family Household, Mishino, Russia, 1782-1858," *Journal of Family History* 7 (1982): 6, 10–11.

54. George M. Foster, "Peasant Society and the Image of Limited Good," *American Anthropologist* 67 (1965): 296, 298 (italics in original).

55. A. Bolotov, "Opisanie svoistva i dobroty zemel'," 162.

56. Ibid., 171–72.

57. Confino, *Domaines et Seigneurs*, 128–29.

58. Kahan, 45.

59. Klingshtedt, "Iz"iasnenie voprosa," *Trudy* 16 (1771): 240.

60. Ibid., 242–43, 244–46.

61. Ibid., 238, 247.

62. Ibid., 242, 246.

Chapter Three

Patrons and the Peasant Question

The Free Economic Society's topographical survey passed over the topic of serfdom, and for good reason. In the minds of many, Russia's peculiar institution lay at the foundation of the service hierarchy that framed its civilization. Like medieval Europeans, whose social theory distinguished between nobles who fought, clergy who prayed, and the rest who worked, the Society tacitly believed that the privileges and obligations of an individual corresponded to the rank and function of one's social estate, or *soslovie*, in the larger order. Even before the reign of Peter the Great, the nobility's control of land and labor depended on military and administrative service to the ruler. Merchants and craftsmen, for their part, operated their businesses in exchange for providing the government with the goods and services necessary for administering the realm. Peasants knew mainly duties: food production, extraction of raw materials, the poll tax, and, for the truly unlucky, military conscription, which spanned twenty-five years.

Like any paradigm, universal state service displayed contradictions that undermined its core assumptions. After 1725, it became government policy to favor noble aspirations and interests, particularly regarding serfdom. The Legislative Commission of the 1750s not only reaffirmed the right of nobles to own serfs, but authorized them to inflict corporal punishment, break up peasant families, arrange marriages, and exile refractory serfs to Siberia.[1] Peter III's manifesto of 1762 empowered the nobility even more, making available to them a world of possibilities hitherto unimaginable—most importantly the right to live free of the constrictions that applied to most everybody else. When Catherine II's Legislative Commission convened in Moscow five years later, noble delegates sought to strengthen their prerogatives at the expense of the other estates. The most intense debates pitted nobles against merchants as the latter defended their commercial interests while trying to infringe on the privileges of the former. Meanwhile, provincial noble delegates insisted that serf ownership remain an exclusive noble monopoly.[2] In light of the nobility's opposition to curbing their own privileges, the prospects for limiting serfdom—their most prized privilege of all—seemed dim indeed.

Although Catherine personally opposed serfdom, and had even once outlined a plan for gradual emancipation before coming to power,[3] most scholars agree that her reign marks the low point for the Russian peasantry. According to the pre-revolutionary historian V. I. Semevskii, under Catherine "serfdom was intensified in depth and extent." In a similar vein, A. S. Lappo-Danilevskii concluded that "the right to hold serfs, long related to slave-holding, came more and more to resemble a private property right."[4] Instead of improving the position of serfs, so the argument goes, Catherine implemented landmark reforms designed to transform the Russian nobility into a ruling class of landlords and serf owners as well as state servants. For this reason, some believe it premature to trace the origins of the Russian peasant question back to her reign.[5] There would be no peasant legislation under Catherine's watch comparable in scale or substance to Joseph II's agrarian reforms in the Habsburg Empire of the 1780s. The first piece of real agrarian legislation came in 1803 with the Free Cultivators Law, which permitted nobles to manumit serfs on a voluntary basis. This was only after the French Revolution had compelled Tsar Alexander I to begin limiting serfdom lest the Romanovs meet the same fate as the Bourbons in France.

Yet in ending mandatory service for the nobility, Peter III had unintentionally left the door open for redefining the status, privileges, and obligations of the other social orders. In March 1762 he decreed the secularization of monastic estates, placing nearly 1,000,000 male souls under state jurisdiction with the expectation that their higher status would make them more diligent farmers. Catherine continued her late husband's unfinished business, finalizing the reform of monastic peasants with the creation of the Economic College and charging it with the administration of this new class of "economic" peasants.[6] She also opened vast stretches of territory in the south to foreign settlement, luring colonists with cheap land grants, self-government, and exemption from taxes and military service.[7] This policy resulted in the creation of a small but significant free farming population in the steppe, offsetting the decline in the eighteenth century of the free homesteaders (*odnodvortsy*) and portending similarly far-reaching agrarian legislation in the future.

In the meantime the Empress began to solicit proposals from her intimate circle of friends and advisors for the reform of serfdom in the heart of Russia itself. At first the discussion centered on peasant land tenure and property rights. Certainly its best known participant was the great aristocrat Dmitrii Alekseevich Golitsyn. While serving as Russia's Minister to Paris in the

1760s, Golitsyn became a convert to the ideas of the French physiocrats, the famous school of economists who insisted that private property in land formed the basis for agricultural abundance and national wealth. In correspondence of 1765 and 1766 with his brother (but read by Catherine nonetheless), Golitsyn praised the supposed benefits of private property for peasants: social stability, commercial prosperity, and advancements in the arts and sciences. While clinging to the common prejudice that Russian peasants were inclined to idleness, he also held that they could be enlightened before winning their freedom. Golitsyn even sketched out a reform for the gradual introduction of peasant landownership, first on Crown estates and later on the demesnes of the nobility, who, so he assumed, would voluntarily follow her example. His vision of the vast Russian countryside teeming with private homesteads and independent farmers calls to mind Thomas Jefferson's agrarian dreams for the young United States. Catherine's response, scribbled in the margins, showed more common sense: "Magnanimity comes easily and cheaply to Golitsyn and those like him. It is nothing for him to give his peasants landed property rights, but rich landowners, whose peasants number in the many thousands, will think and act differently."[8]

Others came forward with less far-fetched proposals. Jakob Sievers, one of the leading members of the Free Economic Society, had implemented fixed rents for the peasants of Korostina, a court estate near Novgorod city. Emulating Baltic Germans in the province of Livonia, Sievers believed that rational and paternalistic administration could eliminate peasant destitution and reinforce noble power.[9] While Sievers was busy at Korostina, the Lutheran Pastor and future Society member Johann Georg Eisen was making his own waves at court. Originally from the German state of Franconia, Eisen first came to the attention of Peter III and later the Society member Grigorii Orlov, who in 1764 hired him to administer his northern estate at Ropša. Little is known about Eisen's activities there, and he was dismissed after only two years. But he did manage to circulate his ideas in a number of abolitionist tracts, including one published in 1764 just as Catherine was attempting to institute a modest land reform in Livonia.[10] Eisen advocated personal freedom for serfs and a system of land tenure called hereditary leasehold, which, while not the same as private property in the modern sense, afforded peasants some measure of legal protection from their lords. Like other cameralists, Eisen favored cautious reform that maintained the nobility's privileges. As he described this system, the "peasant shall own his land as property" and the "nobility shall possess overlordship over the peasant farms and shall enjoy in addition to the other noble rights and freedoms an hereditary rent."[11] Significantly, the Livonian nobles who assembled in the Landtag at Riga in early 1765 to debate land reform resisted any intervention in the landlord-serf relationship by the state. After three months of debate, the Landtag reluctantly agreed to regulate all manorial dues, to grant peasants access to lower courts, and to permit them ownership of moveable property. Yet the terms of the new law still favored the nobility: it obliged peasants to settle all debts with their masters before selling their moveable property and preserved the landlords' power to fix labor dues. Corporal punishment and hard labor, the most dehumanizing features of personal bondage, remained fully in force.[12]

Catherine and the Free Economic Society also heard related proposals for the reorganization of peasant villages. By far the best known came from Ivan Perfil'evich Elagin, Catherine's personal secretary and a prominent St. Petersburg Freemason, who suggested reorganizing the traditional husband-wife *tiaglo* into much larger units consisting of four married couples and their dependents. Under his plan, land allotments would be large enough to meet all of the tiaglo's needs and under no circumstances could they be transferred or alienated.[13] A similar project was presented before the Free Economic Society at the same time by Fedot Udolov. Like Pastor Eisen, Udolov was the client of Grigorii Orlov, who had him accepted into the Society in October 1765 on the strength of Udolov's magnum opus, a massive mishmash of instructions entitled "Collection of Economic Regulations."[14] Udolov shared the prevailing opinion that agriculture had fallen into decline, but, unlike Eisen, attributed it to obrok, which he claimed encouraged peasants "to live and do as they please" and resulted in the "misfortune that the very farmers who should be feeding everyone else are taking grain from society."[15] Waxing nostalgic for the "old way" of estate management, which, as he said, "counted, numbered, and forced [peasants] to live in large families," he urged landowners to establish a "new rural order" characterized by large *tiagla* (plural of tiaglo), permanent land allotments, intensified supervision of peasants, and the expulsion from the village of all misfits and stragglers—the so-called *bobyli*. As he phrased it, peasants should be content with handing over their surplus and following the selfless example of "the fighting men who throw themselves in harm's way and sacrifice their lives for the fatherland."[16]

Udolov took micromanagement to unprecedented extremes—his proposal exemplifies what Richard Stites has called the "administrative utopia" of eighteenth-century Russian reformers.[17] He envisioned an enormous *barshchina* regime in which peasants were evenly distributed across the Russian plain, living in perfect balance with each other and their environment. Each village would consist of 20 tiagla devoted exclusively to farming and animal husbandry and located far away from all highways, navigable rivers, and markets. In contrast to the traditional husband-wife tiaglo, Udolov's labor team consisted of six adult men and their spouses who received exactly 60 *desiat-*

iny of inalienable land directly from the estate.[18] Superimposed on this village was a revamped administration under the authority of the *nachal'nik*, a functionary appointed by the lord whose responsibilities included everything from overseeing plowing to resolving petty domestic squabbles. The nachal'nik in turn worked closely with a village elder (*sotskii*), elected directly by the masters of the tiaglo. Udolov's administration formed a pyramid structure of authority as orders flowed down from the lord through the nachal'nik and elder to the master of the tiaglo. The commune obviously had no function in this scheme: all unauthorized meetings of the village assembly were banned on the grounds that "rowdy" and "shiftless idlers" would use it "to break all the rules" and "disturb the peace." It fell to the village elder to extirpate these "evildoers" and "troublemakers."[19]

Amidst the flurry of activity and discussion over the peasant question, an anonymous letter arrived at the Free Economic Society in November 1765 that summarized the status of the debate thus far and requested the assembly to break the deadlock. Its author was almost certainly the Empress:

> Many intelligent authors have shown, and experience itself demonstrates, that there can be neither skilled handicrafts nor firmly established commerce where agriculture is shunned or practiced carelessly, and that agriculture cannot flourish where the farmer (*zemledelets*) owns no property. All this is based on a very simple rule: every man cares more about that which is his own than that which he fears another may take away from him. Having established the certainty of this rule, it remains for me to ask you to resolve [the following question]: for the sake of encouraging agriculture, of what does and should the farmer's landed property and inheritance consist? Some claim that it consists of land belonging to a father, his son, and his descendents, along with acquired moveable (i.e., personal) and immoveable property (i.e., land) of any kind; others by contrast recommend assigning a single parcel of land to four to eight people from different families and making the eldest member of this unit the chief or so-called master (*khozianin*). From this it follows that the son is not the father's heir. Consequently, he does not own any property, but rather property belongs to the unit, and not the individual. I have found myself in great confusion not knowing whether the word "property" is used here in an exact or speculative sense. Hitherto I have considered property to be that which cannot be taken away from either me or my children without legal cause, and in my opinion that should make me industrious. But my views on this are not finalized and I, having great respect for you, await an explanation for me and my descendents of your resolution of this.[20]

The Society's immediate reaction to the letter is revealing. In the preface to the first volume of the *Trudy* Klingshtedt had written that "speculative knowledge" fell outside the Society's field of expertise.[21] Since defining property qualified as speculation, the assembly chose to file the letter away and concentrate on projects that promised more tangible results: competitions for exporting wheat, storing grain, and distilling vodka, to name only a few.[22] Thus matters stood until a year later when another communication appeared, this time signed by a mysterious "I.E.," acknowledged by most historians as the initials for "Imperatritsa Ekaterina" (Empress Catherine). Nartov presented it to the assembly on November 1, 1766:

> It has come to my attention that you have insufficient funds for distributing your rewards to the public . . . [For] this reason, I am asking you to accept 1,000 gold pieces, which I have enclosed for those needs which you deem necessary. But I would be pleased if you would first present a question to the public with promise of a reward to whomever explains the following: What does the property of a farmer consist of—the land which he works or his moveable property, and how can he be granted the right to one or the other for the good of all society?[23]

When flattery failed, a chest full of gold succeeded. Nartov speedily reworded the question to read: "Would it be more useful for society for peasants to own immoveable property or only moveable property, and how far should this right be extended?" Two weeks later the notice was printed in the *St. Petersburg Vedomosti* and appended at the last minute to the *Trudy*.[24] It soon was announced in publications across Europe. Offering a first-place prize of 100 gold pieces in addition to a medal, the Society set the cutoff date at November 1, 1767, a deadline it later extended by nearly five months. As was the custom during the eighteenth century, authors were required to conceal their identities with mottos. Although the Society made no plans to publish the winning entries, it resolved at the time to destroy the others. Fortunately for historians, they changed their mind. Nearly all of the essays have been preserved in the manuscript division of the Russian National Library in St. Petersburg. Uncovered in 1996 by the French and Russian scholars Georges Dulac and V. A. Somov, they still await publication.[25]

Judging by the enormous volume of entries—162 in six different languages—it was assumed by all that the Empress had some hand in initiating the contest. No other Society competition before or after elicited such an impressive response.[26] Participants viewed it as an opportunity to project onto Russia their dreams of social reform in their own countries, while Catherine used it to reinforce her carefully crafted image as an enlightened monarch at home and abroad.[27] As a result, it became something of an international event. Nearly all of the entries were written in foreign languages, 129 in German alone, including one by Pastor Eisen. Prominent contestants included Voltaire (who actually entered not once, but twice), his fellow French philosophe Marmontel, and the physiocrat Du Pont de Nemours. Only seven essays were in Russian, none of them from the Society's provincial correspondents. One scholar has argued that the young Alexander Radishchev submitted an essay which the Society labeled #71, but this is highly doubtful since the letter was postmarked in Moscow and the future author of *A Journey from St. Petersburg to Moscow* was studying in Leipzig at the time.[28]

The meager Russian response to the contest highlighted the nobility's refusal to acknowledge the peasant question as a legitimate issue. In a letter to the Society from November 1766, the playwright Alexander Petrovich Sumarokov stressed the pointlessness of debating property rights for peasants without freeing them first. Not that he supported the latter option. Liberating peasants, he claimed, was like freeing a caged canary or unchaining a rabid dog: "One will fly away and the other will start biting people . . . freedom for the peasant would not only be harmful to society, but ruinous."[29] His friend Mikhail Shcherbatov agreed. In a response to the contest question that he chose not to submit, the future court historian declared that peasants lacked sufficient knowledge of agronomy to produce the grain needed to feed the country. Rather than grant their peasants freedom and property, nobles should return to their ancestral estates as enlightened citizens in order to wean their peasants from the "old ways" of husbandry. He urged the Society to lead the movement: "All of Russia, which looks upon you as sincere friends, awaits your advice, not your orders; all reasonable people will follow it down to the last detail, and the profits they earn from it for themselves will be emulated by others and become the general custom, working for the general welfare of Russia, the glory of our ruling monarch, and also yourselves."[30]

The poor quality of some of the Russian submissions also testified to the primitive conditions of public discourse in the empire. In contrast to foreign contestants who knew natural law theory but lacked knowledge of the real conditions in rural Russia, these writers spouted the kind of homespun wisdom found in the *Domostroi*. One essayist opened with a self-effacing paean to the Society's leaders, who have "inspired this remote [rural] dweller to pick up the uncustomary instrument of the pen." Another employed crude analogical reasoning to endorse limited property rights for peasants: "The peasant who owns land, but not movable property, is like a man who has only one hand but needs to pick up two melons off the ground." A third argued against property rights for peasants using similarly raw language: "Our peasants [are] . . . lazy, stubborn, unzealous, spiteful, and inclined to deceit and brigandage . . . Since [they] are born and raised in slavery and ignorance, they require coercion and restriction to be contained." If the Society really wanted to improve the rural economy, they should pay a visit to "the smallest village" managed by a pomeshchik without the interference of courts, officials, or stewards. Only there would it find "the best correction for the sickness oppressing [rural] inhabitants" without ruining the peasants.[31] The writer did not elaborate on this last point, although we may assume that "the best correction" was a resident landlord who honored local custom and family tradition.

Over the course of the next eighteen months the assembly reviewed all 162 submissions, narrowing the field to a short list of 15 finalists, nine of which were in German and five in French (including one by Voltaire). Only one of the final essays was in Russian; its author was Aleksei Iakovlevich Polenov, a young translator for the Academy of Sciences.[32] We can only speculate on the criteria used to determine the finalists. M. T. Beliavskii, the leading Soviet authority on the subject, once asserted that the assembly favored essays which helped maintain Catherine's "enlightened façade."[33] There is some evidence to support his argument. Although many believed that Polenov's work deserved first-place honors, some "found it to contain utterances which are strong by today's standards, and for this reason think it necessary for someone in the assembly, if he knows the author, to instruct him to make corrections in haste."[34] Ivan Taubert, Polenov's patron at the Academy, conveyed the message to his client. The result was a massively diluted version which deleted or drastically revised two-thirds of the original. Perhaps the assembly regarded Polenov's masterpiece as a thunderous criticism of serfdom and moved to suppress it for that reason.[35] Yet other evidence suggests that the assembly simply wanted writers to follow the directions and answer the question with clarity and style. One of the best essays, for instance, was disqualified for inadvertently divulging its author's name. A second piece which also had many strong points was excluded because it focused "almost exclusively on the condition of peasantries in foreign states." Still another proposal was rejected because its author lapsed into abstract digressions.[36]

One thing is indisputable: the competition opened the floodgates for all the critics of Russian serfdom. Most of the proposals came down in favor of property rights and personal freedom. To be sure, many also endorsed what one historian has recently called "repressive modernization," the belief that private property, like some "magic formula," would reinforce noble hegemony and turn peasants into better farmers.[37] Moreover, none of the contestants seemed aware of the advantages of communal land tenure, and the foreign ones were ignorant of it altogether. Instead, they emphasized the universal legitimacy of private property rights and the need for the state to extend those rights to all subjects. Consider the winning essay, written in French by the Aachen jurist Beardé de l'Abbaye and published in Russian translation in 1768. According to the contest committee, the author approved of "property and freedom" but also "demonstrates from the beginning all the difficulties that come with such an undertaking, and then presents ways of achieving this great objective without disrupting at all the security and peace of the state."[38] Beardé justified property rights for peasants on utilitarian and humanitarian grounds. Unlike the Ottoman Empire, whose system was based on "the equal distribution of slavery," Russia had a free noble elite perched on top of an enslaved mass of peasants. The first casualty of this arrangement was legality itself: "All order is shrouded in a thick fog; no one knows if the children born into slavery belong to their father, their lord, or their sovereign."[39] The second victim was the peasantry: "Poor creatures! They cut wood or till the land at their master's command: the smallest desire, the tiniest enterprise is denied them; great actions are forbidden them; they grow old and die. And what have they accomplished?"[40] Since peasants comprised over 90 percent of subjects, it was in society's best interests to protect them, first in the form of limited property rights and later in the form of gradual emancipation. His ideal arrangement envisioned free peasant proprietors working to improve and extend their small holdings, secure in the knowledge that their children would inherit the land and further enrich themselves. "Freedom and property are linked in an inseparable union," Beardé told his readers, adding that "100 free peasants are more useful to the state than 2,000 slaves."[41]

Beardé urged introducing reform slowly and cautiously, however. Arguing that "it would be senseless to demand from a crude peasant the fulfillment of laws unknown to him," he insisted that educating peasants was a long-term project. He even employed an analogy similar to Sumarokov's: the freed peasant was like an unshackled horse that eats well until winter strikes and then starves.[42] Serf owners had long viewed peasants as wild animals who required naked coercion to perform their "natural occupation." If the lord loosened the reins, so the argument ran, agriculture would decline and result in the destruction of the state. Beardé turned these assumptions on their head. Serfdom was the reason for the decay of agriculture in Russia, and in order to counteract its harmful effects nobles had to educate peasants in the ways of landed proprietors before fully freeing them:

> Thus the lord may tell several slave families: last year you worked only 100 desiatiny and I received only 300 measures of grain from your arable; double your efforts and labor for my benefit, cultivate the land which I entrust you with zeal; and as soon as you bring it to a level which can increase my income by 100 more measures of grain, I will grant you your own land; I will grant you the freedom and power to enrich yourselves through your diligence and labor.[43]

Aside from this call for voluntary manumission, Beardé included few specific recommendations. He advised lords to reward the most diligent serfs with conditional property rights, assuming that other peasants would emulate their example. Full emancipation would be postponed until an unspecified point in the future as nobles steadily Westernized the lifestyles and work habits of their serfs.

Aleksei Polenov's essay also merits attention. As the earliest native critique of serfdom, it prefigured Alexander Radishchev's *A Journey from St. Petersburg to Moscow* and secured Polenov a spot in the small pantheon of progressive eighteenth-century Russian thinkers. Trained in jurisprudence at Strasburg University, well versed in Montesquieu (whose *Considerations on the Causes of Rome's Greatness and Decline* he later translated into Russian), and knowledgeable of labor and life in the Russian village, Polenov discerned the complex ramifications of serf reform on land tenure, noble property rights, and local government.[44] Like Beardé, he condemned serfdom on the basis of natural law theory and outlined modest palliatives for curbing its extension: "[To] find that which gives us absolute pleasure, and to avoid that which is contrary to us is the essence of the two perpetual sources of virtue and vice. It is necessary to know the proper means to turn those passions to good and cleverly encourage them: the results will inevitably correspond to the desire." Property, Polenov continued, would permit the peasant to serve society better and work more diligently for himself and his family: "The household either voluntarily follows his example or properly fulfils its duties through firm supervision; nothing is hidden from his eyes, he sees everything himself; the least little shortcoming cannot stop causing him concern until it is corrected."[45] Serfdom, by contrast, deprived the peasant of his natural rights to property and the fruits of his labor while fulfilling him with "laziness, negligence, suspicion, and fear." While corroding the social fabric, it subjected society to the same threat of rebellion that had plagued the Romans, the Spartans, and, with uncanny presentiment, "our neighbor Poland at the time of the Cossack Revolt."[46]

Similar to Beardé's proposal, Polenov's reform would be voluntary and kindled by the power of the nobility's enlightened example. Peasants would receive an inalienable land allotment, the right to sell surplus grain and cattle, and a maximum of one barshchina day per week. All sales of serfs without land would be prohibited. As compensation, nobles would retain their monopolies over hunting, fishing, and forest reserves and keep the right to administer civil law courts.[47] Like the Society's provincial correspondents, however, Polenov feared a massive peasant *otkhod* followed by a decline of agriculture if peasants were freed without land. Left to their own devices, he predicted a mass migration to the cities where they would become "corrupted by independence and luxury . . . and accustomed to idleness and render themselves incapable of enduring village labor; because of this it must be firmly attempted to keep them from this and to use coercion to make them live according to their [social and occupational] designation." Hence, just as contemporary projects for noble education promoted curricula to mold "patriotic citizens," so did Polenov's plan recommend rural schools for teaching peasants the skills necessary to become good farmers, or as he phrased it, "to live simply, plainly, and with decency."[48] As a further inducement to tie peasants to their villages, he recommended establishing a rural welfare network of hospitals, apothecaries, police forces, and schools.

Other essayists expressed similarly reformist views. Voltaire argued in one of his submissions that private property would benefit nobles, peasants, and the state because "wherever the people work for themselves and their sovereign, the state is wealthy." "Serfs should own property," one Livonian baron declared. "Property should teach them how to love themselves and their occupation, to care for themselves, and to work in order to improve their position." "If we are to consider peasants as members of the state," wrote another essayist from France, "then the highest social good demands that they, like all other citizens, enjoy the benefits that come with the possession of the right to own landed and moveable property . . . The social good always consists of the good of the majority." The Russian essayist from Moscow, known to historians only as #71, believed that private property would lay the basis for a virtuous citizenry as skilled in farming as it was in war: "It is especially necessary to hold agriculture in the highest esteem as did the ancients, for whom farmers were as honorable as fighting men and landed aristocrats as honorable as generals." At the same time, most writers were determined to keep the nobility firmly in power in the countryside. Voltaire and Marmontel urged the government to bar peasants from owning more land than their lords so as to remind them of their rightful place at the bottom of the social hierarchy. Similarly, #71 favored private property because it would encourage the peasant "to live in one place, to provide and enrich oneself . . . and not to start wandering around in idleness and getting used to the vices of the city." And for Baron von Meck of Livonia, the sole purpose of land reform was to encourage the peasant to perform his natural occupation better and "find in it his happiness." "The happy state," he continued, was an orderly hierarchy in which "the noble [serves] in the capacity of the noble, the merchant as the merchant, and the peasant in the capacity of the peasant, and not [one in which] each inhabitant is happy as he sees fit; in the opposite case, every peasant would want to be a craftsman, while the merchant would want to be a noble, etc."[49]

While most finalists were unanimous in their praise for private property and their condemnation of serfdom, their proposals for implementing reform in practice diverged considerably. J.-J.-L. Graslin, Director of the French Royal Treasury in Nantes and recipient of second-place honors, recommended turning all land over to the state, which, in a massive repartition, would then redistribute it to farmers as inalienable property. Far more conservative was Herr Wöllner of Saxony, who proposed that nobles assign permanent allotments to households and replace barshchina with a clearly defined obrok payment.[50] Between these two poles were plans for transitional regimes that prefigured land reform projects enacted in the nineteenth century. Baron von Meck, for example, made an independent court system the centerpiece of his reform. After controlling moveable property for several years, peasants could purchase parcels of land from their lords, notarized by a court and protected by the state. Not even if the peasant abandoned farming could the lord reclaim the land. In these circumstances, ownership rights would revert to the commune "under the supervision of the pomeshchik" until the peasant's children were old enough to take over—an idea anticipatory of the final emancipation settlement of 1861 and the land captains of the 1880s. As we have seen, in Polenov's reform peasants would also receive access to basic education and healthcare, not unlike the network of social services later provided by the *zemstvo*, the network of local governments created in 1864.[51] Secure in property rights and protected from the degradations of poverty, Polenov and Meck envisaged a total regeneration of the serf into a God-fearing, practical, and rational farmer. Like Beardé, they assumed that agriculture was the peasantry's true occupation and that serfdom prevented them from excelling at it. Land reform did not have to trigger social and political disturbances as long as a legal and welfare system existed to guide peasants through the transition from serfdom to freedom.

None of the finalists paused to consider the incompatibility of educating serfs without freeing them first. Pastor Eisen, it is true, entered the competition, but his essay neither made the final cut nor has it survived to the present day. In another piece for a subsequent contest, however, he made his views clear: "It is completely unfathomable that he who talks about a gradual preparation of attitudes would not also feel secretly that this would mean pushing back emancipation for a long time or even forever." Eisen's belated response to Beardé and the Society struck an open nerve. Ivan Taubert lambasted it in a memo to Nartov: "Everything in it is described with such confusion and such little common sense that his work under no circumstances can be considered worthy of respect."[52] In fact, the only truly dissenting opinion among the finalists offered a countervailing argument in favor of serfdom. Written by an anonymous Livonian baron and listed in the register as #97, it spurred one Society member to scribble the words "foolish and funny proposals" (*durnyia i smeshnyia predlozheniia*) in the margins, while his colleague, evidently with more influence, overruled him.[53] Agreeing in principle that the state might benefit from peasant land ownership, the author nevertheless opposed the idea since it would undermine ancient privileges passed down through countless generations of nobility:

The slave, as I understand the word, or serf, who belongs to his master, cannot abandon the latter without his permission; the master may sell him to another with land or without it, and may punish him for offenses—burglary, neglect of duties, etc. The lord inherits this right from his ancestors, or buys it himself, and [this right] should be set on firm and inviolable privileges. If the landowner abuses this right, then the peasant may complain and the [landowner] be punished by the ruling powers.[54]

Responding to the popular argument that serfdom violated natural law, the writer noted that bondage was necessary in a country such as Russia with mediocre soil, a vast interior, and an expanding frontier. Given a choice between freedom and farming—as if the two were irreconcilable—the peasant would invariably elect the former: "[Field work] does not require a great mind," he asserted, "but only a strong body, diligence, and obedience, all of which are possible without freedom."[55] The prospect of freedom, on the other hand, connoted elemental fears of agricultural ruin reminiscent of the Time of Troubles—empty fields and wandering peasants susceptible to brigandage.

True to Sumarokov's prediction, what began as a discussion on the pros and cons of peasant property ownership quickly morphed into the first public debate on serfdom in Russia. It became even more rancorous when the assembly turned to the question of publishing Beardé's essay in Russian translation. When the judges first announced the winner in April 1768, they suggested soliciting the opinions of the most notable members and the Empress before deciding whether or not to publish it: "[The] issue is important itself and touches upon fundamental state institutions . . . the arguments are not fit for publishing without express permission from the supreme authorities to private individuals [whose opinions] our Economic Society regards as [trustworthy]." In the meantime, they recommended preparing a Russian translation and short extract purged of the more incendiary passages which "may cause people who are insufficiently enlightened or filled with callous, deceitful opinions to commit offensive deeds or [which] may serve as grounds for false and harmful thoughts."[56] Of all the translators in St. Petersburg, they made the mistake of selecting the same Aleksei Polenov whose essay on peasant property had generated such controversy only a few weeks before. Not surprisingly, they found his rendition of Beardé's work to be unnecessarily "forceful" and "flowery"—virtually the same words the judges had used to describe his own submission. Polenov quickly made the requested changes, and on June 11 the assembly sent the revised translation to Catherine.[57]

The Empress replied on July 2. In a note couriered through Alexander Sergeevich Stroganov, she relayed that there was "nothing in the essay which could not be published."[58] Had the topic dealt with anything other than serfdom the assembly probably would have done her bidding. Instead, the lower-ranking members rebelled. Only two weeks after Catherine had expressed her approval, the assembly decided by a vote of twelve to two not to publish the essay. More ballots came in later through proxy, and when the meeting finally adjourned, the results were sixteen against publication and five in favor. The following week six more members—all of them Russian aristocrats—cast their votes with Catherine. In the end, out of 27 who voted, a minority of 11 favored publication, including the Empress herself.[59] None of the notables explained to their colleagues why they voted the way they did—Catherine's support was evidently enough. Roger Bartlett has stressed the magnetic influence that Catherine had over certain members: "[Due to] the attraction exerted by the charisma and political authority of the Imperial dignity in itself, where the Empress gave positive approval and showed the way on a sensitive issue, lesser people of any persuasion, and especially her intimates, might follow."[60] Most Society members remained fiercely opposed to publishing the piece. At stake was nothing less than the Society's autonomy from the court and the power to frame its agenda. At the height of the debate, the Frederick von Wol'f reproached his associates for agreeing to sponsor the contest in the first place:

> [Not] a single one of these pieces is worthy of a prize, and for this reason should not be published. It is common knowledge that if a man knows of another means of making a living, he will not choose the most difficult one—and arable farming is the most difficult work; thus it is necessary to use the law to force him into performing this hard labor, and no other type of work. Consequently, we must not grant the peasant complete landownership, for once he is free, he will use the freedom granted to him to work only for his own household, and not for the general welfare.[61]

Wol'f's deterministic argument reflected the practical sensibilities and narrow vision of most of his fellow members in the Society. Russia had no choice but to depend on forced labor. If Beardé had spoken of the price of freedom for peasants, Wol'f now saw serfdom as the price Russia had to pay for civilization itself.

The rebellion soon fizzled out. By the end of the July 23 meeting, three German members—Taubert, Klingshtedt, and Staehlin—announced that the assembly had no choice but to reverse its decision. Their reasoning was remarkably blunt. First, they reminded their associates that the assembly was comprised mainly of foreigners who should have known better than to disagree with the "most notable Russian members of our Society [who] have made known their opinions that they considered it useful to publish the essay in Russian." Second, they drew a distinction between the "political" competence of high-ranking Russian aristocrats and the "economic" expertise of civil servants and provincial landowners:

> It is more becoming . . . for those Russian members who hold important govern-
> ment posts to judge what appears to be more of a political task than an economic
> one; as for other persons who perhaps do not possess sufficient knowledge of
> the matter, they are not in so important a position [as high-ranking Russians] to
> cast judgment on the imperceptible or important effects that might come from
> publishing [the essay]. And so we defer to the enlightened opinion of the most
> notable Russian members of the Society, even though a majority of voices have
> expressed resolute disagreement [with them] through the ballot.[62]

Few could argue with this kind of decree. Within a month Beardé's essay appeared as the leading item in the next volume of the *Trudy*.

The peasant property competition cast a long shadow over the Free Economic Society for the remainder of the century. Although the rank-and-file
members lost the battle over publishing Beardé's essay, they won the war
over the *Trudy*'s editorial policy. In the decades following the contest, the
Society consistently avoided the legal and political dimensions of the peasant
question. On occasion it received proposals for land reform or even gradual
peasant emancipation, yet rather than discuss the merits of these ideas, the
assembly routinely deposited these proposals into its archives. Thus, when
the Economic Director of Polotsk in 1786 reported on peasant leaseholders
in his province, the assembly informed him that "the Society in no way is
authorized to comment on state-related matters . . . correspondence with the
Society is to consist of information pertaining to agriculture in his province
and other matters relating to it."[63] Two years later the Society member August Huppel presented a similarly "political" description of the condition of
the Crown peasants in his native Livonia in 1788. The assembly responded
by having all the "indecent" portions deleted before publishing it. Soon after
that, Mikhail von Bork of Polotsk submitted two proposals for alleviating the
poverty of Belorussian serfs. Although the assembly invited him to join the
Society, both of his projects were rejected for publication on the grounds that
they meddled in thorny legal matters.[64]

Having taken the politics out of political economy, the Society instead sought
a grand solution to the peasant question that was technical and administrative.
In October 1771 the great magnates Ivan Chernyshev and Peter Grigor'evich
Demidov launched an essay competition on the theme of determining land allotments for a "typical" Russian peasant household sufficient for "meeting all
dues and state taxes without falling into poverty or debt."[65] The project took
almost seven years to complete. This peasant question was far more difficult
to answer than the previous one—it required detailed knowledge of farming

conditions in all parts of European Russia, not just mastery of natural law theory. The prize went to Gottfried Grasman, a pastor from the Prussian province of Pomerania who had already won a medal from the Society in 1769 for his work on clover and other forage crops.[66] His latest work was just as impressive. The judges praised him for his "sufficient command of the best writers," in other words the same scientists and seigneurs who had contributed to the *Trudy* and made it such an indispensable source for agronomists. More important, they believed that his innovations applied everywhere. "Pastor Grasman," the committee declared, "has arrived at a general principle so that all of the gentlemen who are participating in this task may glean from his essay satisfactory rules for the improvement of land with which his question is concerned." The patrons who sponsored the contest exhibited similar satisfaction. They paid for the medal with unusual punctuality, and Ivan Cherynshev requested a copy of the treatise for his personal library.[67]

The book's sheer comprehensiveness made its publication in April 1778 a culminating point in the Society's history. Here finally was a meticulous and coherent criticism of traditional Russian agriculture in its entirety. Like Beardé, Grasman acknowledged the economic advantages of peasant property ownership, but stopped short of recommending such a reform for Russian serfs. In his estimation, serfs lacked the intelligence and responsibility to use freedom and property rights for the common good:

> These treasures [i.e., freedom and property] in and of themselves are not as profitable to the state as they are harmful to society when they fall into the wrong hands. Freedom may produce unbridled conduct, while property may become grounds for their liberation from dependence. I regard most enserfed peasants [i.e., serfs] as youths who, having escaped from the stringency and supervision of their peasants, immediately seize their freedom and property and do with them as they please.[68]

Grasman discerned a disturbing pattern of behavior in peasants who had earned surplus income. Instead of reinvesting it in their farms, he claimed, they wasted it on food, drink, festivals, and other forms of "voluptuousness."[69] As we shall soon see, the Society favored generous measures of leisurely excess, but only for the leisure class. Peasants were held to a different standard: "[It] has been proven that when a peasant household has more or less land than it needs, then from this there is harm to the pomeshchik and society." Grasman advocated a strict maximum on peasant landholdings, thus reinforcing the social distinction between nobles and peasants while perpetuating economic equilibrium among farmers at the village level. If peasants could manage their land as if they owned it and as if they were free, then the decay of agriculture would fade away for good.[70]

Grasman's model peasant household (Table 3.1) closely corresponded to the subsistence ideal in many European agrarian societies: a multi-generational family; a healthy allotment of livestock; and a tax burden equal to 20 percent of the annual harvest. Few Russian peasants were able to approach this ideal: on most barshchina estates employing the three-field system, families paid half of their annual harvest in rent and dues alone.[71] Moreover, they lacked enough land and cattle to feed themselves, let alone to generate a surplus. Fidgeting under these constraints, Grasman instead proposed that Russians begin employing the "English system" where "everybody owns their own arable, pasture, and meadow." In this system, the household would enclose all adjacent land on which it would raise forage crops alongside the customary grains as it gradually reduced the common grazing land and stabled livestock permanently. The final result would be an English-style village, teeming with modestly prosperous families, who used their land "without interference and as they please."[72]

Just how were Russian peasants supposed to put Grasman's English system into practice? Grasman believed his system could succeed as a program for peasant resettlement in the sparsely populated black soil region.[73] Instead of transplanting the traditional practices of communal land tenure and triennial field rotation, he urged landowners to defy custom and establish an entirely new order. Households were to be set up on separate homesteads measuring 16 desiatiny. All arable land was to be enclosed, divided into 11 fields of equal proportions, and sown alternately with grains and English clover. To increase fertilizer production, livestock would be stabled on a permanent basis and fed with clover. While feasible on paper, Grasman's southern project ignored the realities and limitations of peasant farming in Russia. At no point did he explain why Russians should start using manure under his system when they hardly ever used it under their own, or why they should sow clover and stable their cattle—on virgin land no less. Nor did he clarify how landowners would introduce a system that threatened to disrupt every aspect of the peasantry's communal life.

Fifteen years later, a *Trudy* writer who identified himself as "K" tried to apply Grasman's system to the steppe lands recently annexed from the Ottoman Empire. According to the author, orderly agriculture required an independent family farm with clear boundaries "so that [the peasant] may have complete freedom to use it as he pleases."[74] Like Grasman, "K" recommended assigning 16–20 desiatiny to each household, assuming that enclosure would transform them into productive tenant farmers: "No matter how untamed the country, if only it has soil of good quality and a suitable climate, it can be turned into a paradise if the eyes and hands of the worker can be applied to it on a daily basis."[75] Yet practical considerations compelled "K" to scale back

Table 3.1.   Annual Consumption Requirements for a Russian Peasant Household

Winter grain (Rye)	*chertverty**
2 male workers	6
2 female workers	4
6 children	6
2 seniors	4
For priests and teachers	1
6 head of horned cattle	0.5
3 horses	0.37
12 pigs	0.25
25 sheep	0.25
2 cows	0.13
For feeding pigs	6
For suckling pigs	1
Taxes, rent, miscellaneous	16
Total for winter grain	**45.5**
Spring grain	
Barley	
4 working adults	6
2 seniors	2
6 children	3
Poultry feed	1
Oats	
3 horses	18
12 geese	1.5
For groats	4.5
Peas and buckwheat	2
Total for spring grain	**38**
Total for all grain	**83.5**

*One *chertvert* equals 5.95 bushels or 210 dry liters.
Source: Grasman, "Opredelenie zemli," 46-49.

his expectations. Scarcity of workers on the steppe demanded that peasants pool their labor and resources, much as they had done in the past. Meanwhile, the lord made all the managerial decisions, particularly regarding land use, in order to inspire peasants "to come around to the correct rural economy." Most important, all land under this system still belonged to the lord who simply redistributed it from time to time. "K" imagined taking 1,000 desiatiny of open land and dividing it between 50 households, who cultivated it rent-free for a three-year grace period, after which the lord imposed the customary barshchina payment of three days per week.[76] Inevitably, Grasman's "new order" in the south replicated the old one from the central regions, complete with commune, the three-field system, and serfdom.

Along with new agronomical techniques, the Society also began promoting a style of estate management called protective tutelage (*popechitel'stvo*). It was essentially a publicity campaign for noble self-regulation. Its practitioners liked to think they were rescuing their serfs from poverty and superstition while furthering the progress of enlightenment in the countryside. Emblematic of the new trend was Baron von Zaltse, a Baltic German Society member who had managed a small estate in Livonia for eighteen years and reported his achievements in an article from 1770. Its portrayal of an enlightened seigneur in action complemented the theories of the finalists in the Society's peasant property contest. When Zaltse first settled in the village, 27 out of 31 families "were found in the most impoverished condition." Plagued by debt, poor housing, and shortages in cattle and grain, the village seemed on the verge of collapsing.[77] Trying to eliminate the "mutual suspicion between pomeshchik and peasant," he attributed the disintegration of the village to destitution, not the lord's "tyranny" or the peasant's "idleness." "Extreme poverty produces idleness and negligence," he wrote, "because the peasant cannot tell whether or not the land can ever become his own property."[78] Zaltse first assigned each household a new master, knowledgeable in farming and a paragon of diligence and sobriety. If the master proved his worth, Zaltse left him and his land alone so long as he performed all his services. When the master's sons reached adulthood and were ready to begin their own households, Zaltse subsidized them for the first three years with land, seed, cattle, tools, and sometimes housing.[79]

Interestingly, Zaltse's practice of protective tutelage resembled the patronage system that kept the Free Economic Society dependent upon Catherine for so long. In neither case was "freedom" a natural right which its recipients had earned through struggle or negotiation, but a gift dispensed by someone far above who also had the power to take it away. In fact, his drastic restructuring of village life was extremely invasive from the peasants' perspective. He strictly regulated the amount of land and cattle households could accumulate: as they expanded and contracted, he reshuffled their members and established new ones on vacant land or dispersed "dilapidated" families as circumstances dictated. He frequently intervened in their daily lives, especially when they owed him money. And if peasants slipped back into their old ways of idleness, he had them whipped—one of the few endorsements of corporal punishment published in the *Trudy* during Catherine's reign.[80] Nevertheless, Zaltse liked to think that his system "treated peasants as free people":

> There is nothing so onerous to mankind than the continual lack of freedom that comes with dependence on the will of a single man . . . The harm that comes from this is almost as great as that which comes from the complete absence of law. In the latter case, no one is secure in his property, and hence secure in

his life; and in the former case, no one would try to acquire an estate since he would be constantly in danger of losing it. Consequently, [both cases] produce laziness, poverty, and destitution.[81]

Subsequent events made the Society's talk of reforming peasant culture sound naïve. Pugachev's rebellion of 1773 and 1774 quickly smothered public enthusiasm for any kind of peasant reform, while Russia's annexation of the enormous southern steppe from the Ottoman Empire put an end to all the grumbling about the "decay of agriculture." Beginning as a Cossack jacquerie on the Central Asian frontier, Pugachev's uprising spread deep into the Volga region, where it was joined by thousands of Russian peasants. It was the most violent domestic conflict since the Time of Troubles as Pugachev's soldiers marched almost unopposed into the heartland. By the time the rebellion was finally suppressed in 1774 and its leader captured, more than 1,500 serf owners and 1,000 state officials had been killed. The crisis finally convinced Catherine of the need for an effective government apparatus in the provinces as well as a corps of reliable noble officials for staffing it.[82] Working closely with Jakob Sievers, in 1775 Catherine issued the Statute on the Provinces, which provided for the most comprehensive reorganization of the Empire down to the Bolshevik Revolution. It divided the existing *gubernii* into smaller units, each under the control of a royally appointed governor-general. While creating an extensive local administration, independent courts, and municipal institutions for provincial towns, the reform permitted the establishment of assemblies at the district and provincial levels whose members were elected by the wealthiest landowners and chaired by a noble marshal.

The historian John LeDonne sees Catherine's reform of provincial and local government as evidence of a growing political alliance between the autocracy and the landed nobility intended to strengthen the hold of the ruling class over the Russian peasantry.[83] Whatever reservations the Empress had previously harbored about sharing power with serf owners clearly collapsed in the wake of the Pugachev rebellion. According to this view, Catherine's Charter to the Nobility of 1785 finalized the terms of this special relationship. Twenty-two years after Peter III had freed Russia's nobles from mandatory service, Catherine confirmed their right not to serve while still holding on to their titles and privileges. Many of the freedoms, immunities, and benefits that they had accumulated since the time of Elizabeth were now guaranteed by the state: due process before the law, exemption from corporal punishment, the right to sell and purchase whole villages, and the right to association through the noble assemblies. The Charter moreover confirmed their right to own "not only the fruits of the land belonging to them, but also all resources found beneath the surface and in waters." As

Robert Jones has written, the "state now looked upon the Russian noble-man as an estate owner who was expected to spend several years in the service rather than as a servitor supported in part through the ownership of an estate."[84] Just as important is what the Charter left unsaid. Making no mention of the serfs living and working on the lord's property, it implicitly expected Russian nobles to regulate themselves and to offer their peasants the benefits of protective tutelage. True, Catherine had prepared a draft document for state peasants comparable to her Charters to the Nobility and Towns, which may have set in motion a gradual process of general emancipation had it ever been enacted. Like nobles and townsmen, state peasants would have been guaranteed a few basic rights (and many obligations) commensurate with their low status. Except in parts of New Russia, it remained stillborn. Finding qualified personnel to staff the growing bureaucracy in the provincial towns was hard enough; extending an additional layer of bureaucracy deep into the villages was virtually impossible.[85]

Yet the Charter to the Nobility must be situated within the larger context of Catherine's reform program. While fulfilling the nobility's desire to exercise greater power, the Charter defined noble status in relation to the other social estates of her realm and pressured nobles to follow the Empress's example in governing the provinces and ruling over their serfs. The Free Economic Society had been propagating the same message since its founding, and the reform of provincial government gave them the opportunity to promote a culture of noble enlightenment and gentility in the provinces. When Vologda held the first election for its noble assembly in 1780, for instance, their choice for Marshal of the Nobility fell on Aleksei Oleshev, the long-time provincial correspondent for the Society whose writings continually stressed the need for a class of enlightened lords residing on their estates. Enormously popular with the local gentry, Oleshev embodied all the virtues that Catherine wanted her provincial leaders to possess. In an ode commemorating his election, the Society member and poet Vasilii Grigor'evich Ruban specified three virtues displayed by the retired pomeshchik:

> He was raised on love for the fatherland
> In spring he was raised on science
> In summer he served the monarch
> And in winter, or his old age,
> He is still filled with love of life
> And strives to be of use,
> Making the best of his days, until the end.[86]

Science, service, and purposeful, independent activity initiated by the nobility—here was the Society's solution to the peasant question. Their logic was as circular as it was self-serving. Since peasants were like children and incapable of managing their own affairs, responsibility for their well-being fell to men like Zaltse and Oleshev. If more lords would follow their example, then tyranny, ignorance, and poverty would eventually disappear, leaving in their wake an agrarian regime in which lords and peasants knew their rightful place and performed the tasks nature had assigned to them. When Russian nobles spoke of reforming their peasants, they were really speaking about reforming themselves.

*****

For all the Free Economic Society's rhetoric emphasizing the general welfare, public service in practice was a rather low-stakes venture. Indeed, the patron-client relationships that laced the Society were significantly weaker than those that prevailed in officialdom. Patronage in state service provided real rewards—promotions, salary increases, political loyalty—all of which worked to strengthen the bonds of mutual dependence between the two parties. And unlike patronage in the arts and sciences, whose visible and tangible results helped to enhance the patron's status, support for the Society produced few benefits of lasting value. Few Russian landowners ever acted on the technical and managerial advice offered in the *Trudy;* and when they did, they discovered that the "new agriculture" was unfeasible under Russian conditions, or, to paraphrase Michel Confino, not even all that new.[87] Nor did the public status conferred by the Society prove particularly advantageous. As we have already seen, membership symbolized forfeiture of one's status before the public—valuable for rank-and-file members seeking access to the court, but unnecessary for the aristocrats, favorites, magnates, and courtiers who already had it.

Signs of a new understanding between the Society's great patrons and its regular members emerged several weeks after the controversy over the publication of Beardé's essay. Reminding his colleagues that the statute required each member to submit "at least one" essay or translation annually, Russian Secretary Andrei Nartov admitted that most high-ranking members were "too occupied with important matters" to write economic reports and conduct experiments. Rather than expel them, however, he suggested that they either pay for translations of useful books or sponsor essay contests for which they would put up the prize money.[88] Nothing immediately came of his proposals, and by the end of 1769 it became obvious that the Society had reached an impasse. In November of that year Vladimir Grigor'evich Orlov, brother of Catherine's favorite, announced that "urgent action" was necessary if the association was to continue. "Out of this [crisis] such harmful consequences may occur that the Society established for the general welfare and with her

Imperial Majesty's approval will enter first into disorder, then into decline, and finally, to the chagrin of all ardent patriots, will be subjected to inevitable destruction; and thus not only will the glory of the Free Economic Society turn into nothing, but the [Society] itself will not be worthy of any praise."[89] Orlov's appeal had a galvanizing effect. The following week, President Alexander Ivanovich Glebov declared that the Free Economic Society was "in decline" and ordered that a committee be formed to study the problem.[90]

The result of the committee's work was a revised statute that drastically reduced membership requirements and in effect transformed the Society into an agricultural advisory board for its aristocratic patrons.[91] Candidates simply had to be nominated and accepted into the association by majority vote, after which they could decide for themselves how to serve. The statute also made attendance at meetings optional, reminding members to inform the assembly of their economic activities "from time to time." Relations between the patrons and regular members improved, at least for the time being. At an extraordinary meeting in September 1770, 13 members, all of them notables, pledged annual contributions ranging from 30 to 500 rubles for the next five years.[92] Never before had the Society's leading members performed so magnanimously. Keeping with the spirit of renewed goodwill, the next month Zakhar Chernyshev offered his palace for the Society's first formal jubilee celebration. After coffee and dessert, the veteran general paraded a group of Turkish prisoners of war before the packed assembly.[93]

These extraordinary celebrations allowed notable members to announce new essay competitions and monitor the assembly's progress on other details. Many of the questions reflected the patrons' preference for comprehensive policy manuals tailor-made to suit their personal needs as absentee lords and career state servitors. At the jubilee celebration in 1770, for instance, Kirill Grigor'evich Razumovskii, the last hetman of Ukraine, proposed a contest for the best handbook on managing large urban households. At 200 and counting, Razumovskii's domestic staff was one of the biggest in St. Petersburg.[94] Needless to say, the very notion of a household staff was anathema to the agrarian ideal. As early as 1767, Peter Rychkov had lambasted his fellow nobles in the *Trudy* for taking peasants away from the fields to build mansions, gardens, and other frivolities. In the past, he claimed, landowners were content with unassuming homes, modest equipages, and "two or three personal servants in plain but clean clothes."[95] Rychkov failed to see that conspicuous consumption was all in a day's work for the aristocrat, and, like any other job, came with its own set of dilemmas that seem irrational from a modern perspective. In his classic study of court society in seventeenth-century France, the sociologist Norbert Elias once argued that luxury was a necessary structural feature of aristocratic life in the pre-industrial age. Beginning with the monarch, it radiated across the larger society, embedding, as in stone, the symbolic distinctions that determined one's place and left in its wake the "ineradicable distance" separating the elite from everyone else. The rank-conscious rituals of the court extended deep into society. Through the title he inherited and the powdered wig he wore on his head, through his sumptuous banquets, table settings, horse-drawn carriages, and personal servants, the aristocrat announced to the world his own dependence on the monarch while reinforcing the hierarchies of dependence beneath himself. "A duke who does not live as a duke has to live," writes Elias, "who can no longer properly fulfill the social duties of a duke, is hardly a duke any longer."[96]

All this held as true for the eighteenth-century Russian nobility as it did for French bluebloods under Louis XIV. To be sure, the two winners of Razumovskii's contest tried to reconcile the conspicuous consumption of aristocrats with basic accounting practices. Joseph Regensburger, a magistrate from St. Petersburg and Society member since 1771, claimed to write his booklet for aristocrats who enjoyed displaying their immense wealth while still counting their kopecks. Eberhardt Johann Schretter, author of the other prize-winning essay, likewise stressed "orderly and correct allocation of small, middling, and large expenses."[97] Yet for all the fuss over frugality, they only sidestepped the issue. Schretter imagined hundreds of domestics performing an enormous variety of decorative functions: door openers, lackeys, and the "spice commissar," to name a few. There was also the "negro," whose duties included clearing empty glasses and setting up card tables.[98] Behind this elaborate façade lay an almost Platonic unfolding of talents and inclinations which predetermined individuals for performing specific tasks and gave them essential supporting roles in the presentation of wealth and power. Since the lord was only as good as his help, Schretter cringed at the slightest imperfection that tarnished the master's image: spots on a wineglass, bowing excessively, not laughing at his jokes.[99] In return for faithful service, each servant received some insight into the lord's personality: the valet knew his taste in prostitutes, the cooks his palate, the bartender his personal problems.[100] The steward who managed the household had the hardest balancing act of all—at one and the same he had to be "humane and conscientious," and never "ignoble, mercenary, biased, angry, hot-tempered, peevish, malevolent, envious, or bored." Schretter admitted that he had never come across a steward who approached his ideal.[101] Why should it have been otherwise? The dearth of capable and trustworthy men for performing their tasks would remain a constant problem so long as there was no material incentive for people to excel at them. When Schretter rhetorically asked what the steward received in return for years of faithful service, he gave an evasive response: the "trust and respect" of his master, as if the sort of personal fealty that linked a lord to his vassals somehow applied to the relationship between the master and household staff.[102]

Regensburger and Schretter believed that a lord could flaunt his wealth and still live within his means. Assuming an annual income of 20,000 rubles, an extraordinarily large sum available only to a handful of people, Regensburger divided expenditures into 26 categories (Table 3.2). Not surprisingly, the lion's share (6,180 rubles, or 31 percent) went for supporting domestics and livery. The steward naturally earned the highest salary—400 rubles plus an extra 200 for his own table, followed then by the head chef and home secretary, whose specialized skills earned them 300 and 200 rubles respectively.[103] Most servants had to settle for much less, typically between 50 and 100 rubles depending on the job. By contemporary standards, these were still generous salaries—no wonder so many peasants in the north wanted to abandon farming for work in St. Petersburg. The second largest expense was for food and

Table 3.2. A model annual budget for a Russian aristocrat

Items	Rubles	Kopecks
Rent	1,200	
Firewood	440	
Food and kitchen ware	3,594	10
Beverages	1,505	85
Confections	973	
Salaries for domestics	3,267	50
Salaries for livery	1,767	
Dining linen	422	
Cuffs and lace	150	
Livery expenses	774	
"Free" livery expenses	372	33
Horses and stables	1,087	60
Artisan expenses	150	
Carriages	254	50
Candles	176	
Hunting dogs	18	
House dogs	14	60
Pipe cleaning	18	
Medical expenses	160	
Church donations	44	
Alms	150	
Clothing	2,000	
Bed linen	100	
Pocket change	1,000	
Stationery	200	
Remainder	161	52
Total	20,000	

Source: J. Regensburger, "O razdelenii," 223-24.

drink. On any given day, guests were treated to multicourse lunches and dinners and a well stocked wine cellar. Regensburger reserved more than seven
percent of the master's income for alcohol, enough to buy 3,290 bottles of
French wine every year, not to mention vast quantities of champagne, Bur-
gundy, and English and Russian beer.[104] All told, the Society's model aristocrat spent 12,253 rubles—two-thirds of his annual income—on servants,
food, and alcohol alone. Virtually everything he brought in—and this was a
great deal—he and his friends consumed on the spot.

Society aristocrats also attempted to codify the sumptuary practices for
Russians "of middling circumstances." (*posredstvennoe sostoianie*). According to the academician Johann Georgii, winner of another contest sponsored
by Zakhar Chernyshev on this theme, the man of "middle calling" (*srednoe
zvanie*) stood between "a count and a common citizen," similar to the "third
estate" that Catherine had tried to legislate into existence.[105] If aristocrats
were encouraged to indulge in foreign luxuries, then Russians of the middle
were expected to reduce the "abundance of imported luxuries in our homes,"
while at the same time stimulating native arts and industries.[106] The man of
average means served traditional Russian foods at his table, supplemented by
the exotic fruits, spices, oils, and wines produced in the southerly reaches of
the Empire. In place of imported luxury items, he found homegrown substi-
tutes: honey and fruit syrups for sugar; kvass and flavored vodka for French
wine and English beer; sassafras for tea, coffee, and chocolate. "With regard
to food," Georgii assured his readers, "it is easy to see that a man of middle
rank can have a table almost as good as a rich man, and incomparably better
than a poor one." Nor were the elaborate English gardens enjoyed by the aristocracy necessary for average Russians: "Their maintenance has as their object
not the use of the household economy, but only amusement and enjoyment of
good taste. For this reason they are really only the property of notables and
the owners of great villages."[107] The same rule applied to clothes, housing,
kitchen and tableware, carriages and horses, artists and entertainers, books,
curiosity collections, medicine, and tombstones. Just as aristocrats had their
dress, their banquets, and their amusements—all imported from Europe—so
did those below them have native versions equivalent to their station in life.
Unlike Razumovskii, imprisoned in his palace, or the peasant, doomed by
nature to scrape by at subsistence level, the "average Russian" enjoyed the
flexibility and the means to be modest and independent.

Just who wanted to read these kinds of handbooks, nobody could say. Perhaps that was the point. The notables' attitude towards public service calls to
mind the words of Habermas, who long ago observed that Renaissance courtiers "kept men of letters as [they] kept servants, but [whose] literary production
based on patronage was more a matter of conspicuous consumption than of

serious reading by an interested public."[108] The real purpose of such contests, it seems, was for notable members to serve the Society in ways that symbolized their higher status and calling.[109] As a consequence, it proved difficult for the Society to inspire them to participate in its activities beyond lending their names to it. For the duration of Catherine's reign, only five members from the top four ranks published substantial pieces of work in the *Trudy:* Roman Vorontsov, Jakob Sievers, Stepan Ushakov, Peter Petrovich Konovitsyn, and Alexander Mikhailovich Lunin.[110] As for attendance at the assembly (see Table 3.3), out of 110 high-ranking members who joined between 1765 and 1796, only four appeared at meetings frequently enough to make any impact upon the Society's day-to-day activities.[111] Thirteen others turned up regularly for four or five consecutive years, yet most of these men were active only during the 1760s.[112] After the revision of the statute in 1770, it became a rare event indeed for a notable to attend a meeting. Most of them appeared at the assembly hall once or twice after their induction and then vanished, never to be seen or heard from again. Anniversary celebrations became the only forum during which most of the Society members residing in St. Petersburg actually met together.

Table 3.3 further attests to the steady removal of notable members from the assembly over the course of Catherine's reign.[113] In the 1760s, when the Society drew nearly half of its members from the Empress's closest advisors and her court, the notable presence at meetings reached its peak at 35 percent. From 1770 through 1777, it hovered at around 20 percent before evaporating for the next 11 years. Even the apparent upsurge in aristocratic attendance in the mid-1780s and early 1790s is illusory: virtually the only members from the top four ranks to attend during these two periods were two presidents, Adam Ivanovich von Bril, who served from 1783 to 1785, and Count Fedor A. Angal't, who presided over the assembly on a regular basis between 1788 and 1794. In the wake of Angal't's sudden death in May 1794, however, the notable presence dropped to the same low levels of the early 1780s.

The scarcity of representatives from the highest ranks clearly increased their prestige value to the Society, and the assembly reciprocated by reserving the office of president for them. A position of ceremonial significance, the president's primary responsibility was to chair meetings which were usually so quiet, if not boring, that he had little to do.[114] The limited powers and duties of the post made it a good fit for men whose high-level governmental and court responsibilities prevented them from participating more energetically in the Society. With the passing of time, the president's mere presence at meetings became its own kind of service. When Bril stepped down from the post in 1785, for example, the assembly awarded him a gold medal and hung his portrait in the hall, even though he had done nothing but show up for all the meetings.[115]

Table 3.3. Attendance at Assembly Meetings of the Free Economic Society, 1767–96

Year	Number of Meetings	Attendees per Meeting (average number)	Total Number of Attendances	Ranks 1-4 (Number of Attendances and % of total)	Ranks 5-8 (Number of Attendances and % of total)	Miscellaneous* (Number of Attendances and % of total)
1767	31	6.8	212	32 (15 %)	180 (85 %)	0 (0 %)
1768	42	10.6	445	154 (35 %)	291 (65 %)	0 (0 %)
1769	34	9.1	310	99 (32 %)	211 (68 %)	0 (0 %)
1770	38	12.6	477	121 (25 %)	353 (74 %)	3 (1 %)
1771	39	10.3	402	67 (17 %)	328 (82 %)	7 (2 %)
1772	30	8.3	250	72 (29 %)	157 (63 %)	21 (8 %)
1773	21	8.0	168	36 (21 %)	121 (72 %)	11 (7 %)
1774	29	7.8	227	68 (30 %)	139 (61 %)	20 (9 %)
1775	31	7.7	239	27 (11 %)	201 (84 %)	11 (5 %)
1776	23	8.2	189	18 (10 %)	163 (86 %)	8 (4 %)
1777	14	14.5	203	51 (25 %)	143 (70 %)	9 (4 %)
1778	10	10.0	100	10 (10 %)	82 (82 %)	8 (8 %)
1779	23	8.0	185	9 (5 %)	158 (85 %)	18 (10 %)
1780	14	9.4	131	3 (2 %)	123 (94 %)	5 (4 %)
1781	6	7.2	43	0 (0 %)	40 (93 %)	3 (7 %)

1782	14	10.4	145	9 (6 %)	114 (79 %)	22 (15 %)
1783	35	10.9	380	37 (10 %)	278 (73 %)	65 (17 %)
1784	36	9.8	351	36 (10 %)	237 (68 %)	78 (22 %)
1785	29	9.6	277	21 (8 %)	180 (65 %)	76 (27 %)
1786	32	7.9	252	1 (0 %)	176 (70 %)	75 (30 %)
1787	32	7.4	236	1 (0 %)	182 (77 %)	53 (22 %)
1788	42	8.3	349	14 (4 %)	280 (80 %)	55 (16 %)
1789	44	11.7	514	75 (15 %)	367 (71 %)	72 (14 %)
1790	46	11.7	535	65 (12 %)	388 (73 %)	82 (15 %)
1791	42	12.9	540	63 (12 %)	385 (71 %)	92 (17 %)
1792	51	17.6	899	119 (13 %)	640 (71 %)	140 (16 %)
1793	52	20.6	1072	126 (12 %)	699 (65 %)	247 (23 %)
1794	47	21.7	1020	97 (10 %)	652 (64 %)	271 (27 %)
1795	45	16.0	719	34 (5 %)	465 (65 %)	220 (31 %)
1796	44	15.8	696	15 (2 %)	470 (68 %)	211 (30 %)

*Includes ranks 9-14, merchants, clergy, foreign nationals, and members of undetermined status. Source: RGIA, f. 91, op. 1, d. 4-8, 10-18, 22, 25, 27-30, 32, 35, 38, 41, 44, 47, 50, 53.

To be sure, a charismatic patron-president had the power to make even the most mundane business interesting. Such was the case during the lengthy presidency of Fedor Angal't. A blood relative of Catherine II, Angal't is known to historians as the most beloved Director of the Army Cadet Corps, which he administered from 1786 to 1794.[116] His tenure there sheds much needed light on the dynamics of patron-client relations in the Free Economic Society. Angal't was less an administrator over the cadets than he was their "father" and resident "wise man."[117] Although enormously popular with his pupils, Angal't's approach elicited sharp criticism from conservatives who believed he should be preparing his students for the real world of military command and desk jobs.[118] Among his innovations were the school's "recreational hall," essentially a reading room filled with Western newspapers, and the "talking walls," hallways painted with inspirational tips from ancient sages. In its egalitarianism the school was a utopia, far removed from St. Petersburg's service culture. Angal't guided the Free Economic Society between 1788 and 1794 with the same paternalistic benevolence he employed in managing his cadets. While satisfying all the requirements of Society presidents specified in the statute, Angal't plunged into every detail of the organization's work. At his first assembly meeting he commenced an audit of the Society's account books. Several weeks later he reactivated a stalled campaign initiated two years before to involve provincial economic directors more closely in the Society's work.[119] In January 1789, Angal't pledged to set aside part of the Cadet Corps' garden for economic experiments so that "from their earliest years [the students] might have an understanding and knowledge of estate management."[120] Nor was his activism a mere novelty that wore off with the passing of time. Angal't clearly had a proprietary interest in the Society's welfare and developed an effective partnership with the core members in the assembly. The results were impressive. Working closely with Russian Secretary Nartov and Foreign Secretary Ivan Zakharovich Kel'khen, Angal't's recruitment efforts nearly doubled the Society's membership base by the time of his death in May 1794. His constant presence at meetings served as a magnet for both aristocrats and members of less exalted status who otherwise would have stayed away from the assembly hall. For a few years the Society's lived experience corresponded to the egalitarian promise of its original statute.

Or did it? The assembly was aware of the glass ceiling separating regular members from notable patrons like Angal't. In a speech of 1793 commemorating his fifth anniversary as president, the long-time member Albrecht Euler expressed thanks to the assembly's leader for renewing "the close ties that have existed between you and us." With words calling to mind Angal't's administrative methods at the Cadet Corps, Euler credited him with transforming the assembly's walls into a "pleasant and useful preserve for us." As a result of "this mutual attachment, which your Highness expresses to us at every meeting," Euler declared, "our fellow citizens thank us . . . foreigners read our essays and promise to reciprocate . . . and the Free Economic Society receives the glory that places it on an equal footing with the most notable and most ancient societies."[121] At an extraordinary meeting summoned in June 1794, 10 days after Angal't's sudden death, Nartov further described the late president as a "friend and companion," whose dedication to the assembly and tireless activity made the Society such a notable success.[122] The Society's fond memories of Angal't were fundamentally no different than those of his students at the Cadet Corps. For both institutions, he was a powerful outsider assuming an insider's identity, agreeing to limit his own power for the good of his students and colleagues.

The preponderance of evidence suggests that the Society did not promote sustained and substantial interaction between members of different social status. Instead, it had become the nerve center for a group of academicians, civil servants, and literati responsible for publishing the *Trudy*. Many of these men came from the German states, having relocated to St. Petersburg to work for the Academy or civil administration.[123] After 1770, when editorial committees were formed to review and edit submissions for the *Trudy*, a growing number of Russian writers and translators also gravitated toward the Society's meeting hall to offer their services.[124] Judging by its regular work and routines, the Society had practically gone full circle to constitute the "agricultural class" of the Academy initially outlined by Catherine in 1763.

Standing in the center of the assembly's activities was the Russian Secretary and cofounder Andrei Nartov. He possessed the intellectual qualities and personal connections that the Society required in its day-to-day operations. With multiple ties to the German academic community and the young literati circles at the Cadet Corps, Nartov was a scholarly and affable writer of considerable talent who moved through a variety of social groups with chameleon-like ease.[125] And although he inherited from his father a small estate with 153 male souls in Novgorod province, he evidently had no interest in managing it.[126] Nartov was a creature of St. Petersburg. Like his fellow literati, he was committed to spreading enlightenment and possessed the social skills, literary talent, and work ethic to make it happen.[127] As Russian Secretary it was his job to edit and publish the *Trudy*, to draft the Society's official announcements, to petition the Empress and other patrons, and to circulate the weekly reminders of assembly meetings. Effectiveness in these networking tasks necessitated the kind of slick sociability that the Russian Secretary seemed to exude, but in the long run the Society became as depen-

dent upon his services as it was on Catherine's protection and the patronage
of its notable members. When he resigned from his post in February 1779,
the Society teetered on the verge of collapse. Following his departure, his
former colleagues admitted that "one and the same member [could not be]
burdened" with so much secretarial responsibility, for in his absence the
Society would cease to function, "as has happened in the case of his Excel-
lency Mr. Nartov."[128] Their words proved to be prophetic. For much of the
next decade, the Society languished in a comatose state as it wrestled with
stagnating recruitment, declining attendance at meetings, and a dramatic
slowdown in the publication of its journal.

When Nartov returned to his old post in December 1787, the assembly
rewarded him for his services with an annual gold medal.[129] By 1794 his
remuneration had increased to three medals a year.[130] Although Nartov's
dedication and diligence certainly merited special recognition, his public
service may have had a shadier side. J. H. Brown has speculated that Nartov went so far as to embezzle funds from the Society's treasury, a pos-
sibility given his modest salary at the Mining College, his lack of a large
supplementary income from his estate, and, if the memoirist Anna Labzina
is correct, his penchant for gambling and drinking.[131] More significantly,
all his work was for naught without an effective patron at the helm. In a
speech delivered before the assembly in July 1794 to Angal't's successor,
Peter Bogdanovich Passek, Nartov spelled out to him his chief duty as
president: "Our work will be made so much easier, pleasant, and glorious
if we are encouraged by your example, and, finding in you a defender and
representative at the throne of our wise autocrat, we shall merit her attention. That is our reward! That will satisfy all of our desires!"[132] The Society
certainly grabbed Catherine's attention, but not as it had expected. Writing
to Baron Friedrich Grimm in April 1795, the Empress ridiculed the Society
for taking advantage of her patronage, wasting her money on printing "useless books" which no one bought, "handing out prizes left and right," and
proposing contest questions, "each one more stupid and useless than the
other."[133] Deprived of Angal't's high-caliber protection, the unwritten rules
of disengagement that had governed patrons and clients in the Society for
decades returned with full force, reaching a low point in the months following Catherine's death in November 1796. Despite repeated efforts to secure
the personal protection of Paul I, Nartov and the assembly failed even to get
a nod out of him. The patrons were quick to follow suit: Passek immediately
resigned from his post, and no other notable accepted the assembly's offer
to assume leadership.

The party was over. On December 20, 1796, the regular members decided to give themselves medals and cash prizes in recognition of their

long-term service to the Society. All told, 17 members received some form of compensation. Nartov was singled out for his work with correspondents, governors, and aristocratic patrons; for editing the *Trudy;* and for his "patriotic encouragement of other members . . . to spread economic information in our fatherland."[134] Two weeks later, the assembly took the next logical step and unanimously approved him as president.[135] He held the post until his death in 1813. Although the Society never regained the glory it had enjoyed under Catherine II and Angal't, to Nartov's credit the Society never folded either. Having adapted to the unpredictable and unforgiving environment of patronage and public service, the Society had located a niche in Russia's social and cultural landscape, poised to offer its services to its next patron.

NOTES

1. A. N. Medushevskii, *Proekty agrarnykh reform v Rossii (XVIII-nachalo XXI veka)* (Moscow: Nauka, 2005), 46.

2. Dukes, 115, 117, 123: Augustine, 388–89, 396–405; Farrow, 103–6.

3. Kamenskii, *Ot Petra I do Pavla I*, 356.

4. V. I. Semevskii, *Krest'iane v tsarstvovanie Imperatritsy Ekateriny II*, volume 1, second edition (St. Petersburg: Tipografiia M.M. Stasiulevicha, 1903), XXV–XXVI; A. S. Lappo-Danilevskii, "Ekateriny II i krest'ianskii vopros," in *Velikaia reforma: Russkoe obshchestvo i krest'ianskii vopros v proshlom i nastoiashchem*, volume 1, ed., A. K. Dzhivelegov (Moscow: Izdatel'stvo I. D. Sytina, 1911), 181. For a dissenting view, see Isabel de Madariaga, "Catherine II and the Serfs: A Reconsideration of Some Problems," *Slavonic and East European Review* 52 (1974): 34–62.

5. Susan P. McCaffray, "Confronting Serfdom in the Age of Revolution: Projects for Serf Reform in the Time of Alexander I," *Russian Review* 64 (2005): 4–5.

6. Leonard, 87–88.

7. Roger Bartlett, *Human Capital: The Settlement of Foreigners in Russia, 1762–1804* (Cambridge: Cambridge University Press, 1979), 47–48.

8. *Izbrannye proizvedeniia russkikh myslitelei vtoroi poloviny XVIII veka*, volume 2, ed. I. Ia Shchipanov (Moscow: Izdatel'stvo moskovskogo universiteta, 1952), 33–36. See also Kamenskii, *Ot Petra I do Pavla I*, 354.

9. Roger Bartlett, "J.J. Sievers and the Russian Peasantry under Catherine II," *Jahrbücher für Geschichte Osteuropas* 32 (1984): 17–18; Jones, *Provincial Development in Russia*, 152–53.

10. J. G. Eisen, "Eines livländischen Patrioten Beschreiben der Leibeigenschaft, wie solche in Livland über die Bauern eingeführet," in *Sammlung Russischer Geschichte*, ed. G.F. Müller 9 (1764), 491–527.

11. Quoted in Roger Bartlett, "Russia's First Abolitionist: The Political Philosophy of J.G. Eisen," *Jahrbücher für Geschichte Osteuropas* 39 (1991): 167–68.

12. Semevskii, *Krest'ianskii vopros*, volume 1, 14–19; Madariaga, *Russia in the Age of Catherine the Great*, 63–65.

13. "Proekt D.S.S. i chlena dvortsovoi kontsiliarii Ivana Elagina ob opredelenii v neot"emlemoe vladenie dvortsovym krest'ianam zemlii i o razdache kazennykh dereven, za izvestnuiu platu, na vremennoe i opredelennoe vladenie vol'nym soderzhateliam," *Sbornik kniaza Obolenskago* 12 (1859): 31–41.

14. A. R. Barsukov, "Zhizneopisanie Kniazia Gr. Gr. Orlova," *Russkii Arkhiv* 2 (1873): 51; RGIA, f. 91, op. 1, d. 1, ll. 21–21ob,l. 25.

15. F. Udolov, "Sobranie ekonomicheskikh pravil," *Trudy* 15 (1770): 165; idem, "Pokazanie o sel'skom domostroitel'stve i zemledelii," *Trudy* 23 (1773): 118.

16. "Sobranie ekonomicheskikh pravil," 166, 178–79.

17. Richard Stites, *Revolutionary Dreams: Utopian Vision and Experimental Life in the Russian Revolution* (Oxford: Oxford University Press, 1989), 19–20.

18. "Sobranie ekonomicheskikh pravil," 168–72.

19. F. Udolov, "Ekonomicheskikh pravil chast' tretia o skotovodstve," *Trudy* 20 (1772): 188–98.

20. Quoted in Khodnev, 20–21.

21. "Preduvedomlenie," *Trudy* 1 (1765), no pagination.

22. RGIA, f. 91, op. 1, d. 1, ll. 27-28; d. 3, l. 4, ll. 9–10.

23. RGIA, f. 91, op. 1, d. 3, l. 43.

24. RGIA, f. 91, op. 1, d. 3, ll. 43-45; "Ob"iavlenie," *Trudy* 4 (1766): 201-3.

25. V. A. Somov, "Dva otveta Vol'tera na Peterburgskom konkurse o krest'ianskoi sobstvennosti," in Karp and Mezin, 150, 164.

26. The register of all essays received by the Society is found in RGIA, f. 91, op. 1, d. 388, ll. 111–13.

27. Bartlett, "The Free Economic Society," 205–09; Shovlin, 114–17; M. T. Beliavskii, "Frantsuzskie prosvetiteli i konkurs o sobstvennosti krepostnykh krest'ian v Rossii," *Vestnik Moskovskogo Universiteta* series 9 (1960): 26–51.

28. On Eisen, see Bartlett, "Russia's First Abolitionist," 163; on Voltaire, Marmontel, and du Pont de Nemours, see Somov, "Dva otveta Vol'tera na Peterburgskom konkurse o krest'ianskoi sobstvennosti," 152–63. See also Semevskii, *Krest'ianskii vopros*, volume 1, 61–64; for excerpts of Voltaire's essay, see M. T. Beliavskii, "Novye dokumenty ob obsuzhdenii krest'ianskogo voprosa v 1766–1768 godakh," *Arkheograficheskii ezhegodnik za 1958 god* (1960): 412–14; on Radishchev's unlikely authorship of #71, see V. Oreshkin, "Problemy chastnoi krest'ianskoi sobstvennosti na zemliu v krepostnoi Rossii XVIII v.," *Voprosy ekonomiki* 1 (1992): 149–50.

29. RGIA, f. 91, op. 1, d. 3, l. 50; reprinted in Khodnev, 24–25.

30. M. M. Shcherbatov, "Zapiski po krest'ianskomu voprosu," in *Neizdannye sochinenii* (Moscow: Ogiz, 1935), 8–11, 14. See also Roger Bartlett, "Defences of Serfdom in Eighteenth-Century Russia," in di Salvo and Hughes, 69–71.

31. Beliavskii, "Novye dokumenty ob obsuzhdenii krest'ianskogo voprosa v 1766–1768 godakh," 410–11; M. T. Beliavskii and L. A. Loone, "Dokumenty ob obsuzhdenii krest'ianskogo voprosa v vol'nom ekonomicheskom obshchestve v

1767–1768 gg.," *Arkeograficheskii ezhegodnik za 1960 god* (1962): 350; Semevskii, *Krest'ianskii vopros v Rossii*, volume 1, 89.

32. Two essays, Marmontel's among them, were later added to the fifteen finalists, bringing the total to seventeen. Compare the original list from the meeting of March 19, 1768 in RGIA, f. 91, op. 1, d. 5, l. 16 with the finalists announced on April 9, 1768 in RGIA, f. 91, op. 1, d. 388, 11. 114–16, reprinted in Beliavskii, "Novye dokumenty," 404–6.

33. Beliavskii, *Krest'ianskii vopros v Rossii*, 284–85. Many other Soviet historians advanced the same argument. See I. S. Bak, *Antifeodal'nye ekonomicheskie ucheniia v Rossii vtoroi poloviny XVIII v.* (Moscow: Nauka, 1958), 42–43; N. K. Karataev, *Ocherki po istorii ekonomicheskikh nauk v Rossii XVIII veka* (Moscow: Nauka, 1960), 55; Oreshkin, *Vol'noe ekonomicheskoe obshchestvo*, 64; Shtrange, 164–65.

34. RGIA, f. 91, op. 1, d. 388, ll. 115–16, reprinted in Beliavskii, "Novye dokumenty," 405–6.

35. Beliavskii, "Novye dokumenty," 399–400. See also I. S. Bak, "A.I. Polenov (filosofskie, obshchestvenno-politicheskie i ekonomicheskie vzgliady)," *Istoricheskie zapiski* 28 (1949): 198; Beliavskii, *Krest'ianskii vopros v Rossii*, 292–93; Shtrange, 166–68; Karataev, 63–65; Semevskii, *Krest'ianskii vopros*, volume 1, 82.

36. RGIA, f. 91, op. 1, d. 5, ll. 4–5; d. 388, l. 125, reprinted in Beliavskii and Loone, 359.

37. Esther Kingston-Mann, *In Search of the True West: Culture, Economics, and the Problems of Russian Development* (Princeton, NJ: Princeton University Press, 1999), 44–46.

38. RGIA, f. 91, op. 1, d. 388, l. 114, reprinted in Beliavskii, "Novye dokumenty," 404.

39. "Perevod sochineniia, prislannago v Vol'noe Ekonomicheskoe Obshchestvo v otvete na zadannyi v 1766 godu vopros: *'Chto poleznee dlia obshchestva, chtob krest'ianin imel v sobstvennosti zemliu, ili tokmo dvizhimoe imenie, i skol' daleko ego prava na to ili drugoe imenie prostirat'sia dolzhni," Trudy* 8 (1768): 30–32.

40. Ibid., 29.

41. Ibid., 23–25.

42. Ibid., 37–38, 52. See also Bartlett, "Defences of Serfdom in Eighteenth-Century Russia," in di Salvo and Hughes, 69–70.

43. "Perevod sochineniia," 42.

44. Medushevskii, 55. On Polenov's translation of Montesquieu, see N. Iu. Plavinskaia, "Kak perevodili Montesk'e v Rossii?" in Karp and Mezin, 281.

45. A. Polenov, "O krepostnom sostoianii krest'ian v Rossii,:" in Beliavskii, "Novye dokumenty," 414–30. A full translation appears in Ralph Blanchard Jr., "A Proposal for Social Reform in the Reign of Catherine the Great: Aleksei Polenov's Response to the Free Economic Society Competition of 1766–68" (PhD diss., State University of New York, Binghamton, 1972), 304–44. Unless otherwise noted, all references and citations come from Blanchard's translation.

46. Blanchard, 309, 310.

47. Ibid., 331–42.

48. Ibid., 325. See also J. L. Black, *Citizens for the Fatherland: Education, Educators, and Pedagogical Ideals in Eighteenth-Century Russia* (Boulder, CO: *East European Quarterly*, 1979), 86–88.

49. Beliavskii and Loone, 352, 353–54; Semevskii, *Krest'ianskii vopros*, volume 1, 63–65; Beliavskii, "Novye dokumenty," 408, 409, 413.

50. Semevskii, *Krest'ianskii vopros*, volume 1, 65–66, 69; Beliavskii, "Novye dokumenty," 408.

51. Beliavskii and Loone, 353–55; Blanchard, 321–42; Medushevskii, 61–64.

52. Beliavskii and Loone, 364, 366.

53. Semevskii, *Krest'ianskii vopros*, volume 1, 72.

54. Ibid., 73.

55. Ibid.

56. RGIA, f. 91, op. 1, d. 388, ll. 115, reprinted in Beliavskii, "Novye dokumenty," 405.

57. RGIA, f. 91, op. 1, d. 5, l. 29.

58. Ibid., l. 32.

59. Ibid., ll. 34–36. The eleven members in favor of publishing the essay included G.G. Orlov, V. G. Orlov, L. Euler, A. Euler, I. G. Chernyshev, Z. G. Chernyshev, R. L. Vorontsov, G. N. Teplov, I. I. Melissino, J. Sievers, and I. A. Taubert. The following fifteen members voted against publishing: A.S. Stroganov, A. V. Olsuf'ev, A. A. Nartov, A. V. Oleshev, T. von Klingshtedt, C. Peckey, Model, F. von Wol'f, I. P. Falk, Ekleben, A. I. Cherkasov, W. von Pol'man, F. Udolov, F. Epinus, J. J. von Staehlin. The minutes to the meeting do not clarify which member cast the sixteenth vote against publishing the essay.

60. Bartlett, "The Free Economic Society," 204.

61. RGIA, f. 91, op. 1, d. 5, l. 35. Shcherbatov made the same argument before the Legislative Commission. See Dukes, 125.

62. RGIA, f. 91, op. 1, d. 5, ll. 36–37, reprinted in Beliavskii, "Novye dokumenty," 406.

63. RGIA, f. 91, op. 1, d. 399, ll. 63–64; d. 28, ll. 47–47ob.

64. RGIA, f. 91, op. 1, d. 30, ll. 20ob-21, 28, 32ob, 92, 98ob; d. 35, ll. 47ob–50.

65. RGIA, f. 91, op. 1, d. 8, l. 61. One year later, five other notable members (K. G. Razumovskii, G. N. Teplov, Z. G. Chernyshev, A. I. Cherkasov, I. S. Boriatinskii) offered additional prize money with the stipulation that the winning answer apply to four provinces in the non-black-earth region and one in the steppe. See RGIA, f. 91, op. 1, d. 10, l. 49.

66. G. Grasman, "Otvet na zadachu o udobrenii zemli bez szheniia kubyshei," *Trudy* 19 (1771): 1–91.

67. RGIA, f. 91, op. 1, d. 12, l. 30; d. 14, l. 25, ll. 27–28; d. 15, l. 2.

68. G. Grasman, "Opredelenie zemli na odno krest'ianskoe tiaglo," *Trudy* 29 (1775): 40.

69. Ibid., 36–37.

70. Ibid., 32, 42–43, 45.

71. Grasman estimated that a household employing the three-field system required 36.5 desiatiny (the equivalent of 98.5 acres) to meet subsistence levels: six desiatiny each for winter grain, spring grain, and fallow; nine desiatiny for grazing land; and an additional 9.5 *desiatiny* for hayfields. See ibid., 58–61, 67.

72. Ibid., 73–75, 81, 84–86.

73. Significantly, in 1772 the Society almost approved holding a major essay competition on precisely the same theme: "In Russia's vast empire," the question began, "there are places which are so densely populated with peasants that, owing to their multitudes, there is insufficient land for cereals, hayfields, etc. By contrast, there are few people in those places where there is much land. And so, the Society promises a gold medal to the person who reports the easiest method of correcting this imbalance and of resettling peasants without entailing loss for either the peasant or pomeshchik." See RGIA, f. 91, op. 1, d. 10, l. 46.

74. "O zavedenii novago sel'skago domostroitel'stva, dlia khlebopashestva, skotovodstva i lesovodstva pri novozavodimykh selakh ili poseleniiakh, na sovershenno odichaloi, ne obrabotannoi, otdalennoi, no pri tom plodonosnoi pochve," *Prodolozehnie Trudov* 45 (1792): 260–61.

75. Ibid., 263–64.

76. Ibid., 282–83.

77. "O popravlenii dereven'," *Trudy* 17 (1770): 113–21.

78. Ibid., 115, 122–23.

79. Ibid, 126–32, 140–41.

80. Ibid., 133–34.

81. Ibid., 154–55.

82. Jones, *Emancipation*, 203–4.

83. Le Donne, *Ruling Russia*, 62, 66, 75, 78, 82.

84. Jones, *Emancipation*, 283.

85. Roger Bartlett, "Catherine II's Draft Charter to the State Peasantry," *Canadian-American Slavic Studies*, 23 (1989): 42–43, 45, 53–54; Jones, *Provincial Development in Russia*, 93.

86. Aleksei Oleshev, *Vozhd' k istinnomu blagorazumniiu i k sovershennomu shchastiiu* (St. Petersburg, 1780), 166–67.

87. Confino, *Domaines et seigneurs*, 134.

88. RGIA, f. 91, op. 1, d. 5, ll. 51–52. There is a discrepancy between the statute, which required members to submit three pieces a year, and Nartov's less-demanding condition of a single piece annually. In any case, the vast majority of members failed to meet either requirement.

89. RGIA, f. 91, op. 1, d. 6, l. 40.

90. Ibid., l. 41.

91. "Ustav Vol'nago Ekonomicheskago Obshchestva s populneniiami k prezhnemu, utverzhdennyi obshchim soglasiem chlenov Fevralia 24 dnia, 1770 goda," *Trudy* 17 (1771): 190–213.

92. RGIA, f. 91, op. 1, d. 6, l. 42. The donations came from the following men: G. G. Orlov, A. S. Stroganov, R. L. Vorontsov, I. G. Chernyshev, V. G. Orlov, A. P. Melgunov, A. I. Cherkasov, K. F. Kruze, J. Sievers, G. N. Teplov, W. von Pol'man.

Subsequent contributions in the next two years came from six more members of varying social status: A. G. Demidov, K. von Sievers, A. F. Turchaninov, Pavel G. Demidov, K. G. Razumovskii, I.S. Boriatinskii. See RGIA, f. 91, op. 1, d. 7, ll. 46–47; d. 8, l. 2; d. 10, 1.11, 1.49, 1.57.

93. M. E. Gize, "Andrei Andreevich Nartov (biograficheskii ocherk)," *Krae-vedcheskie zapiski: Issledovaniia i materialy* 4 (1996): 14–15.

94. Munro, 60.

95. P. Rychkov, "Primechaniia o prezhnem i nyneshnem zemledelii," *Trudy* 6 (1767): 61–63. Shcherbatov made the same criticism in his unpublished essay for the peasant property competition. See "Zapiski po krest'ianskomu voprosu," 4–5.

96. Norbert Elias, *The Court Society*, translated by Edmund Jephcott (New York: Pantheon, 1983), 48, 52–56, 64.

97. J. Regensburger, "O razdelenii izvestnoi summy na godovoi prozhitok," *Trudy* 21 (1772): 118; E. J. Schretter, "Opyt' domostroitel'stva i planov na ekonomi-cheskuiu zadachu 1770 i 1771 godu," *Trudy* 22 (1772): 4.

98. Schretter recommended at least 45 different positions: chief supervisor, home secretary, steward, head chef, assistant chef, pastry chef, bartender, wine steward, cof-fee master, gardener, valet, stallmaster, treasurer, silversmith, interior decorator, silver cleaner, purchaser, handyman, storage guard, spice commissar, page, kammerlackey, lackeys, negro, huntsman, footman, door openers, porter, floor polisher, head driver, coachmen, horseman, stableman, teachers and nannies, stokers, water-carriers, kitchen help, laundress, servants for lackeys, wardrobe keeper, linen-keeper, washerwoman, bed-makers, seamstress, kitchen-maid. See "Opyt' domostroitel'stva," 105–216.

99. Ibid., 131, 147–48, 172, 181, 229–30, 234.

100. Ibid., 110, 118, 134, 139.

101. Ibid., 80, 83.

102. Ibid., 88.

103. Regensburger, "O razdelenii," 165–66, 171.

104. Ibid., 137–64.

105. I. Georgii, "Otvet na zadannuiu Vol'nym Rossiiskim Ekonomicheskim Obshchestvom v Sanktpeterburg na 1783 god zadachu: 'Kak Rossiianin posredstven-nago sostoianiia, po vvedenomu teper' obrazu zhit'ia, vse svoi nuzhdy, v razsuzhdenii pishchi, napitkov, odezhdy i zhilishcha, ne tol'ko s kraineiu nuzhdu, no i sootvetst-venno blagopristoinosti, spokoistviiu, udovol'stviiu i zdraviiu, odnimi Rossiiskimi neobdelannymi produktami udovol'stvovat' mozhet,'" *Prodolzhenie Trudov* 5 (1784): 5. See also David Griffiths, "Eighteenth-Century Perceptions of Backward-ness: Projects for the Creation of a Third Estate in Catherinian Russia," *Canadian-American Slavic Studies* 13 (1979): 452–72.

106. Georgii, "Otvet," 66–67.

107. Ibid., 28, 62–63.

108. Habermas, 38.

109. David Griffiths, "Catherine II's Charters: A Question of Motivation," *Cana-dian-American Slavic Studies* 23 (1989): 62.

110. R. Vorontsov, "O zavedenii zapasnogo khleba," *Trudy* 1 (1766), 1–10; "O spo-sobakh k: ispravleniiu sel'skago domostroitel'stva," *Trudy* 5 (1767), 1–12; "Priglashenie

sel'skikh domostroitelei," *Trudy* 13 (1769): 1–6; S. Ushakov, "Delo sovershenno," *Trudy* 23 (1773): 1–28; "Dopolnenie o plodorodii ozimago khleba," *Trudy* 23 (1773): 29–40; "O dernovoi krovle," *Trudy* 23 (1773): 41–50; J. Sievers, "O razplod zemlianykh iablok," *Trudy* 5 (1767): 201–5; P. Konovitsyn, "O proizrastenii kyrlyka," *Trudy* 40 (1790): 39–48; "Izvestie o mashine dlia riazlomaniia l'da," *Trudy* 40 (1790): 49–53; A. Lunin, "Opisanie novoi kirpichnago zavoda pechi," *Trudy* 47 (1793): 90–124.

111. P. S. Svistunov, Adam von Bril, Fedor Angal't, and A. I. Svechin.

112. R. L. Vorontsov, A. V. Olsuf'ev, A. I. Cherkasov, G. N. Teplov, W. von Pol'man, V. G. Orlov, A. S. Stroganov, P. N. Trubetskoi, T. I. Ostervald, S. F. Ushakov, K. A. von Bok, S. I. Viazemskii, I. F. von Lipgard.

113. The Society did not begin to record attendance at assembly meetings until late 1766. Table 3.3 begins with 1767, the first year for which there is complete data.

114. For a useful description of assembly meetings in the 1760s and 1770s, based on the correspondence of Society member Albrecht Euler, see Bartlett, "The Free Economic Society," 189.

115. RGIA, f. 91, op. 1, d. 25, l. 62; d. 27, l. 9, 1.34 ob.

116. N. N. Aurova, "Idei prosveshcheniia v 1-m kadetskom korpuse (konets XVIII-pervaia chetvert' XIX v.), *Vestnik Moskovskogo Universiteta* series 8, 1 (1996): 35.

117. Alexander Viskovatov, *Kratkaia istoriia pervago kadetskago korpusa* (St. Petersburg: Voennaia tipografiia glavnago shtaba, 1832), 46.

118. Aurova, 36-37; Fedor Glinka, "1-I kadetskii korpus volyn' i dal'neishiia snosheniia moi s Miloradovichem," *Moskvitianin* 1 (1846): 35–38.

119. RGIA, f. 91, op. 1, d. 30, l. 164ob. ll. 170–72.

120. RGIA, f. 91, op. 1, d. 32, ll. 21–22; see also "Raznyia proizshestviia s 28-go Oktiabria 1788 goda, vo vremia prezidentstva Grafa Angal'ta po 28-e Oktiabria, 1789 goda," *Prodolzhenie Trudov* 10 (1790): 249–50.

121. "Privetstvie k Prezidentu Ekonomicheskago Obshchestva, govorennoe Nad-vornym Sovetnikom i Kavelerom A. Eulerom 10 Dekabria 1793 goda," *Prodolzhenie Trudov* 19 (1794): 336–39.

122. RGIA., f. 91, op. 1, d. 47, ll. 188–89ob., 1, 191.

123. So extensive was the overlap between the Academy and the Society that out of the 52 persons admitted into the Academy between 1750 and 1796, 22 joined the Society. Many of them became active members. See *Akademiia nauk SSSR: Personal'nyi sostav* (Moscow, 1974), 17–29.

124. Among them were many leaders of Russia's first generation of literati: M. M. Kheraskov, G. V. Kozitskii, N. N. Motonis, P. I. Pastukhov, V. I. Maikov, I. I. Glebovskii, and V. G. Ruban, to name only a few.

125. Gize, 7–13; N. Novikov, *Opyt istoricheskago slovaria*, 145–47.

126. F. N. Zagorskii, *Andrei Konstantinovich Nartov, 1693–1756* (Leningrad, 1969), 52.

127. Gary Marker, "The Creation of Journals and the Profession of Letters in the Eighteenth Century," in *Literary Journals in Imperial Russia*, ed., Deborah Martinsen (Cambridge: Cambridge University Press, 1997), 14–16; Gleason, 76–77; Gareth Jones, *Nikolay Novikov: Enlightener of Russia* (Cambridge: Cambridge University Press, 1984), 170–71.

128. RGIA, f. 91, op, 1, d. 17, ll. 10–11, 1.26. Bolotov confirms that the organization's troubles in the late 1770s were caused in part by Nartov's resignation. See *Zapiski Andreia Timofeevicha Bolotova, 1737–1796*, volume two, 346.

129. RGIA, f. 91, op. 1, d. 30, ll. 77ob.–78.

130. RGIA, f. 91, op. 1, d. 47, l. 240.

131. J. H. Brown, "The Publication and the Distribution of the *Trudy* of the Free Economic Society, 1765–1796," *Russian Review* 36 (July, 1977): 347–49. In a brief autobiographical note dating from the mid-1780s, Nartov gives his salary as 2,375 rubles. See A. A. Nartov, *Rasskazy o Petre Velikom (po avtorskoi rukopisi)* (St. Petersburg: Istoricheskaia illiustratsiia, 2001), 55. On Nartov's lifestyle, see Anna Evdokimovna Labzina, *Days of a Russian Noblewoman: The Memories of Anna Labzina, 1758–1821*, trans. and ed. Gary Marker and Rachel May (DeKalb, IL: Northern Illinois University Press, 2001), 65.

132. RGIA, f. 91, op. 1, d. 47, l. 237ob.

133. *Sbornik imperatorskogo russkogo istoricheskogo obshchestva* 23 (1873): 627–28.

134. RGIA, f. 91, op. 1, d. 53, ll. 275ob–277ob.

135. RGIA, f. 91, op. 1, d. 57, l. 2.

Chapter Four

Voices from the Provinces

The Free Economic Society presented a cosmopolitan façade to its public. Glancing at a membership register published in 1779, 154 names appear in chronological order of admittance with scant reference to places of origin and residence.[1] Casual observers had no way of knowing that "Mr. Beardé" came from Aachen and never met any of his comembers while "Magistrate Regensburger" lived in St. Petersburg and hardly ever missed a meeting. It was even harder to tell apart the ones who had retired to their country estates or worked in the provinces from those who spent their lives and careers in the capitals—the names of provincial members turn up only with their service rank and title just like all the others. As one scholar has recently noted, as late as the mid-nineteenth century most educated Russians collapsed all the provinces into an enormous and homogenous "not capital" bereft of any meaningful regional identities.[2] That was the Society's intention as well. Whether one lived in the capital or the tiniest village, Society membership signified a larger commitment to serving the general welfare that transcended local allegiances.

At a practical level, however, cosmopolitanism presented certain problems. If the Society's leaders regarded retirement on the estate as a temporary condition likely to be disrupted by the pomeshchik's return to state service, how could they ever really bring Russian agriculture to perfection? In an early attempt to balance the reality of noble absenteeism with the Society's dreams of enlightening the countryside, Klingshtedt in 1766 urged the great magnates in the assembly to invest in the training of competent estate managers. Traditionally recruited from the ranks of the peasantry, these stewards had a reputation for indolence and corruption. Frustrated with this system, lords had begun to transfer increasingly large numbers of serfs from barshchina to obrok. While this may have eliminated the need for stewards, it also lured

101

peasants away from the estate, which, in Klingshtedt's view, diminished agriculture's appeal and exacerbated fears of its decay.[3] Unwilling to accept either incompetent stewards or wandering peasants, Klingshtedt proposed a solution conceived in the Petrine spirit: recruiting the best and brightest peasants in their teens for a lengthy term of study in the Baltic provinces where they would study scientific agriculture, later returning to Russia as qualified managers.[4]

It was highly unlikely for pomeshchiki to make this sort of investment. The best peasants belonged behind a plow, not a desk, and shipping them off to study at the height of their physical strength defied common sense. The following year President Alexander Stroganov proposed an interesting alternative: holding a competition for the best "model instruction to a steward in the absence of his lord."[5] Its timing was no coincidence—coming immediately on the heels of the peasant property contest, the Society probably intended the winning submission to serve as a blueprint for reforming peasant behavior, just as Beardé had recommended. Only five submissions trickled in by the deadline, four in German and one in Russian.[6] The lackluster response compelled the assembly to extend the deadline and urge its members "who are absent from St. Petersburg" to participate, a message no doubt intended for Peter Rychkov and Andrei Bolotov.[7] In the meantime, after much hand-wringing the contest committee agreed to give the prize to Baron von Wol'f.[8] His essay showed how quickly and completely the rational housekeeper bowed before the time-honored customs of the peasantry. Its eight chapters covered all the components of the traditional manorial economy—cereals, animal husbandry, forestry, side-work, labor management, inventory and accounting, and the selling of village products. Not once did he advise disrupting the peasantry's work routines and techniques—quite the opposite in fact: he explicitly urged the steward to follow the example of the wealthiest peasants in sowing and harvesting.[9] Only in forest maintenance did Wol'f try to rationalize his methods, rotating his reserves over a 15-year period, systematically replacing felled trees with new seedlings, and barring peasants from slash-and-burn practices.[10] Another entry submitted by Fedot Udolov displayed an equally profound aversion to risky technical innovations, advising lords to tighten the managerial reins in order to extract greater revenues. Just as he had done several years before in his "Economic Regulations," Udolov organized large estates into twelve-person labor units under the authority of a steward who oversaw all farming tasks and maintained detailed inventories.[11] Aside from the expansion of arable and a renewed emphasis on fertilizing the winter fields, the agricultural methods in Udolov's instruction revealed nothing new.

Roman Vorontsov also weighed in on these debates, suggesting that lords leave estate management entirely to peasants. Agreeing with Klingshtedt on the inherent corruption of stewards, who "consider it their chief objective to despise the peasants," he advocated stripping away most of their managerial authority and leaving them only bookkeeping responsibilities. Under Vorontsov's plan, peasants would elect their "most able and diligent leaders" to courts responsible for overseeing all aspects of village life: agricultural work, justice, military conscription, land distribution, child welfare, and arranging marriages.[12] Michel Confino once noted the incompatibility of Vorontsov's proposal with the servility of the manorial system. The research of Edgar Melton has further demonstrated that the great families who attempted to put Vorontsov's "enlightened seigneurialism" into practice encountered the fiercest resistance from the most "upstanding" peasants who used their powers to loot the village treasury and to compel poor peasants into the army against their will.[13]

Yet Vorontsov also saw the link between noble residency and real improvements in farming. In May 1769 he offered his seaside dacha on the Gulf of Finland to the assembly for experiments with a new threshing machine. It was the first time since the Society's establishment that one of them proposed doing something with their hands. Events conspired to thwart his plans: first the machine broke, then in October the Society itself almost fell apart.[14] Two months later, as the Society was teetering on the brink of total collapse, Vorontsov again tried moving his colleagues in a more practical direction. First he sponsored a competition for the best fertilizing alternative to slash-and-burn practices employed by the peasants of Koporsk, a district near St. Petersburg where some of his estates were located. The winner was the same Gottfried Grasman who later earned a gold medal for his book on land allotments for peasant households.[15] At the same meeting Vorontsov delivered a rousing exhortation to pomeshchiki from all provinces to move back to their estates and conduct agricultural experiments. His address appeared in the next issue of the *Trudy*. "The majority of our rural housekeepers think that they have done everything and are worthy of praise if they have sown a great amount of grain," he announced, "but do not think whether it was done at the right time, or whether it was tilled and fertilized." To eradicate these "old-fashioned" ways, he proposed that the Society recognize those "zealous agricultural improvers" who forged a culture of experimentation and innovation in the provinces.[16]

For many historians, these debates testify to the stubborn persistence of noble absenteeism after 1762 and the inability of Russian landowners to refashion themselves into agricultural improvers. Most notably, Peter Kolchin has argued that an "absentee mentality" was the inevitable result of the nobility's service orientation. Dependent on their state salaries for income, these men existed for their service careers and regarded the ancestral estate as an outpost for exiled aristocrats who had fallen out of favor at court. Hardly ever did nobles feel at home there, and those who did were ridiculed by the service elite as "grubby" country bumpkins. Since so few nobles sank deep roots in the country, they never developed a truly agrarian way of life independent of Russia's service culture.[17] While Kolchin's thesis certainly holds true for the wealthiest nobles whose serfs numbered in the thousands, it ignores the steady emergence of a class of residential nobles after 1762. Using records from the Imperial Heraldmeister Office, I. V. Faizova has uncovered a "flight of officers" from the military in the decade following their emancipation in 1762. Most were petty and middling nobles who hoped to scratch out a living on their estates.[18] Catherine's Statute on the Provinces of 1775 reinforced the steady growth of the provincial gentry. Topographical reports from the 1790s indicate that more than half of all Russian nobles resided in their native localities, dividing their time between newly created administrative posts in the provincial capitals and their family estates. Unlike their fathers and grandfathers who had served for life, these men spent relatively brief periods in military service before retiring.[19]

Certain provisions of the Statute on the Provinces proved difficult to implement. The creation of new towns and self-governing institutions from scratch was especially challenging; many turned out to be overgrown villages while others existed only on paper. In the cultural sphere, the results were somewhat more encouraging. One of the reform's institutional centerpieces was the provincial noble assembly, whose members were elected by local landowners and chaired by a noble marshal for a three-year term. The assemblies did not act as a check on the power of the governors. Instead, they involved local gentry more closely in the administration of their home provinces and brought a certain measure of European culture to Russia's hinterland. In this sense, the reform was more successful. By the end of the century Tula guberniia alone had more than 200 noble authors, most of them writing for a local audience. Meanwhile growing numbers of writers across Russia produced hundreds of works of local history (*kraevedenie*) catering to the antiquarian curiosity of their family, friends, and neighbors.[20] In her history of the Russian country estate, Priscilla Roosevelt has reconstructed the patterns of life for these people in great detail: constant travel and visiting between estates; elaborate tables, parties, and dances; elections for noble assemblies in the district and provincial capitals; and the numerous trade fairs where nobles stocked up on provisions and hobnobbed with other members of their class.[21]

The Free Economic Society hoped to mold these masses of retired gentry into agricultural improvers. Ever since its foundation it invited them to participate in the project, and hundreds responded to the call. Most turned out to be fly-by-nighters who petitioned the assembly for special favors and privileges in exchange for so-called "secrets" before scurrying back into the woodwork. Thus, the author of one letter offered to divulge a cheap and easy method of manure preparation for an undisclosed price, only to learn that the assembly recognized men "who further the general welfare out of zeal alone." Another pomeshchik tried to convince the assembly to give him the money to purchase 86 peasant households in a nearby district in exchange for revealing his own method for harvesting rye. And then there was Fedor Kalugin, the inventor of a perpetual motion machine. The Society returned his letter by order of Catherine herself.[22]

Others fared better. A few managed to win formal recognition for their efforts, and still a smaller number became regular contributors to the *Trudy* and members of the Society. One of the assembly's first decisions was to recruit such men as "lovers of farming and domostroitel'stvo" provided they first inform a member of their intentions and pay a fee of 10 rubles.[23] The campaign ended in disappointment. By 1770 the Society counted only six provincial members: Baron von Wol'f of Ingermanland, who regularly attended meetings of the assembly; the geographer Peter Rychkov, then in retirement on his Orenburg estate; Grigorii Orlov's client, Fedot Udolov; Aleksei Oleshev of Vologda; Andrei Bolotov of Tula; and Baron von Zaltse of Livonia.[24] Although a few other rustics ventured to submit their work, they all drifted back into obscurity and were never invited to join. Clearly, the Society would have to cast its net more widely. In August 1771, it resolved to use governors to comb their respective provinces for zealous nobles who might be interested in joining the organization. This campaign produced only two new members and underscored the futility of appealing to the provinces.[25] Fifteen years later, the Society targeted the 42 directors of "domestic science" (*domovodtsvo*) established by the Statute on the Provinces of 1775. These men formed a ready-made set of contacts.[26] Inviting them all to join, the assembly promised in return to divulge "useful information which only it [i.e., the Society] possesses or can obtain."[27] Fourteen responses to the assembly have been preserved. Most of them expressed interest in the Society's mission and were flattered by the invitation, but they also understood that membership required a lot of unpaid work. Only a handful accepted the Society's offer.[28]

Recruitment in the provinces remained unsystematic (and discriminatory) to the extreme. When the young Tula writer Vasilii Alekseevich Levshin first contacted the assembly in 1772, he included with his letter his own translation of the classic seventeenth-century work *Lifland Economy*. He was not invited to join until 19 years later, long after his translations, plays, and stories had made him a famous man.[29] Not even wealth and royal connections guaranteed acceptance. Astrakhan governor and former courtier Nikita Afonas'evich Beketov won public acclaim in 1771 when the academician and scientific explorer Samuel Gmelin published a brief description of his model estate, but only in 1793 did he finally become a corresponding member.[30] Often new recruits were discovered by accident. One correspondent from Mogilev informed the assembly of a local pomeshchik who had operated a successful textile mill on his estate for twenty years, an achievement which earned the neighbor membership in the Society and praise from the assembly "for not being a sponger." That same year the academician Peter Simon Pallas met Dmitrii Agafi, a Greek globetrotter whose experiments with sesame and cotton seeds impressed the assembly so much that he was immediately asked to join.[31]

For enterprising country gentry, discovering the Society was like an act of God that gave them the chance to rise above their station and mingle with Russia's most notable people. When the Yaik Cossack Vasilii Tambovtsov won a silver medal for his experiments with hemp oil he compared the award to "the deity breathing new life into me."[32] Writing many years later, Bolotov recalled his first encounter with the *Trudy* in 1766 at a Moscow kiosk as a magically transformative experience:

> The booklet's title sparked my curiosity. For many, such an economic society was foreign and the booklet might as well have been written in Double Dutch. But to me, who had already read a sufficient amount of foreign economic works, these matters were already known. I had enough understanding of economic societies in other lands and all their statutes that, seeing from this booklet that now we too had established such a [society], and moreover that it was distinguished to have been taken under the special protection of the empress herself, I nearly jumped for joy, reading it with enormous greed from cover to cover. My satisfaction deepened still more when I saw that all of us nobles who resided in villages, regardless of title, were invited by the Society to send in economic observations following the example of foreign [societies]. In order to guide us along this most suitable path there was attached at the end of the booklet 65 questions of such a kind and about such matters that required neither great intelligence nor strain to answer, if only someone who had an understanding of the rural economy and knew how to write would pick up a pen.[33]

No wonder that recruiting provincial correspondents was so difficult—the halo of royal authority frightened them away. Rychkov implied as much in a letter to Gerhard Müller: "Here in Orenburg I can lead the best people to [the Society] if it recommends that I do so . . . It is only necessary that a skilled man review their essays, for though many of them think well, not all of them write well enough for the public or for such a distinguished assembly."[34]

The Society's Statute on Correspondents, approved and published in 1790, formalized the unequal and hierarchical relationship between town and country. In order to be admitted, correspondents had to publish a minimum of two pieces a year or be nominated by five members and then approved by two-thirds of the assembly. To maintain their status, they had to submit at least one piece annually and respond to all correspondence. Although they could attend meetings, they did not have voting privileges.[35] Just as the Society's leadership had to internalize the etiquette of court society, so were its provincial affiliates expected to submit to rules of public behavior that highlighted their dependency on the leading members in the capital.

These men were different. Perceived by regular members as self-made exiles, they lacked the connections that sustained cultural life and intellectual exchange in the cities. They tended to be an insecure and resentful lot. As Michael Kugler has argued in a thoughtful study of European provincial intellectuals during the Enlightenment, their reliance on urban culture for sustenance and direction collided with their rural isolation, leaving them in a mental limbo that typically found expression in rigid dichotomies. Most obviously they functioned as intermediaries between the "public-minded" metropolis and the "chaotic and medieval" countryside, producing an uneasy blend of dueling identities that Kugler sees as a clash between "barbarism and civilization."[36] While the Society's correspondents belonged to Russia's public sphere, they also regarded themselves as voices from the interior, mindful of their subordinate status yet proud of their practical, hands-on experience in the country. And in contrast to their St. Petersburg colleagues, they claimed to possess inside knowledge of Russia's rural economy and the limitations inherent in the Society's projects for enlightenment. Few Russians understood better than they that public culture was virtually nonexistent in the countryside. When it did appear, the service culture of the capitals provided the stimulus.

Yet the anxieties deriving from their geographical remoteness also generated considerable creativity. By interfacing with the Society, rural correspondents developed a discourse of enlightened otherness that elevated them above their immediate surroundings but never quite earned them equality with their urban colleagues. Certainly its most distinctive feature was the representation of long-term residence in the countryside as an achievement in and of itself. When Oleshev, Rychkov, and Bolotov first contacted the assembly, they rattled off the years spent on their estates as their main qualification for inclusion in the Society. Baltic German correspondents also liked to specify the length of their residence in the country and never tired of reminding the assembly that practical experience always trumped scientific theory. "Above all I must inform [this assembly] with submissiveness," wrote one Lifland baron with 47 years under his belt, "that all the fine and useful theoretical essays notwithstanding, it is practice which for the most part comprises the heart of the matter." Frederick von Wol'f, the first provincial lord to join the Society, likewise made the distinction between the "physicists and chemists" in the assembly and the "practitioners of agriculture [who] know so much better."[37] Stating the duration of one's residency in the countryside became a kind of validation stamp, no matter how long it was and even if it produced only failure or frustration.

Of course, the Society had its regular members who knew the hinterland very well, academicians like Pallas, Gmelin, and Ivan Ivanovich Lepekhin, who had explored the empire, reported back to the assembly, and published their findings.[38] But like many absentee lords visiting their estates, these men were just passing through. They lived and worked in the capital, appearing regularly at assembly meetings and representing Russian intellectual life to their counterparts in Europe. The experiences of provincial members reversed this process. In his recent study of the mythology surrounding Mikhail Lomonosov, Steven Usitalo has argued that Russian intellectuals of low and insecure status tended to present their life paths as an ascent from darkness and ignorance to the shining heights of enlightenment.[39] Like Lomonosov, the prototypical self-made intellectual, the Society's provincial correspondents had to work hard to prove their worth. As the Karelian geologist and Society member Samuel Alopeus wrote, local peasants were simply not intelligent enough to discover and develop the wealth of natural resources lying at their feet.[40] In his topography of the White Sea, the Archangel merchant Alexander Fomin echoed these sentiments, claiming to uncover a "new world" discernible "only to a few minds."[41]

Although wanting to activate public discourse in the countryside, provincial correspondents still regarded peasants and petty nobles as antique curiosities, virtually immune to the kind of reasoned argument and debate that appeared in the *Trudy*. In 1769 Bolotov informed the assembly of a local pomeshchik who refused to divulge to his neighbors his secret for treating cattle fever during a particularly calamitous outbreak of the epidemic.[42] Condemning the neighbor's behavior, he announced to the Society his own treatment for the illness, setting an example of openness for other nobles to publicize their own cures.[43] In a similar vein, the Livonian writer Wilhelm Fribe likened the Society's opponents in the countryside to primitives who were content with subsistence farming instead of following the innovators "at the highest stage of enlightenment who seek perfection."[44] It is fitting that Fribe wrote these words in response to one of the Society's essay contests, for he and other correspondents liked to believe that enlightenment inevitably sprang from the open exchange of ideas facilitated by such events. Although they admitted that peasants and poor nobles could be inventive at the microlevel of their villages, laziness and stupidity locked most of them into a permanent dark age. "It is very rare to find here any locals who think about draining swamps, even though it would not require that much labor," wrote Tobolsk's economic director in 1793. "Its cause is both the excess of land and the resulting laziness of the locals, who in all justice can not be called diligent." Or one Baltic baron's lament: "[The] local peasant ignoramus rejects all novelties, for to him they seem laborious and useless." And for Herman von Rading, the economic director of Astrakhan province, "commoners care little about what came and happened before them."[45] In sum, public life demanded the revelation of secrets, which otherwise went to the grave with their makers. "Reason does not permit us to wallow in silence," Oleshev wrote in his first communication to the assembly. "[We] will soon see how the Free Economic Society proves itself to be filled with true patriots and devoted sons of the fatherland."[46]

*****

Peter Rychkov's name was bound to appear on the membership lists of the Free Economic Society. Before entering, he had already established a national reputation as the geographer and historian of the Orenburg frontier. He was also known in government circles for his expertise in industry, mining, and commerce. His writings publicized and celebrated the transplanting of European civilization into the Russian Empire under the watchful eye of its reforming monarchs. In his debut article, he argued that Peter I's protectionist policies had enabled Russia's merchants to harness the Empire's resources "to the amazement of Europe."[47] A few years later he justified Russia's expansion into Central Asia with the same logic. As he asserted in *History of Orenburg*, God had ordained the Russians to Christianize the barbarians and idolaters of the steppe who were too lazy and unimaginative "to enlighten" (*prosvetit'*) themselves.[48] Now in retirement after a long and exhausting career, Rychkov similarly sought to harness the resources and productive forces of his estate, bringing profit to himself and practical enlightenment to his peasants. Nominated for membership in 1765 along with Aleksei Petrovich Melgunov, Zakhar Chernyshev, and Frederick von Wol'f, he was admitted into the Society on the strength of his "efforts to improve agriculture and estate management in Russia."[49] Rychkov dutifully reciprocated by submitting an essay entitled "Observations on Past and Present Farming." Its central theme anticipated much of his later work for the *Trudy*.[50] Linking the widespread use of obrok to the decay of agriculture, Rychkov blamed Russia's supposed economic crisis on the nobility's loss of virtue. Following the end of mandatory service in 1762, he claimed, many landowners had chosen to live in the country, yet instead of devoting themselves to farming, they opted for idleness. To Rychkov, this demonstrated that nobles had deviated from their traditional roles and responsibilities. "Our ancient Slavic forefathers," he opined nostalgically, "were glorious in war through their bravery, glorious in domestic and international commerce, and glorious in every type of estate management (*domostroitel'stvo*) through their great efforts in agriculture, animal husbandry, and apiculture." A robust agricultural economy started with masters and serfs performing their natural occupations. The peasant's "natural knowledge" of farming required him to remain in the fields and behind a plow, just as the nobleman's privileged status obliged him to eschew idleness, live modestly, and keep a "full granary."[51]

Here Rychkov embodied the agrarian virtues that the Society wanted to cultivate in its public. Unlike many of its own members, who postured as modern-day Cincinnatuses, Rychkov actually resided in the country. Writing to his friend and patron Gerhard Müller in June 1760, one month after leaving service, he described his retirement with joyous relief: "I take pleasure in and enjoy the country life. My domestic economy gives me as much to do as the chancellery, but here there is tranquility like I never see in the city."[52] And in contrast to his neighbors, who, as he claimed, whiled away the hours in idleness and luxury, he led a life of rustic simplicity worthy of the leading citizens of ancient Rome. Or so he wanted people to believe. As early as 1761 he began fighting desperately to return to state service in order to escape the frustration and drudgery of what he called "my country life." Membership in the Society helped to offset the disastrous consequences of his decision, but only a little bit. Truth be told, Rychkov failed miserably as a country squire: his peasants hated him, his stewards embezzled his money, and his house and factories burned to the ground. Yet through all his travails he maintained his lifeline to the Free Economic Society. In the end, it was Russia's rising public culture that gave his life meaning, not the country estate which his writings for the *Trudy* made famous as a model farm for peasants and nobles alike.[53]

Born in Vologda in 1712 to a merchant family, Rychkov was one of "12 or 13" children and the only son to survive to adulthood. For this reason, perhaps, his father made sure he received the best possible education for someone of his station. By his teenage years he was apprenticing at the Moscow textile factory of the English entrepreneur John Paul Thomas. There he continued his schooling, concentrating on foreign languages, mathematics, and accounting before moving to St. Petersburg, where in 1730 he promptly landed a position with the glass manufacturer William Elmsel, another Englishman who owned a factory 100 miles outside the city. Impressed by Rychkov's work ethic, Elmsel entrusted him with all the managerial responsibilities. Yet Rychkov was too ambitious to remain a factory manager for very long. Soon after, he secured another job with the St. Petersburg Customs House as a translator and bookkeeper. Although the position paid a paltry 150 rubles a year, it did secure him a foothold at the bottom of the Table of Ranks as well as the patronage of its director, Senator I. K. Kirilov. When Kirilov was appointed director of the newly organized Orenburg expedition in 1734, he recruited Rychkov as its bookkeeper.[54]

Aside from a few trips to Moscow and St. Petersburg, Rychkov would spend the rest of his life on the Orenburg frontier, working to establish the Russian presence in the region and to integrate its Bashkir, Kirghiz, and Karakalpak tribes into the imperial power structure. His competence, dedication, and ambition became immediately apparent to his superiors. Vasilii Tatishchev, who served as governor from 1737 to 1739, often left the entire chancellery in Rychkov's hands, no mean achievement considering Rychkov's youth, low rank, and lack of military experience. Tatishchev was equally impressed with the young man's scholarly potential, enlisting him to assist in the collection of topographical information for his posthumously published magnum opus, *History of Russia from Ancient Times*.[55] As A. A. Sevastianova has emphasized, Tatishchev envisioned a comprehensive history of Russia that assimilated regional perspectives into the national narrative, and his example inspired Rychkov to produce a similarly exhaustive study of Orenburg province.[56] Throughout the 1740s and 1750s he traveled extensively across the region, assembling data for his most famous work, *Orenburg Topography*, whose publication in 1762 sealed his reputation as a scholar and administrator. For Rychkov, the Russian conquest of the steppe signaled the triumph of "enlightenment," at least as he understood it: orderly government, efficient development of natural resources, and the establishment of Christianity. While most of his coworkers in the chancellery looked upon the nomadic peoples of Orenburg as wild animals fit for violent expulsion, Rychkov advocated their peaceful conversion to what one scholar has called "the Russian way of life based on agriculture." This would be accomplished through scientific study of the province as well as a steady influx of Russian settlers whose presence would encourage the Bashkirs and other tribes to settle permanently and begin farming.[57]

In 1743, after nine years of service on the Orenburg line and thanks to Tatishchev's tireless petitioning on his behalf, Rychkov finally earned hereditary noble status. That same year he capped his success by purchasing a village of 172 serfs on 1,040 desiatiny of land in Ufa province, 300 miles north of Orenburg near the town of Bugul'ma. He named it Spasskoe. Over the next 15 years, Rychkov acquired additional property eight kilometers away from Spasskoe and a third village near Moscow.[58] Throughout this time he did his best to balance state service with his own economic pursuits at Spasskoe—distilling, apiculture, and metallurgy especially—and it may have been in the 1750s that he first got the unusual idea of leaving service and living as a private man off the profits of his enterprises.[59] In a pastoral essay of

1757, appropriately entitled "Letter on living the country life," he exhorted his fellow nobles (and presumably himself) to emulate the ancient Romans by rejuvenating themselves occasionally by gardening, hunting, and fishing.[60] Still, at this point Rychkov clearly saw Spasskoe mainly as a status symbol—suitable for relaxation, retirement, and burial, but not much else. In a personal testament addressed to his sons, Rychkov faithfully documented his steady ascent up the Table of Ranks to College Counselor, using his many promotions as pegs on which to hang the rest of his life—marriage, friendships, the births and deaths of children. Of Spasskoe there is hardly any mention.[61]

While not working at the Orenburg chancellery or relaxing at Spasskoe, Rychkov was striking out on a literary career. Since 1755 he had been publishing in *Monthly Compositions*, whose editor Müller soon became his most faithful patron, friend, and correspondent. Over the course of the next decade, the journal published 10 articles by Rychkov, not including serialized versions of *History of Orenburg* and *Orenburg Topography*.[62] Rychkov's success as a writer prompted Müller to praise him as the exemplary provincial intellectual—"if only there was a man in every province as artful and diligent as Counselor Rychkov of Orenburg" were his exact words.[63] While fueling Rychkov's literary ambitions, this first taste of fame also aggravated his frustration of having to work around men of higher status and noble lineage but (in his mind) inferior intelligence. As he counseled his sons: "Always render service to the fatherland and do not enter into disputes or conversations about your family, no matter how much they reproach you. I consider such arguments useless because only the greatest harm and dishonor can come from them, especially to young people."[64]

After two years of correspondence with Müller, he felt sufficiently comfortable to petition him for protection from the indignities meted out to him at the chancellery: "Is it possible [for you]," he began, "on the strength of the Imperial Charter of the Academy of Sciences to include me as one of its titled members . . . and to inform the Orenburg chancellery about it? Then not only would it provide me with better and more comfortable means to fulfill everything . . . that the Academy wants me to do, but I would be completely free from every reproach and indignation."[65] Müller lobbied successfully for Rychkov before his colleagues, and in August 1759 the Academy admitted him as its first corresponding member. As Müller informed him in the letter accompanying the diploma:

> You are the first in Russia to receive this honor; you have received it not through your title, nor through the connections of your friends, for you yourself are personally unknown to the Academy; rather, you are known strictly on the strength of your letters, which you have written in order to spread science and to further the general welfare, and also through the correspondence which you

have conducted with me up to this time, and which the Academy has found useful in various ways.[66]

Rychkov's induction into the Academy of Sciences was his greatest personal and professional triumph. As he told Müller upon receiving his diploma, membership in such an "elite club" of scholars obliged him to prove his worth even more.[67] This emphasis on lifelong service to a higher ideal typified Rychkov's style and resurfaced again in the public record of his everyday life at Spasskoe.

Nestled between snow-peaked mountains and fed by rivers bursting with salmon, Spasskoe offered Rychkov many advantages: sleeping in late, long dinners with friends and neighbors, drinking tea with the family, and plenty of time "to raise three sons who will serve the fatherland."[68] On his daily rounds he visited his bronze works and distillery before inspecting the village and its surrounding fields.[69] The slow and monotonous rhythms of life there facilitated the economic experiments which he dutifully recorded for the *Trudy*. But these were mere hobbies—Rychkov craved intellectual companionship more than anything else. In September and October 1768, he hosted the famous naturalists Lepekhin and Pallas, who at the time were exploring the Empire's borderlands for the Academy of Sciences. Rychkov relished his role as Orenburg's leading citizen—giving his guests the grand tour, leading them on long hikes through the mountains and woods, and letting them inspect his beehives, goat herds, fishing pond, and forest reserves.[70] The high point of his retirement came in March 1767 when he traveled to Moscow for an audience with the Empress, who personally praised his scholarly achievements and thanked him for years of dedicated service. As he later recalled: "For more than an hour . . . she asked me about the town of Orenburg, about the condition of its local places, about agriculture and commerce, conversing with me so kindly and indulgently that I have to consider that day to be the finest and happiest of my life." Ever the good subject, he presented to Catherine a copy of his latest work, *History of Kazan in Ancient and Medieval Times*, which he also dedicated to her, the great monarch who "considers the reading of historical books one of the most pleasant pastimes."[71]

Yet these were only brief respites from an otherwise abysmal experiment in country living. Catastrophe first struck in December 1761 when his house went up in flames, destroying nearly 800 books, including all his manuscripts and personal papers. Writing to Müller, he described the loss as "irretrievable."[72] For the next year he was forced to live in Orenburg while rebuilding his manor house at Spasskoe, an additional expense that he could barely afford. Two years later a group of peasants, including his most trusted elder, fled to Orenburg where they petitioned the chancellery to release them from their obligations to Rychkov on the grounds that they were actually state peasants and not serfs. The case was thrown out, but his reputation never fully recovered from the damage.[73] The worst was still to come. In April 1766 his steward absconded with all his funds, and at the end of the year another fire gutted his factories, eventually forcing him to close them down for good. Rychkov's failure was now complete. Once the epitome of success in the world of service and scholarship, he had become a "useless invalid" on his own estate.[74]

Such was the stuff of life on the Orenburg frontier: boring garrison towns, prairie fires, ornery serfs, double-crossing stewards, that sinking feeling of futility. The ancient Greek farmer-poet Hesiod called these kinds of tests the "good strife."[75] Three weeks after his manor house burned down in 1761, Rychkov began to channel his energies toward "getting back into service and serving the fatherland."[76] He first tried to win an appointment as Director of the recently established Kazan Gymnasium, a position for which he was over-qualified and which paid 600 rubles annually, modest by the standards of the time. Unsuccessful at that, he then thought of using his connections with Mül-ler to secure a seat on the elite Commerce Commission, established in 1763 by Catherine to advise her on national economic policy. Rychkov believed his expertise on Central Asian trade would guarantee him the job, but Mül-ler, a hardened veteran of St. Petersburg politics, persuaded him otherwise: "Why do you want to do this? Isn't it better to spend your old age in peace and at home with your family?"[77] Peter Kolchin has written that even nobles who physically resided on their estates displayed a strong absentee orienta-tion,[78] and Rychkov's self-imposed exile at Spasskoe vividly illustrates this mentality. He sulked there for ten long years before landing a job in 1770 as Director of the Iletskii Salt Works near Orenburg.[79] It paid only 1,000 rubles a year, but Rychkov was elated anyway. He stayed in state service until his death in 1777, continuing his historical and geographical research, occasion-ally publishing in the *Trudy*, and garnering accolades from his peers—in his *Dictionary of Russian Writers*, Nikolai Novikov called him a "hardworking and zealous man deserving eternal praise."[80] During Pugachev's six-month siege of Orenburg, Rychkov was forced to take refuge in the fortress while the rebel leader set fire to his estate yet again. He approached the whole ordeal with stoic indifference, keeping a detailed, day-by-day account of the siege and surviving on a jelly that he made from cow hides.[81]

Rychkov's unlucky predicament helps put his association with the Free Economic Society in proper perspective. Although by no means an outsider, he knew that membership in the Society had introduced him to a world of networking opportunities hitherto unimaginable. Wasting no time, Rychkov appealed to cofounder Grigorii Orlov in March 1766 to grant him a stipend in recognition for his work, even though the Society had just formed the year before. Then in 1767 he disclosed the location of some coal deposits in Oren-burg province to Adam Olsuf'ev, hoping that the Society's first president would return the favor and help him back into service. The petition to Orlov was rejected and his overture to Olsuf'ev went unanswered. In his letters to Müller from this period, Rychkov constantly pouts about getting the silent treatment from the Society: Why is Nartov so uncommunicative? Who is the new president and why have I not been informed? A year has passed and still no word from Klingshtedt! Be sure to tell Olsuf'ev that I am now living in my wife's village—she owns only 70 serfs![82] In the meantime, Rychkov produced a long string of essays for the *Trudy* on virtually every aspect of the rural economy: cereal cultures, forestry, distilling, apiculture. He exemplified all that the Society had hoped for in its provincial members, yet in the end had so little to show for it.

The assembly viewed things differently. Rychkov had certainly earned his stripes, but they rewarded distinguished service with prizes and praise, not money and jobs. In 1769, after four years of experiments and numer-ous articles for the *Trudy*, Rychkov finally received a lifetime achievement award—a gold medal featuring the Empress on one side and a laurel wreath on the other with an inscription reading "recompense for labor." The next year the assembly presented to his wife Elena a gold medal for her own household experiments with caps and sackcloth.[83] It was one of the rare occa-sions in the eighteenth century that the Society paid tribute to a woman who was not the Empress.

Rychkov's most notable award came in 1770 when he won a gold medal (along with Andrei Bolotov) for his model instruction to an estate manager. The contest came at an opportune moment, for it spurred him to synthesize all he had learned from his country experiment before his return to service. Declaring in the opening pages that farming constituted the most useful oc-cupation for peasants and society, Rychkov exhorted his new manager to make the arduous business of agriculture more attractive and profitable for peasants.[84] Rather than grant peasants more freedom, however, the steward was to tighten control over the labor force in order to ensure peace and pro-ductivity. With the cooperation of the most reliable peasant elders, he was to monitor village elections, survey the property, and make a record of all land transfers.[85] His administrative responsibilities reached well beyond office work. In addition to policing field work "with an unslumbering eye," he made sure that all arable was sown and that "lazy and roguish peasants" commit-ted no "dirty tricks" against the lord. He was to serve as village matchmaker, promoting population growth by encouraging adolescents to marry young and start families as quickly as possible.[86] On paper at least, this was an exacting regime administered through strict police ordinances.

Yet Rychkov's instruction also left considerable room for improvisation by the steward and even some peasant initiative. This is especially evident in his ordinances on the management of peasant work teams, or the tiaglo system. In contrast to Udolov, whose twelve-man tiaglo would have destroyed independent village institutions, Rychkov advocated few substantive reforms of the traditional system of labor organization. The tiaglo on his estate still contained two able-bodied adults, preferably a married couple. All the steward had to do was maintain the census records and take measures to promote the formation of large families. And although it always fell to the individual lord to determine the number of barshchina days on his own estate, Rychkov insisted that it was more humane, patriotic, and prudent to employ the traditional practice of three barshchina days.[87] He even permitted the use of obrok when circumstances rendered it the only viable option, despite his misgivings about the practice.[88] Nor did he consider introducing drastic technological improvements that threatened to upset the balance of the three-field system. Indeed, the most radical measure he ever advocated was sowing winter grain two weeks in advance of the customary time.[89] Rychkov filled his instruction with provisos on forest management, the prevention of cattle plague, establishing grain reserves, and medical treatment. In many instances he simply referred his steward to official governmental decrees or relevant articles from the *Trudy*, recommending that the "best" peasant children learn to read and write so that they too might learn the principles of orderly farming.[90]

In practice, all that Rychkov could do was set an example for his peasants and hope that some of them might try to follow it. He typically performed what he called his "economic experiments" on the margins of the estate, using women, seniors, and children while leaving the most essential male workers to tend to the fields. Sometimes he employed Bashkir and Kirghiz nomads whom he believed were not fit for agricultural work.[91] Many of his experiments were attempts to make ends meet: recycling old towels and dishrags for caps, stockings, and wallpaper; or growing nettle on mediocre soil and using its fiber for sackcloth.[92] Michel Confino once wrote that even the most progressive lords lapsed into the same mind-set of subsistence and scarcity that afflicted their serfs, and Rychkov presents no exception to this rule.[93] Similar considerations guided him in his award-winning response to the Society's essay contest on distilling.[94] Rychkov russified an old Tatar recipe for fermenting mare's milk by adding a pinch of whey to the brew and boiling it for three hours. Finding its taste no less pleasant than grain alcohol, he heralded it as a vodka substitute whose cheesy residue could even be used in cabbage soup.[95] At other times, Rychkov's ideas were more conventional. Observing that his peasants rarely used goat fur (*pukh*) for clothing, he ordered several women and children to comb their goats and sell the fur at the local market. Rychkov calculated that four goats could produce enough fur to pay the poll tax for one person.[96] Best of all, it employed children who, as he later wrote, "would otherwise roam idly around the streets and farmyards all day from dawn to dusk."[97] This simple and practical solution benefited both peasant and lord, for it alleviated the peasant's tax burden and developed hitherto untapped resources on the estate.

In the 1840s, the Moscow Slavophiles criticized men like Rychkov and the generation of the "Russian Enlightenment" for making so little impact on Russia and its traditional institutions. While he may have led an exemplary private and public life, the fact remains that everything he did at Spasskoe was jarringly superficial from both an administrative and technological standpoint. In this respect his experience was a microcosm of the Westernization project launched by Russia's rulers. Yet Rychkov was also his own harshest critic. In a footnote to one of his articles, he spoke with remarkable candor:

> It is quite evident that the only practices which enter quickly into our customs and take root are those which qualify as luxury and promote dissipation, not requiring from us any great labor or work. In contrast, those practices which are linked with labor and the vital interests of the people always require strong incentive or special encouragement. Without them, not even a century is enough to bring these practices into everyday circulation, no matter how useful and necessary . . . Upon entering the local Orenburg expedition . . . I observed that almost none of the natives did any farming; and today, no matter how hard we try to encourage them to do so, there are still very few of them who have taken it up. As for the Kirghiz, who became subjects 30 years ago, they too have made no progress, although they have seen how the Russians and others farm and profit from it . . . Yet when it comes to their clothing, then the luxuriousness and dandyism of their men and women have been on the rise year in and year out . . . We ourselves are no less susceptible to the same thing, but I will keep silent on that matter . . . .[98]

So much for trying to reform peasants through education and example! If the Kirghiz nomads were still missing their cue to begin farming after a generation, why should Russian peasants behave any differently within a few years? Even the gentry, who the Society had hoped would spread enlightenment in rural Russia, displayed little interest in becoming agricultural improvers. As Rychkov and others wrote time and again, these men were quick to embrace the outward trappings of European culture—food, wine, clothing, and servants—but not its rational, scientific, and humanistic core.

As a geographer, Rychkov knew that farming routines and technologies resulted from adaptations to climate, soil quality, population density, and access to markets—all variables largely beyond individual human control. In light of Orenburg's chronic labor shortage, the resettlement of Russian farmers and their traditional institutions offered the most feasible option for the

improvement of agriculture there. By the late eighteenth century, the colonization process was well under way. Consider the experiences of Stepan Mikhailovich Bagrov, another landowner who lived not far from Spasskoe. Bagrov was
the grandfather of the nineteenth-century writer Sergei Timofeevich Aksakov
and protagonist of the latter's nostalgic memoir, *The Family Chronicle*. Moving his family and peasants to a large estate on the Buguruslan River less than
100 miles from Bugul'ma, Bagrov helped spearhead the Russian colonization
of Bashkiria in the last quarter of the eighteenth century. He possessed little
in the way of enlightenment: "It is true that he, like all his contemporaries of
the Russian landed gentry, had little or no education; he could scarcely read
or write Russian, and when he first entered on his military service he had only
learnt the first four rules of arithmetic and the use of the counting board."[99] He
was also prone to arbitrary and uncontrollable fits of rage. Yet Bagrov made
up for these deficiencies with many of the personal qualities that Rychkov had
hoped to find in the Russian nobility of his frontier province. As Aksakov recalled in one chapter, he instinctively knew how to establish an orderly regime
without abusing his patriarchal authority. He granted his peasants a wide degree of latitude, intervening mainly to offer occasional advice and instructions:
"In a few short words my grandfather gave the necessary orders respecting the
management of the estate to the steward, and then hurried to the dining room
where supper was waiting for him." If his serfs came by the manor house to
ask for a favor, he made sure each one left "well content" and bearing a "silver cup filled with the strongest home-brewed brandy." On his daily rounds,
he carefully inspected the stables, poultry yard, meadows, plow land, and the
fallow "to test the accuracy of the plowing." Come evening, he liked to visit
his grinding mills. "My grandfather was very expert in all branches of country
industry," Aksakov reminisced. "He knew all about the working of a mill and
. . . could instantly detect any fault in the wheels or defect in the adjustment
of the millstones."[100] And like Rychkov, Bagrov avoided all luxuries, keeping
domestic servants to a bare minimum, wearing homespun linen, and serving
only traditional Russian dishes at his table: cabbage soup, sturgeon, crawfish,
strawberries, kvass, and home-brewed beer.

Published in 1856 when Aksakov was sixty-five, *The Family Chronicle* reflects its author's Slavophilic biases and must be treated with caution. Aksakov
likens his grandfather's tyranny to a violent force of nature—everyday the fate
of his peasants hinged on his capricious mood. Had they been free, his mood
would have been irrelevant. But his presence on the estate also helped to produce the material abundance Rychkov and the Free Economic Society wanted
to see from Russian agriculture. As Bagrov left his manor house, "he rejoiced
at the sight of so many beautiful animals, which bore witness to the prosperity
of his peasantry." Surveying his fields, "[he] was pleased with everything he

saw. He looked at the blooming rye, which stood erect, the height of a man, in a solid wall . . . Such a crop was a veritable joy for the owner's eye." And at supper time, "[my] grandfather shared every dish generously with his folk, and as there was about five times as much food on the table as he and his family could eat, there was plenty to spare."[101] All this without ever reading the *Trudy*. The name of the chapter is "One of Stepan Mikhailovich's Good Days."

*****

We last saw the young Andrei Bolotov at a Moscow book vendor early in 1766. He was poring over the first volume of the *Trudy*, considering whether to respond to Klingshtedt's economic questionnaire. Intimidated by such a daunting task, he went back home and turned to a neighbor for advice. As he reported in his memoirs: "Never before had I ventured into what was for us such an unusual matter . . . [My] neighbor Ivan Grigor'evich Polonskii not only did not dissuade me, but still more encouraged me to do it, advising me not to dawdle lest others beat me to it." Yet by Bolotov's own admission, he knew little about farming. Since returning to his estate in 1762, his improvements included renovating his house, improving his garden and building a writing desk—hardly the agenda of a serious agronomist. To respond to the questionnaire, he consulted one of his peasant elders: "Now I admit that my knowledge of rural housekeeping was still not sufficiently far-reaching, and that I was still unknowledgeable on many points, and so as a last resort I was compelled to seek clarification from the elder Fomich—my steward—and having called him to me, asked him about much and took into consideration that which he told me."[102]

Back in St. Petersburg, the assembly praised the pomeshchik from Tula for his "detailed observations over the course of his three-year residence in the country" and promptly published his answers in the next volume of the *Trudy*.[103] Two years later he was voted into the Society, launching a literary career that turned out to be one of the most productive in the history of Russian letters. When Bolotov finally passed away in 1833 at the age of 94, his effects included a collection of published and unpublished papers numerous enough to fill 350 volumes.[104] Of all his writings, his autobiography has attracted the most attention from scholars. Debuting in print between 1871 and 1873, most of its four volumes cover his life as a private nobleman from the moment of his retirement in 1762 to 1796.[105] As we have seen, Rychkov also produced an autobiography of sorts. Reflecting the Petrine values of an earlier era, it submerges family, friends, and social networks in a record of service and promotions. In a radical turnaround, Bolotov's story reverses Rychkov's priorities: state service was merely the gestation period for a private life that epitomized enlightenment and usefulness.

The enormity and complexity of Bolotov's literary legacy render a definitive assessment of his life and work challenging, if not impossible.[106] In the 1940s, the Soviet historian A. P. Berdyshev launched the revival of Bolotov's scientific reputation, emphasizing his contributions to Russian agronomy that his achievements as a memoirist had overshadowed for so long. Since then, agrarian historians have mined Bolotov's extensive publications for insight into traditional Russian agriculture; nowadays no study of the eighteenth-century rural economy is complete without serious attention to him.[107] Similarly, Bolotov's accomplishments in estate design shed valuable light on Westernization in the countryside. In her history of the Russian country estate, Priscilla Roosevelt has shown how great aristocrats emulated the displays of power at Catherine's court through their own gardens, orchards, and landscape architecture. Bolotov played a critical role in this process of cultural transmission. As editor of the journals *Sel'skii zhitel'* (*The Villager*) and *Ekonomicheskii magazin* (*Economic Magazine*), he skillfully recast the ornate designs so popular with the aristocracy to fit the scarce resources and tight budgets of modest gentry nests.[108] Most recently, Thomas Newlin has reexamined Bolotov's memoirs to demonstrate what he calls the "anxieties of Russian pastoral," the deep-seated insecurity caused by a combination of the elite's dependence on the autocracy, fear of a hostile peasantry, and bitter disillusionment with real life in the provinces.[109]

Bolotov's life and work are inseparable from his native Tula. For much of his life he milled around his ancestral estate there, a phenomenon unthinkable earlier in the century but which after 1762 began to lose some of its stigma. Like Rychkov in Orenburg, he valued his privacy but felt isolated from the cultural life of Moscow and St. Petersburg. As Ol'ga Glagoleva has documented, Tula was close enough to Moscow to absorb its aristocratic ethos but still lacked the infrastructure to participate in its life all year long. People traveled easily between the two towns in summer and winter, but during the rest of the year the mud and muck made the roads impassable, stranding villagers on their estates.[110] The provincial reform of 1775 improved the situation, but progress was still uneven. By the 1790s the royal settlement of Bogoroditsk where Bolotov lived and worked for twenty years developed into a respectable provincial town with the fabulous parks designed by him as its main attractions. After he left Bogoroditsk in 1796, the arcadia fell into disuse and the town deteriorated, leaving in its wake several hundred huts and a palace soon to become a ruin. The provincial capital of Tula fared better. As Bolotov later recalled, the Charter to the Towns of 1785 helped transform it from a rickety administrative center into a hub of commerce and culture. By the early nineteenth century, the town began to bustle with the same people, books, ideas, and fashions found in the two capitals.[111]

Bolotov was born in 1738 on his modest family estate, Dvorianinovo, in Kashirsk district. His father, an army officer, tried to provide his son with a rudimentary education, hiring several tutors and placing him for a brief while in a St. Petersburg pension. By the time of his father's death in 1750, Bolotov had received a smattering of instruction in mathematics, physics, geography, French, and German, but failed to manifest much interest in any of his subjects. Like most noble youths, he was preoccupied with the specter of mandatory state service looming like a prison sentence in the near future. For the next five years, he successfully evaded the call-up, using family connections in St. Petersburg to keep him out of the army while he divided his time between Dvorianinovo and his brother-in-law's estate. Bolotov experienced his first taste of ordinary country pleasures during these years: hunting, fishing, carpentry, and visiting with neighbors. Eagerly anticipating the day when he would take over Dvorianinovo, his plans were cut short when the authorities finally caught up with him and sent him to an army unit stationed near Riga.

His time in service was short and uneventful, at least from a military standpoint. The Seven Years' War had just begun, and Bolotov witnessed the Battle of Gross Jägersdorf in August 1757, but saw no action. More significant for his career than soldiering was his growing mastery of German. Earning the notice of his superior officers, he landed a job as a translator in the Königsberg chancellery of Nikolai Korf, the military governor of East Prussia. The undemanding nature of the work gave him time to cultivate friendships with like-minded officers and civil servants who reappeared later in his life as leaders and comembers of the Free Economic Society: Grigorii Orlov, soon to become Catherine II's favorite; Timothy von Klingshtedt, cofounder and German Secretary; and Fedor V. Passek, another provincial correspondent for the *Trudy*.[112] He also had the freedom to soak up the scholarly atmosphere of this college town, "enlightening himself" (*prosveshchat'sia*) with hundreds of books he picked up in stores and at the public library. Although he attended lectures at the university delivered by its "many famous people" and devoted his nighttime hours to copying their texts word-for-word, his memoirs do not mention Immanuel Kant, the most famous of them all.[113]

Transferred to St. Petersburg in 1761, he returned to work for Korf as the general's personal adjutant. Although his duties were light—all he had to do was accompany Korf to social engagements—he never really adjusted to life in the capital. This was a matter of personal choice. Bolotov had the talent and connections to rise in the world of St. Petersburg. As he later wrote, Grigorii Orlov even considered inviting him to join the conspiracy to overthrow Peter III, an offer which, had he accepted, might have resulted in rapid promotions, monetary rewards, and other demonstrations of royal favor.[114]

Lacking the inclination for any of these perquisites, he instead petitioned for a discharge from service. As his memoirs make plain, he was elated with the "complete freedom" that Peter III had granted the nobility in February 1762: "Being a lover of science and inclined to scholarship, I had long since come to hate the noisy and restless life of war, and in my heart I wanted nothing more than to withdraw to the country, to dedicate myself to the peaceful and quiet of country life and to spend the rest of my days amidst my books and in the company of the muses, but until that time I did not tempt myself with the slightest hope of it."[115]

Bolotov finally submitted his paperwork to the War College in June after hearing the rumors of impending war with Denmark. At first the War College refused on the grounds that he was too young to leave service.[116] Fortunately, an old friend of Bolotov's father intervened on his behalf, claiming that the young man would be of more use to Russia on his estate than off it. The argument succeeded. On June 14, less than four months after the manifesto's promulgation, Bolotov became a "liberated and forever free man." His memoirs vividly convey his unbridled joy:

> I myself almost did not believe that I was then no longer a state servitor, and, walking forward, almost did not hear my legs moving beneath me; it seemed that I was walking in the air a full arshin [28 inches] above the ground, and I do not recall if ever in the course of my whole life I had been so happy and cheerful as on that memorable day, and especially in the first moments after receiving the release. I was running from Vasilevskii Island, not looking around and shoving the envelope forcefully into my pocket so as not to lose that invaluable slip of paper.[117]

His brush with state service had lasted seven years. The rest of the time remaining to him can be divided into three phases. First, between 1762 and 1774 he hobnobbed with the muses at Dvorianinovo: marrying a local girl fourteen years his junior; beginning a family with her; trying to improve and extend his properties; corresponding with the Free Economic Society; and earning the praise of his friends in the capital. During this period he wrote nineteen articles for the *Trudy*, including pioneering works on potatoes, fertilizer, forest management, and field rotation. Second, from 1774 to 1796 he reaped the paradoxical rewards of being an agricultural prodigy in a country renowned for dismal agriculture. After much begging and haggling, his fellow Society member Prince Sergei Vasil'evich Gagarin coaxed him out of retirement to direct a pair of Crown estates for the royal family in Tula province. At first he managed the village of Kiiasovka, close enough to Dvorianinovo for him to administer both properties simultaneously. He then was transferred to the town of Bogoroditsk, considerably further away, where he oversaw 20,000 royal serfs.[118] These years turned out to be the most productive of his life. In addition to providing the setting for his work as a gardener and landscape architect, Bogoroditsk also served as the base of operations for his own publishing ventures, *Sel'skii zhitel* and *Ekonomicheskii magazin*.[119] Third and finally, he returned to Dvorianinovo in 1796 and focused on writing and rewriting his memoirs while continuing to garner recognition from the public. In 1821 he earned membership in the Moscow Agricultural Society, Russia's second great agricultural society, which, like its St. Petersburg equivalent, survived until World War I.

Bolotov first acquired a taste for the intellectual lifestyle while serving in the military. As other junior officers spent idle time playing billiards and reveling in taverns, he preferred to be alone with his books.[120] His experiences exemplify what modern scholarship has called an eighteenth-century "reading revolution" whose active ingredient was the "extensive" consumption of books, newspapers, and periodicals. Books were no longer regarded as revealed truths, but as catalysts for personal emancipation and intellectual development.[121] Bolotov later revealed in his memoirs that he read everything that "dropped into my hands," reflecting on it and recording his own impressions before moving on to the next item.[122] As a soldier in St. Petersburg he purchased dozens of books from the Academy of Sciences, sewing the unbound pages together himself, a pastime he found no less edifying than reading them. Later, while quartered in a tiny village in Courland, it was his "thirst for science and the reading of useful books" that saved him from going out of his mind. Once he was transferred to Königsberg, Bolotov immersed himself in science and secular philosophy, which, for a while, led him to doubt his Christian faith and nearly become a "freethinker." What saved him was still another book. Filled with Pietism and neo-stoic philosophy, it sold Bolotov completely on the compatibility of science and religion. Upon finishing it, he fell to his knees, begged "the supreme essence" for more "enlightenment," and then ransacked his bookshelf for additional references and citations on the topic.[123]

One of his notebooks from this intense period reveals the profound influence of these books on his development. Intended for his eyes only,[124] it consists of 365 rules of conduct, one for each day of the year, culled from a variety of moral philosophers. Already an introverted sort, Bolotov hatched his ideas of good and bad conduct in opposition to the fashion, flattery, and fame- and favor-seeking that he perceived all around him. To balance out these vices, he offered examples of everyday virtue that he later tried to emulate at Dvorianinovo: healthy food, physical exercise, respect for the creator, following the rule of nature, and, of course, lots of solitude.[125]

Bolotov's hankering for privacy also found expression in an aversion to toil and drudgery. As Thomas Newlin has argued, he identified all work with

"slavery."[126] Although many other nobles regarded their service duties as
boring, unduly stressful, and demeaning,[127] Bolotov took their disenchant-
ment a step further. He truly loathed being told what to do. In Königsberg he
found himself chained to a desk in a windowless office, copying documents
all day and aching for his "lost freedom."[128] At the time he imagined "how
happy it would make me to be free and far away from all disturbances, to be
at home and with all my friends . . . How I would love for this dream in a
minute to turn into reality . . . But now I return again to Königsberg."[129] His
work for Prince Gagarin in Kiiasovka rekindled all the unpleasant memories
of his service years. At first Bolotov refused Gagarin's offer—the peace and
solitude of his private life at Dvorianinovo were far more valuable to him
than the 400 ruble salary. Yet Gagarin persisted, promising Bolotov that he
would get to enjoy all those things once he "had worked a certain amount and
put everything back in necessary order." The preliminary task of surveying
the property went well enough until he arrived in Spasskoe, a filthy little village built on a swamp and in total disorder after years of neglect:

> Now try to imagine what it was like for us, and especially for me, who not only
> was not used to it but had until then enjoyed the peaceful and cool country life,
> to sit in that unbearable atmosphere and work on letters that were not only not
> interesting but were most boring and arduous. We had to transcribe multitudes
> of notebooks, then to collate all of them, then to check them against our own ca-
> dastral register, and then against the records of the revision census. "My God,"
> I repeated over and over," if only I could get away from this scorching heat and
> from all these accursed flies."[130]

Bolotov found an alternative to service in what he called the "philosophical life." During his time in the military, he had mingled with Baltic German
landowners whose simple yet productive lifestyle had aroused his admiration.
Inspired by their example, Bolotov tried to duplicate their routines on his own
estate. Rising with the sun, he would take his tea in the garden while reading
a book. After consulting with his gardener on the day's tasks, he ate breakfast
and then spent the morning inspecting the fields. At noon he partook in a
simple dinner before retreating with book in hand to the shade of his garden
where he remained until dusk—reading, drawing, and thinking. As before, his
notebooks from this period consist mainly of his translations from European
moral philosophers. They reveal the influence of the pastoral ideal that had
begun to appear in the literary journals of the time.[131] In one of them Bolotov
tried to define ephemera like felicity and beauty, determining that their qualities reflected the order and proportion found in God, reason, and nature. [132]
This was a lonely life, especially since his peasants and neighbors—"stupid
people" as he called them—lacked the intellectual capacity to share it with

him: "I almost completely forgot about visiting neighbors, but was always more willing to remain alone at home, busy with my gardens and books, than to spend time with neighbors and people, of which there was not one with whom I could say a rational word and converse with in a friendly way."[133]

His discovery of the Free Economic Society in 1766 helped put an end to his isolation—as he later wrote, it sealed his future as "an economic writer."[134] But it portended much more than that. In converting his private experiences into public discourse, Bolotov brought the Petrine Revolution to the Russian countryside, endeavoring to dispel ignorance and superstition while promoting his idea of a good society. Let us first consider his view of the provincial gentry. Bolotov admitted that most landowners "do not care at all about the rural economy or about its improvement, nor are bothered by the decay of agriculture." Their apathy and negligence knew no bounds. For the typical noble, estate management consisted of knowing how much land was sown and if the peasant had stolen anything from him. Most believed, like their peasants, that the mere extension of arable would yield a satisfactory increase.[135] Nobles lacked knowledge of basic agronomy and regarded even low-risk experiments in gardens as a waste of time. Rather than try to improve the overall quality of farming, they typically handed the technical aspects of production over to peasants, who continued to farm the land "exactly the way their forefathers did."[136] Frustrated with chronically low productivity, the great landowners of his district had already begun to resettle peasants in the steppe region,[137] proving even more that "the landowner blames all his problems on the land and concludes that it may not be improved, but rather will always languish in the same condition." In an age of enlightenment, the lord's chief concern should be devising an agenda for exploiting and allocating resources most rationally and profitably. "Land may not correct itself and change its own nature," he concluded. "[It] demands the assistance of human hands which the wise creator has anointed to work towards this end, and reason, which may serve in finding the method."[138]

While critical of nobles, Bolotov saved most of his venom for the peasantry. A staunch defender of serfdom to the end of his days, he regarded peasants as superstitious, ignorant, and almost completely resistant to reason. "Our common people come with such an inclination for the old customs, and are so attached to them, that . . . when [the peasant] sees and praises the great use from something new, and admits that he might derive no small profit from it, he still looks upon it with a critical eye and in no way considers applying it."[139] Custom was a catch-all term for explaining everything mysterious and irrational in peasant behavior. For Bolotov, its pervasiveness even blurred the social and cultural distinctions between nobles and peasants. By delegating managerial tasks to their peasants, landowners not only gave a leadership role to the most conservative elements in Russian society, but also perpetuated obsolete farming techniques which then percolated up to the commanding heights of the rural economy.[140] All the negative qualities that Bolotov perceived in his fellow nobles—apathy, obstinacy, negligence, idleness—also appeared in his peasant types.

Bolotov attempted to solve these problems by establishing a distinct culture of noble enlightenment in the countryside and bringing a moral economic order to the village that balanced the subsistence needs of his peasants with the lord's demands for efficiency and profit. As he stated in his prize-winning instruction for an estate manager, the "basic rule" of rational estate administration was to increase the lord's profits without bringing harm to the village.[141] His ideal manager sounded remarkably like the person Bolotov imagined himself to be: "prudent," "honorable," "upright," "virtuous," "good-hearted," "God-fearing," "observant," and impervious to "vice, banditry, drunkenness, and hypocrisy."[142] He was the perfect foil to the lazy, apathetic, and superstitious bumpkins that dot Bolotov's social landscape. More importantly, he functioned as a transmitter of European values, replicating the enlightened social order that Catherine and the Free Economic Society were attempting to institute for the Empire as a whole. Just as the Society coopted the best provincial nobles into its network, so did Bolotov instruct the manager to seek out the "most responsible men in the village" to assist him. The key player here was the peasant elder, whose chief duties included overseeing the orderly execution of plowing, sowing, harvesting, carting, threshing, and grinding of grain.[143] Working in tandem with the elder, the manager enforced a maximum of three barshchina days per week and permitted a limited migration within the general vicinity of the estate. At the same time, the manager was expected to take the traditional measures to stave off peasant destitution: assigning misfit peasants to the strongest and most efficient households; distributing free grain in times of crisis; and spreading the tax burden equitably.[144] Managing an orderly estate resembled governing an empire upon rationalist and activist principles. Even the rewards were similar. Like the participants in Russia's service culture, who measured success and status in terms of their personal proximity to the Empress, so did Bolotov's manager earn the "love and trust of the seigneur" for his "indefatigable diligence, sincere heart, and inviolable faith in his master."[145] Distinguished service to the seigneur belonged in the same category of intangible "virtue" that motivated Bolotov, Rychkov, and other provincial correspondents to offer their services to the Society.

Did Bolotov's regime produce any of the desired effects? Regarding his desire to establish a moral order for peasants, the answer is negative. While he granted peasants a fair degree of autonomy, the fact remains that the structural inequalities inherent in serfdom invariably turned a decent person like Bolotov into a despot and his system into a "police regime." He often exhibited the same vindictiveness that we encountered earlier in the instruction of Rumiantsev, and even employed corporal punishment in variance to the spirit of the times. Emphasizing the dangers of "riffraff," "confusion," and "disorder," he authorized the creation of a police network which promoted an atmosphere of bitter denunciation and mutual suspicion.[146] During the Pugachev rebellion, he just referred to peasants as "the rabble":

> [All] the lowlifes and rabble, especially the enslaved and our servants, in their hearts were secretly on the side of this evildoer; all were rebelling in their hearts, preparing to set the fields alight with the slightest spark as kindling. The example of the recent terrible Moscow [i.e., the plague riots of 1771 revolt] was still fresh in our minds, and we were not only scared of something similar, but expected it to happen at any minute. The stupidity and irrationality of our common people were well known to us, and under the present circumstances we could not even place trust in our servants, who we all looked upon, and not without reason, as the first and most evil of enemies . . . [147]

Serfdom also poisoned his efforts to relieve peasant poverty. In fly-infested Spasskoe, which he managed for the royal family from 1774 to 1776, Bolotov instituted a series of sweeping reforms reminiscent of Baron von Zaltse's improvements of the 1750s and 1760s. Starting with a massive repartition of land that favored the poorest peasants, he cut obrok payments by half. As Bolotov described it to Prince Gagarin, lowering the obrok and allocating resources more equitably enabled smaller families with fewer able-bodied workers to make ends meet. It also freed peasants up for other projects: the building of a hospital and almshouse; increasing livestock reserves; transporting supplies to Moscow; and the construction of a stone office building for Bolotov. Peasants were required to work on these additional tasks six days a year, three in the winter and three in the summer.[148] The results were most unpleasant. One group of peasants submitted a petition to Gagarin accusing Bolotov of extortion, bribery, and other deeds of corruption. In his rejoinder to Gagarin, Bolotov claimed that the petitioners came from the wealthiest stratum of peasants in the village who possessed "a peculiar inclination for rebellion" and resented his attempts to make them pay their fair share.[149] Bolotov was transferred later that year to Bogoroditsk, where he remained until 1796.

Nor did Bolotov manage to break the back of his toughest opponent of all—peasant economic custom. He admitted that peasants regarded technical improvements as foreign frippery with no real application to their everyday lives. In one article, for instance, he described a strategy for increasing emergency grain reserves—a praiseworthy objective to be sure. There was actually little to it: he had boys and old men retrieve the ears of grain which littered the fields after the harvest with a special rake imported from Pomerania. "I saw," he concluded, "that all this work could be done with . . . very little labor and with such productivity that it was approved by even the local *muzhiki* [peasant men], who, as we all know, look at such novelties with a sidelong glance." More grain at no expense—who could argue with that? He learned that no peasants wanted to be branded "upstarts" by their neighbors. Villagers also informed him that the rake disturbed the stubble that they used as supplementary cattle fodder. "Have you ever heard a more stupid and baseless excuse?" Bolotov asked his audience in disbelief.[150] It is not difficult to visualize peasant reactions to such high-handed interference in their domain: silence, stonewalling, eye rolling—anything to make the master go away.

Beyond reforming the agrarian economy, Bolotov also hoped to spread the culture of enlightenment amongst the provincial nobility, even though few nobles in his province shared his enthusiasm for the rational way of life. In an unpublished collection of satirical stories written in the late 1760s, appropriately entitled "Amusements of Living in the Country," he argued that most Russian nobles identified "enlightenment" with the acquisition of European customs and luxuries. Like Rychkov, he targeted the frivolity, insipidness, and stupidity of his neighbors, lampooning their self-destructive obsession with *moda* (fashion), linking it to Russia's lopsided Europeanization and blaming it for turning virtue into vice, health into sickness, and beauty into vanity.[151] True, Russia had institutions dedicated to genuine learning—the Academy of Sciences and Moscow University—but these were official establishments whose reach did not extend beyond the two capitals. As Bolotov phrased it, why should a provincial nobleman read books? If he had a decent rank, married well, and filled his table with enough food and drink, people would come to his house, books or no books.[152] Even if he wanted to read something serious, he lacked the basic skills that it required. While Bolotov's friends in St. Petersburg cited the "printing revolution" as proof of Russia's enlightenment, freshly emancipated nobles living down the road from him were still struggling to pronounce written letters aloud.[153]

Given the low educational level of the provinces, Bolotov directed much of his work towards the more sophisticated readers of the capital cities. As he said in a landmark piece on the use of potatoes, he wrote for a discriminating audience of "curious and experimental people . . . who care about the general welfare," people who, "out of love for the fatherland" have justifiably earned the praise of enlightened society.[154] Bolotov's ambition to be included in this exclusive club necessitated that he portray the daily grind of agricultural improvement as a morality play pitting virtue and reason against vice and tradition. His self-image calls to mind Oldwise in Denis Fonvizin's *The Minor*, another enlightened protagonist who similarly served as a beacon of wisdom against a backdrop of provincial indolence and corruption. Like Oldwise, Bolotov was fond of sermonizing: peasants plow too deeply and scatter grain seeds indiscriminately; they have no understanding of soil quality; they fail to increase cattle and then wonder why they have no manure for fertilizing their fields. His model instruction reads like an agricultural syllabus of errors—peasants spend too much money on vodka; they steal at any given opportunity; they fight amongst themselves; they shirk and complain; they cuss too much.[155] And although at times he praised a few of them, the longer he lived in the country the more convinced he became of the "stupidity and ignorance of our peasants." The overlap between Fonvizin's Oldwise and Bolotov should come as no surprise—the two wrote for the exact same audience. Yet in contrast to Oldwise, whom Fonvizin mercifully freed from the entanglements of landownership and family obligations, Bolotov was really stuck in the provinces. As he once wrote to himself, his mind had become so immersed in his ideas that he could no longer talk with "normal people about normal things."[156]

Bolotov's treatise on field rotation illustrates the extent of his isolation. Ever since his return to the country in 1762, he had experimented with the "particulars" within the perimeters of the three-field system. Experience had convinced him that "tradition" and "custom" would undermine all his efforts so long as the "fundamental basis" of agriculture remained untouched. Permanent improvement, he concluded, had to be geared towards "the establishment of a completely different order in the economy."[157] In lieu of the traditional three-field division, he recommended an ambitious seven-field system that promised to put an end to the nagging problems of dwindling pasturage, mediocre soil quality, and small harvests. Agrarian historians agree that his proposal constitutes the first "assault" on the three-field system in Russia.[158] His new system first called for re-dividing the three fields into seven smaller ones of equal size. Over the course of a seven-year period, a single field would lie fallow for three consecutive years before being plowed over and fertilized with the freshest manure in the fourth year (See Table 4.1). In contrast to the three-field system, which left one-third of the land fallow, Bolotov's system drastically increased the fallow to 57 percent. The prolonged fallow period would enhance the soil's fertility, so much in fact that Bolotov's smaller fields would eventually become more fertile than the three-field rotation.[159] While consistent with certain aspects of Russian agrarian custom—no artificial grasses and year-round stabling of livestock were necessary—asking farmers to leave more than half of their fields unsown was unrealistic, to put it mildly. One can only imagine how his neighbors and peasants would react to such a scheme. The point, however, is that Bolotov no longer cared what they thought—he even hinted that the new system would be feasible only on seigniorial lands and that peasants should stick with tradition.[160] For the first time in his economic writings, his debating partner was no longer the bearded peasant or the neighbor next door, but the educated public—particularly the academicians and literati in the Free Economic Society.

After 1775 Bolotov began to apply his energies and talent to gardens, orchards, and landscaping—the sort of amusements that had inspired leisure classes ever since the ancient Persians. At least someone was listening. In a letter to the Free Economic Society from 1778, written as he was embarking on his first independent publishing enterprise, *Sel'skii zhitel'*, he thanked his colleagues for "instilling in him the desire to write about economics," which placed him on "the very unusual path . . . of rural housekeeping." Fittingly, he signed the letter not as "Captain A. Bolotov" as he did all his previous pieces, "but as "Editor, *Sel'skii zhitel'*."[161] His apprenticeship with the Society had come to an end, earning him passage out of provincial isolation and into the inner circles of Russia's educated public.

Bolotov revived his association with the Free Economic Society in 1789, sending Nartov intermittent reports for the next two decades. Already well into his middle age, he no longer regarded it as much of a privilege:

> I could easily anticipate that renewing my correspondence and dealings with the Society would only result in the Economic Society from time to time burdening me with some kind of demands and charges . . . and that, in any event, I would be forced to work again, to do a lot of bustling, and sometimes at a loss; and for all this I should have to be satisfied only with praise and empty honor that was meaningless, and nothing else.[162]

Unflattering remarks, to be sure, but ones that should be placed in perspective. The Russian National Library in St. Petersburg has preserved Bolotov's family album. Covering the years 1781 to 1821, it contains an assortment of notes, sketches, poems, and impressions etched on its pages by visitors to Bogoroditsk and Dvorianinovo. Thomas Newlin has argued that these jottings reflected Bolotov's frustrations with real life in the provinces. Seeking freedom and security in the countryside but finding only uncultured landowners and hostile peasants, Bolotov and others like him responded by entrenching themselves in their arcadia and turning a blind eye to the harsh realities of life on the other side.[163] It is also significant that out of 40 entries, only one displays any trace of Russia's official service culture. Filled with references to "sons of the fatherland," "true religion," and "the sweetness of your exploits," (!) the note stands out amidst all the feelings of love, happiness, kindness, peace, and ecstasy that Bolotov induced in people.[164] Bolotov's

Table 4.1.   Andrei Bolotov's Seven-field System

	Field One	Field Two	Field Three	Field Four	Field Five	Field Six	Field Seven
Year one	Fertilized and plowed	Fallow	Winter grains	Fallow	Spring grains	Fallow	Spring grains
Year two	Winter grains	Fallow	Spring grains	Fallow	Spring grains	Fertilized and plowed	Fallow
Year three	Spring grains	Fallow	Spring grains	Fertilized and plowed	Fallow	Winter grains	Fallow
Year four	Spring grains	Fertilized and plowed	Fallow	Winter grains	Fallow	Spring grains	Fallow
Year five	Fallow	Winter grains	Fallow	Spring grains	Fallow	Spring grains	Fertilized and plowed
Year six	Fallow	Spring grains	Fallow	Spring grains	Fertilized and plowed	Fallow	Winter grains
Year seven	Fallow	Spring grains	Fertilized and plowed	Fallow	Winter grains	Fallow	Spring grains

Source: "Prodolzhenie o razdelenii na semi polei," *Trudy*, 18 (1771), 75.

house had become a shrine to pastoralism and domesticity, testament to the
far-reaching influence of the Free Economic Society. As a result of its efforts,
the private lifestyle of the noble agrarian had become an acceptable and desir-
able vocation for the Russian elite, so much in fact that the Society itself had
become redundant. As Bolotov himself put it, "praise and empty honor" were
unnecessary—being a man from the village was good enough.

NOTES

1. *Prodolzhenie Trudov* 1 (1779): no pagination.

2. Anne Lounsbery, "'No, this is not the provinces!' Provincialism, Authenticity,
and Russianness in Gogol's Day," *Russian Review* 64 (April 2005): 264.

3. RGIA, f. 91, op. 1, d. 3, l. 39; Klingshtedt, "O neobkhodimoi nadobnosti v
sredstvakh snabdit' zdeshnikh pomeshchikov sposobnymi prikashchikami ili upravi-
teliami, s nekotorymi kloniashchimisia k semu predstavleniiami," *Trudy* 5 (1767): 61.
See also Confino, *Domaines et seigneurs*, 68–69.

4. Klingshtedt, "O neobkhodimoi nadobnosti," 65, 67–68.

5. RGIA, f. 91, op. 1, d. 5, l. 26.

6. RGIA, f. 91, op. 1, d. 6, l. ll, 1.18, 11, 25–26.

7. "Zadacha," *Trudy* 13 (1769): 121–22.

8. RGIA, f. 91, op. 1, d. 6, l. 18.

9. Wol'f, "Nakaz upraviteliu ili prikashchiku, kak upravliat derevniam v otsutstve pomeshchika," *Trudy* 12 (1769): 9, 14.

10. Ibid., 17–19.

11. F. Udolov, "Nastavlenie prikiashchiku opredelennym v gospodskikh myzakh i
derevniakh okolo Peterburga," *Trudy* 11 (1769): 35–58.

12. R. Vorontsov, "O sposobakh k ispravleniiu sel'skago domostroitel'stva,"
Trudy 5 (1767): 1–12.

13. Confino, *Domaines et seigneurs*, 71–6; Melton, 696–99.

14. RGIA, f. 91, op. 1, d. 6, l. 17, l. 18ob, l. 35ob, l. 36.

15. RGIA, f. 91, op. 1, d. 6, ll. 42–42ob; Grasman recommended the gradual
introduction of clover and other artificial forage crops to increase cattle fodder and
manure production. See "Otvet na zadachu o udobrenii zemli bez szheniia kubyshei,"
Trudy 19 (1771): 1–91.

16. "Priglashenie sel'skikh domostroitelei k chineniiu opytov kasaiushchikhsia do
khlebopashestva," *Trudy* 13 (1769): 2, 3, 6.

17. Kolchin, 58–60, 87, 97–98. See also Raeff, *Origins*, 46, 50, 74, 80; and Robert
Givens, "Servitors or Seigneurs: The Nobility and the Eighteenth-Century Russian
State" (PhD diss., University of California, Berkeley, 1975), 462–65, 472–78. On
noble attitudes towards the court and service to the Empress, see Marisinova, *Psikhologiia elity rossiiskogo dvorianstvo*, 67–71. On pastimes of petty provincial nobles,
especially before 1762, see N. Chechulin, *Russkoe provintsial'noe obshchestvo vo
vtoroi polovine XVIII veka* (St. Petersburg: Tipografiia V.S. Balasheva, 1889), 34.

18. Faizova, 107–10.

19. Leonard, 65–71.

20. Ol'ga Glagoleva, *Russkaia provintsial'naia starina: ocherki kul'tury i byta Tul'skoi gubernii XVIII-pervoi poloviny XIX vv.* (Tula: Ritm, 1993), 82–83; A. A. Sevast'ianova, *Russkaia provintsial'naia istoriografiia vtoroi poloviny XVIII veka* (Moscow: Arkheograficheskaia komissiia Rossiiskoi akademii nauk, 1998).

21. Roosevelt, 174, 193–96, 200–202.

22. RGIA, f. 91, op. 1, d. 35, ll. 24ob-25; d. 53, ll. 61ob–62–ob; d. 12, l. 11ob.

23. RGIA, f. 91, op. 1, d. 3, l. 7.

24. RGIA, f. 91, op. 1, d. 1, l. 17, ll. 21–21ob, l. 24, ll. 31-31ob; d. 3, ll. 8–8ob, l. 12, ll. 24–24ob; d. 4, l. 33; d. 7, ll. 29–29ob.

25. RGIA, f. 91, op. 1, d. 8, ll. 32–3, l. 49; d. 10, l. 14. One Society correspondent who broke the mold was Vasilii Andreevich Priklonskii, a retired pomeshchik from Tver province whose response to Klingshtedt's questionnaire appeared in the *Trudy*. See RGIA, f. 91, op. 1, d. 12, l. 36; and V. Priklonskii, "Otvety na zadannye ot Vol'nago Ekonomicheskago Obshchestva, kasaiushchiesia do zemledeliia i vnutrenniago derevenskago khoziaistva po Kashinskomu uezdu," *Trudy* 26 (1774): 1–91. Priklonskii later pursued a vocation as a translator with minimal success. His correspondence with Ia. I. Bulgakov has been preserved and sheds valuable light on the frustrations of provincial intellectual culture in the 1770s and 1780s. See V. D. Rak, "Perevodchik V. A. Priklonskii (materiali k istorii tverskogo 'kul'turnogo gnezda' v 1770–1780–e gody," *XVIII vek* 13 (1981): 244–61.

26. *PSZ*, volume 20, 240.

27. RGIA, f. 91, op. 1, d. 399, ll. 33–4, ll. 41–43.

28. RGIA, f. 91, op. 1, d. 399, ll. 51–2, ll. 53–4, ll. 60ob, l. 62.

29. "Proizshestviia Vol'nago Ekonomicheskago Obshchestva 1790–91 goda," *Prodolzhenie Trudov* 16 (1792): 288–90; RGIA, f. 91, op. 1, d. 38, l. 84. For Levshin's first correspondence with the Society in 1772, see RGIA, f. 91, op. 1, d. 10, l. 32. See also G.P. Prisenko, *Prosvetitel' V.A. Levshin* (Tula, 1990), 9; Glagoleva, *Russkaia provintsial'naia starina*, 88–91.

30. S. G. Gmelin, *Puteshestvie po Rossii dlia izsledovaniia trekh tsarstv estestva*, part 1 (St. Petersburg: Akademiia nauk, 1771), 1–2; RGIA, f. 91, op. 1, d. 42, ll. 170–4.

31. "Prodolzhenie izvestii 1793 goda," *Novoe prodolzhenie Trudov Vol'nago Ekonomicheskago Obshchestva*, 1 (1795): 34–45, 358–59.

32. "Rech' kotoriu zasvidetel'stvoval Vol'nomu Ekonomicheskomu Obshchestvu blagodarenie svoe Iatskikh voisk Deputat Vasilei Tambovtsov," *Trudy* 10 (1768): 115–16.

33. *Zapiski Andreia Timofeevicha Bolotova*, volume 1, 436–37.

34. Arkhiv Rossiiskoi Akademii Nauk (herafter ARAN), f. 27, op. 3, ed. khr. 236, l. 300.

35. "Ustav o korrespondentakh," *Trudy* 41 (1790): 229–32.

36. Michael Kugler, "Provincial Intellectuals: Identity, Patriotism, and Enlightened Peripheries," *The Eighteenth Century* 37 (1996): 158, 162, 169.

37. "Pis'mo Lifliandskago pomeshchika Reingol'da Georga Vangersgeima," *Trudy* 11 (1769): 60–61; Wol'f, "Prodolzhenie otvetov gospodina Barona Vul'fa

na zadannye v pervoi chasti ekonomicheskie voprosy," *Trudy* 3 (1766): 62; see also Rozenkampf, "O prichinakh," 92–93; and Zaltse, "O popravlenii dereven'," 112.

38. P. S. Pallas, *Puteshestvie po raznym provintsiiam Rossiiskoi imperii*, 3 parts (St. Petersburg: Akademiia nauk, 1773–78); I. I. Lepekhin, *Dnevnye zapiski puteshestviia po raznym provintsiiam Rossiiskogo gosudarstvo*, part 1 (St. Petersburg: Akademiia nauk, 1768–69); Gmelin, *Puteshestvie po Rossii dlia izsledovaniia trekh tsarstv estestva*. Academy of Sciences President V. G. Orlov initiated the correspondence between the Society and the expeditions in 1768. See RGIA, f. 91, op. 1, d. 388, l. 77, l. 80. Two years later, the three explorers were inducted into the organization, along with Academician Gildenshtedt. See RGIA, f. 91, op. 1, d. 7, ll. 16ob–17. Pallas, Lepekhin, and Gildenshtedt later assumed leadership roles in the Society. Gmelin was not so lucky—he was imprisoned in the Caucasus by hostile tribesman and died in captivity in 1774. See Vucinich, 152.

39. Steven Usitalo, *Mikhail Lomonosov: The Making of a Russian Myth* (unpublished manuscript), 23–27.

40. Samuel Alopeus, *Kratkoe opisanie marmornykh i drugikh kamennykh lomok, gor, i kamennykh porod nakhodiashchikhsia v Rossiiskoi Karelii* (St. Petersburg: Akademiia nauk, 1787), 2, 85–86.

41. Alexander Fomin, *Opisanie Belago moria s ego beregami i ostravami voobshche* (St. Petersburg: Akademiia nauk, 1797), 2, 4.

42. RGIA, f. 91, op. 1, d. 6, l. 36.

43. A. Bolotov, "O udobrenii zemel'," *Trudy* 15 (1770): 28–30.

44. V. Fribe, "Otvet na vopros o pol'ze i vrede bolot," *Trudy* 50 (1795): 252.

45. Mylnikov, "Kratkoe opisanie glavnykh vygod trekh lushchikh Tobol'skoi Gubernii okrug," *Trudy* 48 (1793): 251; Rogenbuk, "Primechanii po sluchaiu zdelannago v sobranii Vol'nago Ekonomicheskago Obshchestva voprosa, vredno li posredstvom vyzhiganiia lesa zavodit' novyia pashni, i net li drugago kakogo mesto sego sredstva dlia zemledel'tsa no stol' tsennago," *Trudy* 42 (1790): 176–77; Herman von Rading, "Istoricheskoe opisanie o razvedenii v Rossii vinograda," *Trudy* 45 (1792): 171–72.

46. "Pis'mo Vologskoi provintsii pomeshchika, gospodina Brigadira Olisheva," *Trudy* 2 (1766): 102–3. See also E. J. Schretter's report on the improvements of the late Johann von Fredrick in "Izvestie o uchinnykh rabotakh v myze Riabovoi pri osushenii bolot," *Trudy* 33 (1783): 2, 21–22; Tambovtsov, "O chishchenii konopli-anago masla," *Trudy* 18 (1771): 3–4; A. Fomin, "Opisanie izobretennago poselianami Archangel'skoi Gubernii unavozheniia pashem torfom, nazyvaemym tundroiv," *Trudy* 40 (1790): 123–24.

47. "Prodolzhenie perepiski mezhdu dvumia priateliami o kommertsi. Pis'mo II," *Ezhemesiachniia sochineniia* (April 1755): 332, 335.

48. P. I. Rychkov, "Istoriia Orenburgskaia po uchrezhdeniiu Orenburgskoi gubernii," *Ezhemesiachniia sochineniia* (January 1759): 6–7, 9.

49. "Zapiski Petra Ivanovicha Rychkova," *Russkii arkhiv* 3 (1905): 324 (hereafter "Zapiski Rychkova"). For details on Rychkov's nomination and admission into the Society, see RGIA, f. 91, op. 1, d. 1, l. 17.

50. "Primechaniia o prezhnem i nyneshnem zemledelii," *Trudy* 6 (1767): 56–68. The Society received the essay in January 1766, but waited to publish it until the end

of 1767, precisely in the midst of the peasant property competition. See RGIA, f. 91. op. 1, d. 3, l. 2.

51. "Primechaniia o prezhnem i nyneshnem zemledelii," 57–63.

52. ARAN, f. 27, op. 3, ed. khr. 236, l. 113.

53. The foundational source for Rychkov's life and work remains P. P. Pekarskii, *Zhizn' i literaturnaia perepiska Petra Ivanovicha Rychkova* (St. Petersburg: Akademiia nauk, 1867). Based on Rychkov's 20 year correspondence with Academician G. F. Müller, it contains detailed information on his prolonged job search of the 1760s. For three Soviet and post-Soviet biographical studies, see F. N. Mil'kov, *P.I. Rychkov: zhizn' i geograficheskie trudy* (Moscow: Gosudarstvennoe izdatel'stvo geograficheskoi literatury, 1953); A.V. Efremov, *Petr Ivanovich Rychkov: Istorik i pisatel'* (Kazan: Tatarskoe knizhnoe izdatel'stvo, 1995); and P. E. Matvievskii and A. V. Efremov, *Petr Ivanovich Rychkov, 1712–1777* (Moscow: Nauka, 1991).

54. "Zapiski Rychkova," 291, 299–300.

55. V. N. Tatishchev, *Istoriia rossiiskaia s samykh drevnieishikh vremen* (Moscow: Nauka, 1962–68).

56. Sevastianova, 36–37. See also Matvievskii and Efremov, 52–55; and Black, *G.F. Müller*, 38.

57. Sunderland, 61; Michael Khodarkovsky, *Russia's Steppe Frontier* (Chicago: University of Chicago Press, 2002), 169; P. I. Rychkov, "O sposobakh k umnozheniiu zemledeliia v Orenburgskoi gubernii," *Trudy* 7 (1767): 5–7, 21–22.

58. Efremov, 37, 52.

59. Matvievskii and Efremov, 137.

60. "Pis'mo o uprazhnenii v derevenskom zhitii," *Ezhemesiachniia sochineniia* (November 1757): 411–13, 416, 420, 426, 429.

61. "Zapiski Rychkova," 300–301.

62. For an exhaustive bibliography of Rychkov's publications, see Efremov, 99–101. On the history of *Monthly Compositions* and its writers, see Black, *G.-F. Müller*, 123–27, 142–44.

63. Quoted in Efremov, 26.

64. "Zapiski Rychkova," 292–93, 294.

65. Quoted in Pekarskii, *Snosheniia P.I. Rychkova s Akademieiu nauk v XVIII stoletii* (St. Petersburg: Akademiia nauk, 1866), 6–7.

66. ARAN, f. 141, op. 1, ed. khr. 4, l. 4; ed. khr. 1, l. 1.

67. ARAN, f. 27, op. 3, ed. khr. 236, ll. 55–55ob.

68. For descriptions of Spasskoe, see Pallas, part 1, 148-50; and Efremov, 53–54.

69. Pekarskii, *Zhizn' i literaturnaia perepiska Petra Ivanovicha Rychkova*, 53.

70. Lepekhin, 186–94.

71. "Zapiski Rychkova," 325. See also P. I. Rychkov, *Opyt kazanskoi istorii drevnikh i srednikh vremian* (St. Petersburg: Akademiia nauk, 1767), no pagination.

72. ARAN, f. 27, op. 3, ed. khr. 236, ll. 159–59ob.

73. "Zapiski Rychkova," 323.

74. Ibid., 325; ARAN, f. 27, op. 3, ed. khr. 236, ll. 318–19ob. Lepekhin and Pallas each recalled seeing the ruins of Rychkov's bronze and iron foundries. See Lepekhin, 190–91, and Pallas, part 1, 149–50.

75. David W. Tandy and Walter C. Neale, eds. and trans., *Hesiod's Works and Days* (Berkeley: University of California Press, 1996), 53.

76. ARAN, f. 27, op. 3, ed. khr. 236, l. 318.

77. Ibid., ll. 168–69. See also Pekarskii, *Zhizn' i literaturnaia perepiska Petra Ivanovicha Rychkova*, 51–52.

78. Kolchin, 60.

79. Perkarskii, *Zhizn' i literaturnaia perepiska Petra Ivanovicha Rychkova*, 55–56.

80. For Novikov's appraisal see *Opyt istoricheskago slovaria o rossiiskikh pisateliakh*, 197.

81. "Zapiski Rychkova," 335; "*Osada Orenburga (Letopis' Rychkova),*" in A. S. Pushkin, *Polnoe sobranie sochinenii v shesti tomakh*, volume 4 (Moscow-Leningrad: Akademiia nauk, 1936), 578. For Rychkov's description of the jelly (with all references to Pugachev and the siege of Orenburg deleted), see "O prigotovlenii v pishchu vo vremia krainei nuzhdu, goviazh'ikh i baran'ikh kozh," *Trudy* 25 (1773): 119–29. On his motivations for submitting the recipe, see his letter to the Free Economic Society (March 5, 1775) in RGIA, f, 91, op. 1, d. 394, l. 85.

82. ARAN, f. 27, op. 3, ed. khr. 236, ll. 314–15, 1.318, 1.323, ll. 324–24ob, 1.333, 1.353

83. "Zapiski Rychkova," 330–31. See also RGIA, f. 91, op. 1, d. 7, l. 2.

84. Rychkov, "Nakaz upravitelia ili prikashchika, o poriadochnom soderzhanii i upravlenii dereven v otsutstve gospodina," *Trudy* 16 (1770): 35.

85. Ibid., 18–20, 30–31.

86. Ibid., 21–22, 28–9, 33–34.

87. Ibid., 23–26.

88. Ibid., 23–26, 55–56.

89. Rychkov, "O urozhae khleba," and "O urozhae khleba, dopolnenie k prezhneiu," *Trudy* 13 (1769): 104–5, 110–11.

90. "Nakaz upravitelia ili prikashchika," 15–18, 35, 39–40, 41–43, 48–49, 60–62.

91. "Opyt' o koz'ei shersti," and "O manufakturakh iz khlopatoi bumagi i iz verliuzhei shersti," *Trudy* 2 (1766): 67, 95, 98; "Opyt' o berezovoi vode," *Trudy* 4 (1766): 63; "Opyt' vinnago kureniia na domashnei roskhod," *Trudy* 5 (1767): 51; "O koshenile i chervetse," *Trudy* 6 (1767): 82; "Sposob k vinnomu kureniiu na domashnie razkhody," and "Pribavlenie k sochineniiu o koshenile i chervetse," *Trudy* 9 (1768): 66–70, 166–67; "O travianykh koreshkakh i semianakh, prigodnykh k vinnoi sidke," *Trudy* 9 (1768): 81; "O travianom pukhe i o domashnem ego upotreblenii vmesto khlopchatoi bumagi i prochi," and "O kraske iz travy kipreinika i o pukh iz toi zhe i eshche iz drugoi travy v pribavlenie k prezhnemu," *Trudy* 13 (1769): 47, 52, 61–2; "O priazh iz vetoshek i triapiste, i o upotreblenii onoi v raznyia rukodeliia," *Trudy* 17 (1771): 172.

92. "O priazh iz vetoshek i triapiste," 167–73; "O krapivnom kholste," *Trudy* 18 (1771): 218–19.

93. Confino, *Domaines et seigneurs*, 146–47.

94. RGIA, f. 91, op. 1, d. 3, l. 9; "Predstavlenie VEO ot sochlena onago, Vitse-Prezidenta von Klingshteta," *Trudy* 2 (1766): 268.

95. "Opyt' vinnago kureniia na domashnei roskhod," 48–54, 58.

96. "Opyt' o kozei shersti," 63–68.

97. "Pribavlenie k sochineniiu o koshenile i chervetse," 167.

98. "O krapivnom kholste," 220–22.

99. S. T. Aksakov, *The Family Chronicle*, translated by M. C. Beverly (New York: Dutton, 1961), 6.

100. Ibid., 7, 27–28, 31–33, 34.

101. Ibid., 24, 27, 29.

102. *Zapiski Bolotova,* volume 1, 436–37. Bolotov's recollection here directly contradicts Esther Kingston-Mann's assertion that Bolotov never questioned his peasants about their practices and that he was "certain that they lacked useful knowledge of the land they cultivated." See *In Search of the True West*, 50.

103. RGIA, f. 91, op. 1, d. 3, l. 12; "Opisanie svoistva i dobroty zemel' Kashirskago uezda," *Trudy* 2 (1766): 129–219.

104. James L. Rice, "The Bolotov Papers and Andrei Timofeevich Bolotov, Himself," *Russian Review* 35 (1976): 127.

105. *Zapiski Andreia Timofeevicha Bolotova*, 4 volumes (St. Petersburg: V. Golovin, 1871–73).

106. The most recent biography, published two decades ago by A. P. Berdyshev, is useful but still only scratches the surface. See *Andrei Timofeevich Bolotov: vydaiushchiisia deiatel' nauky i kultury, 1738–1833* (Moscow: Nauka, 1988).

107. A. P. Berdyshev, *A.T. Bolotov: Pervyi russkii agronom* (Moscow: Akademiia nauk, 1948).

108. Roosevelt, *Life on the Russian Country Estate*, 86–87.

109. Thomas Newlin, *The Voice in the Garden*. See also idem, "Rural Ruses: Illusion and Anxiety on the Russian Estate, 1775–1815," *Slavic Review* 57 (1998): 304–5, 307.

110. Glagoleva, *Russkaia provintsial'naia starina*, 11, 14.

111. Ibid., 25–26, 28–29, 33.

112. *Zapiski Bolotova*, volume 1, 232, 238.

113. Ibid., 210, 213, 269–70.

114. Ibid., 364–70.

115. Ibid., 303.

116. Newlin, *The Voice in the Garden*, 66–67.

117. *Zapiski Bolotova*, volume 1, 394.

118. Rice, 128–29.

119. Glagoleva, *Russkaia provintsial'naia starina*, 85–86.

120. Newlin, *The Voice in the Garden*, 21–22.

121. Reinhard Wittmann, "Was there a Reading Revolution at the End of the Eighteenth Century?" in *A History of Reading in the West*, eds., Guglielmo Cavallo and Roger Chartier and translated by Lydia G. Cochrane (Amherst, MA: University of Massachusetts Press, 1999), 293.

122. O. E. Glagoleva, "A.T. Bolotov kak chitatel'," in A. A. Zaitseva, M. V. Kukushkina, and V. A. Somov, eds., *Rukopisnaia i pechatnaia kniga v Rossii: problemy sozdaniia i rasprostraneniia* (Leningrad: BAN, 1988), 141, 157; see also idem, "Imaginary World: Reading in the Lives of Russian Provincial Noblewomen, 1750–1825," in Wendy Rosslyn, ed., *Women and Gender in 18th-century Russia* (Bur-

lington, VT: Ashgate, 2003), 136–37. In 1767 Bolotov also wrote an autobiographical story recounting the development of his reading proclivities in the 1750s and 1760s as well as his own philosophy of reading. It appears as chapter three in the collection of stories "Zabavy zhivushchago v derevene," found in Otdel Rukopis, Rossiiskaia Natsional'naia Biblioteka (hereafter OR RNB), St. Petersburg, fond 89 (Bolotovy), ed. khr. 64, ll. 63–88. A. Iu. Veselova has published the document: "Iz naslediia A.T. Bolotova 'O pol'ze, proiskhodiashchei ot chteniia knig," *XVIII vek* 21 (1999): 358–61.

123. *Zapiski Bolotova*, volume 1, 100–101, 178–79, 198–99, 201, 279–71, 274–75.

124. "Pamiatnaia knizhka im sobranie razlichnykh pravouchitel'nykh pravil: sobstvenno sebe dlia pamiati pri praznykh sluchaiakh," OR RNB, f. 89, ed. khr. 55, ll. 187ob–190.

125. Ibid., ll. 19ob–20ob, ll. 57ob–58, ll. 87ob–88, ll. 134ob–135, ll. 139ob–140, ll. 223–24.

126. Newlin, *The Voice in the Garden*, 24.

127. Marasinova, *Psikhologiia elity rossiiskogo dvorianstvo poslednei treti XVIII veka*, 76–77.

128. *Zapiski Bolotova*, volume 1, 87, 90, 203–4.

129. "Pis'ma k raznym litsam (1760)," OR RNB, f. 89, ed. khr. 110, l. 23.

130. *Zapiski Bolotova*, volume 1, 472, 474, 480–81.

131. Newlin, *The Voice in the Garden*, 27–39.

132. "Razlichnye nravouchitelnyia sochineniia, perevedennye iz raznykh knig A.B.," OR RNB, f. 89, ed. khr. 58, l. ll. 4, 7ob–10ob.

133. Ibid., ll. 6–6ob; *Zapiski Bolotova*, volume 1, 420.

134. *Zapiski Bolotova*, volume 1, 438.

135. A. Bolotov, "Primechaniia o khlebopashestve voobshche," *Trudy* 11 (1768): 37.

136. Ibid., 42–43.

137. "Opisanie svoistva i dobroty zemel' Kashirskago uezda," *Trudy* 2 (1766): 197.

138. "Primechaniia o khlebopashestve voobshche," 48.

139. A. Bolotov, "O sposobe k polucheniiu sel'skim zhiteliam nekotorago kolichestva vsiakago khleba sverkh obyknovennago urozhaia," *Trudy* 30 (1775): 178.

140. "Opisanie svoistva i dobroty zemel' Kashirskago uezda," 172–73; "Primechaniia o khlebopashestve voobshche," 41–42.

141. A. Bolotov, "Nakaz upraviteliu ili prikashchiku, kakim obrazom emu pravit' dereviami v nebytnost' svoego gospodina," *Trudy* 16 (1770): 72.

142. Ibid., 69–71.

143. Ibid., 88–89.

144. Ibid., 185–86, 200–203.

145. Ibid., 209.

146. Confino, *Domaines et Seigneurs*, 263; Aleksandrov, 67; Kingston-Mann, 51.

147. Ibid., 482–83.

148. Rossiiskii gosudarstvennyi arkhiv drevnei aktov (hereafter RGADA), Moscow, f. 10, op. 2, d. 145, ll. 1–1ob.

149. Ibid., ll. 2–3, ll. 4–4ob, 1.6.

150. "O sposobe k polucheniiu," 172, 177–79.

151. "Zabavy zhivushchago v derevene," OR RNB, f. 89, ed. khr. 64, ll. 116–116ob.

152. Ibid., ll. 8–8ob, ll. 11–14.

153. Ibid., l. 109.

154. "Primechaniia o tartofele," 2–3.

155. A. Bolotov, "Primechaniia i opyty, kasaiushchiesia do poseva semian khlebnykh," *Trudy* 9 (1768): 93; "O udobrenii zemel'," *Trudy* 15 (1770): 19–22, 42–45; "Primechaniia o khlebopashestve voobshche," 40–41; "Nakaz upraviteliu ili prikashchiku," 188–97.

156. OR RNB, f. 89, ed. khr. 64, l. 37.

157. A. Bolotov, "O razdelenii polei," *Trudy* 17 (1771): 176–77.

158. Confino, *Systèmes agraires et progrès agricole*, 148–56; Berdyshev, *A.T. Bolotov, Pervyi russkii agronom*, 79–86; K. V. Sivkov, "Voprosy sel'skago khoziaistva v russkikh zhurnalakh poslednei treti XVIII v.," in *Materialy po istorii zemledeliia SSSR*, sb. 1 (Moscow: Nauka, 1952): 581–82.

159. "Prodolzhenie o razdelenii zemli na semi polei, *Trudy* 18 (1771): 51–53, 76.

160. Ibid., 147.

161. RGIA, f. 91, op. 1, d. 394, ll. 124–25.

162. *Zapiski Bolotova*, volume 2, 350.

163. Newlin, "Rural Ruses," 298–99.

164. "Al'bom ego s risunkami i avtografami otdel'nykh lits, 1781–1821," OR RNB, f. 89, ed. khr. 57, l. 11ob.

Chapter Five

"Not Only to Be Read but Fulfilled"

Makers of public culture in Russia often spoke of "useful" books that piqued the natural curiosity of their readers and encouraged them to turn the page, learn more, and pass the reading bug on to others. A sample of some early Russian journal titles underlines the distinctly didactic character of reading in the eighteenth century: *Busy Bee*, *Spare Time Put to Good Use*, *Collection of the Best Essays*, *Useful Entertainment*, and *Leisure Hours*. Catering to many different tastes, these periodicals printed a varied assortment of material, much of it translated from German, French, English, and Latin: history, geography, poetry, fiction, moral philosophy, excerpts from the classics, and heavy doses of rural economics and housekeeping. Aware of their readers' fleeting attention spans, the editors kept the contents brief. As Müller wrote in the preface to *Monthly Compositions*: "When the subscriber receives the next installment, it is rare that he does not wish to read the articles because they are so short that he won't get bored."[1]

To the Free Economic Society, the *Trudy* was the most useful reading of all. It gave purpose and practicality to Russia's public discourse by offering modest doses of moral instruction seasoned with examples of real people who served the greater good while still turning a profit.[2] Beyond that, the Society also nursed hopes that its audience would regard the journal as a summons to join Russia's budding public life, if not as active correspondents then at least as creative readers with serious interests. As it happened, the *Trudy* became one of the most notable disappointments of Russian publishing in the eighteenth century. Robert Darnton has written that a reading public unites agents and consumers of books into a "communications circuit" activated by multiple interactions between anonymous readers and the printed word.[3] While Russia possessed the building blocks needed for laying the circuit— writers, publishers, printers, booksellers and perhaps even sufficient numbers of readers, it lacked the infrastructure to integrate its discrete parts into an operative whole. The difficulties began with the physical location of the readers themselves. In an exhaustive study of hundreds of subscription lists published between 1762 and 1800, the historian A. Iu. Samarin has concluded that nearly three-fourths of the country's reading public resided in Moscow or St. Petersburg, the same places of publication for virtually all books in the eighteenth century. And in fact, most purchases of the *Trudy* were made at the Society's assembly hall in the capital.[4] For the Society, this obviously impeded its distribution in the countryside and prevented its editors from knowing who its rural audience was and what it wanted to read.

The system of patronage compounded the Society's problems. Provided with a blank check from the Empress, easy access to the Academy of Sciences Press through the academicians in the assembly, and free use of the postal service, the editors of the *Trudy* never had to factor the market into their publishing decisions. Here Andrei Nartov was following the example of his father, who earlier had similarly published vast quantities of practical books for the Academy of Sciences.[5] Lacking entrepreneurial instincts, he and his colleagues believed readers would materialize simply because Catherine desired it that way. They had some grounds for optimism at first. The overwhelmingly positive response to the *Household Medical Handbook*, written by Society cofounder Dr. Christian Pecken, suggested widespread popular demand for "useful" literature. As an advocate of popular enlightenment, Pecken took for granted the natural reasonableness of his rural readers. "This book is intended only for the use of the common people (*prostyi narod*)," he stated in the preface, "and for those who, living far away from large cities, languish in their illness without any help at all." Published in 1765 and 1766 with a total circulation of 8,400, the first two editions quickly sold out in large part due to the Medical College's assistance in distributing it.[6]

Pecken's cofounders likewise assumed that their target audience would greedily devour the *Trudy*. It turned out that readers and booksellers had other priorities. Typically published in press runs of 2,400 copies and sold at the relatively low price of 40 kopecks,[7] *Trudy* sales never came close to the phenomenal success of Pecken's *Household Medical Handbook*. From 1767 to 1769, for example, Alexander Fomin's bookstore in the northern port town of Archangel offered over 100 titles, including ten copies of each volume of the *Trudy*. A future provincial correspondent for the Society, Fomin shared its enthusiasm for "useful" books and employed the same supply-side distribution strategy. As he told the Academy of Sciences in 1766: "[From] the increase of books and for the reason of talented [readers] receiving them, an increase in enthusiasts will naturally follow." Still, as a businessman Fomin had to offer dozens of more undemanding titles that stood a better chance of selling—comedies, tragedies, translations of French novels, prayer books, textbooks, grammars, dictionaries, atlases, and calendars.[8] Faced with so many choices, patrons may not have even seen the *Trudy* while browsing bookstore shelves.

While mounting stockpiles of unsold volumes colonized the Society's storage spaces, assembly leaders tried to make the journal more accessible to provincial dwellers by using the empire's governors to help circulate it.[9] In October 1770, they requested 18 governors to give complete sets of the journal to the "most responsible pomeshchiki" in their respective provinces, who in turn would lend them to their neighbors. This attempt met with little success. As news of its failed circulation campaign filtered in from several provinces,[10] the Society in February 1776 turned to Catherine for help:

> The Free Economic Society, having been granted Your Imperial Majesty's protection, has the most humble good fortune to inform Your Imperial Majesty that, making every possible effort to bring rural housekeeping into the best condition, has already printed 27 parts of its works; but given that pomeshchiki living in remote areas of the Russian Empire not only do not use these books, but do not even know about them, the Free Economic Society is obliged to request that Your Imperial Majesty order that the copies of the Society's works be sent as gifts to the governors so that they may distribute them [gratis] to the pomeshchiki who live in the provinces entrusted to them . . . [These pomeshchiki], who undoubtedly have a desire to read them, will then put into practice the instructions contained in them through repeated experiments, and through this they will raise cereal cultures and animal husbandry to higher levels, which in turn will increase the profits of the general welfare, both private and governmental.[11]

The next attempt to disseminate the journal produced better results, a sign, perhaps, that the Empress wanted to see it circulated more widely. In October 1777 the assembly again resolved to use provincial governors to distribute the *Trudy*.[12] Over the next year, reports came flooding in from governors pledging their assistance and detailing their success in finding interested readers.[13] Of course, no measure of royal prodding could force anyone to buy and read books. By the end of the 1770s, the Society finally began to tighten the reins on *Trudy* publication. After 1779, the journal came out irregularly, and between 1783 and 1790 in much smaller press runs of 1,200.[14] That same year the Society completed its first inventory of *Trudy* circulated since 1765 and arrived at the sobering figure of 26,937 out of a total of 72,000 printed, a mere 37 percent.[15] *Trudy* distribution stagnated at approximately the same levels into the middle of the 1790s, after which at long last it found a captive audience in the recently established public schools.[16] Between 1795 and 1805, the quantity of distributed books steadily increased by about one percent annually, an indication that the Society had finally begun to reach a more substantial portion of its target audience.

The Society's overly cautious editorial policies further isolated it from the reading public. Throughout Catherine's reign, the Society was permitted to censor itself, delegating editorial decisions to the president, the two secretaries and elected committees. This kind of decentralization typified secular publishing for most of the eighteenth century: Moscow University, the Academy of Sciences, the Cadet Corps, and the Senate all censored their own publications without any interference by state authorities.[17] Of course, most publishers were government employees themselves and took their responsibilities quite seriously. Müller, for one, refused to run articles in *Monthly Compositions* whose meaning might be easily misconstrued by his readers. "In the interests of decency and preventing unpleasant consequences," he announced, "no arguments or emotional objections to the essays of others will be printed herein."[18] The Society held its contributors to similarly exacting standards, exhorting them to conduct themselves in print with the same decorum that members displayed at meetings of the assembly.[19] Private periodicals were just as careful, as editors tried to meet their readers' demand for topical fare that stopped short of critiquing the established authorities. The writer Nikolai Novikov was the first to test the waters. In his satirical journals of the late 1760s and early 1770s, he poked a lot of good-hearted fun at country squires who abused their power as serf owners.[20] Playwrights also parodied corrupt and ignorant provincial landowners, and Novikov's friend Denis Fonvizin scored the first hit in the history of the Russian theater with such a formula in his famous play *The Minor*, first staged in 1782. Needless to say, debates over state policy and critiques of public figures were not fit to print: Novikov never attacked anyone personally and Fonvizin wisely chose not to criticize serfdom. Like most writers of the time—*Trudy* contributors included—they believed bad morals to be the cause of Russia's social ills, not bad laws or bad political institutions.[21]

Catherine's decree of January 15, 1783 permitting noblemen to own and operate their own printing presses liberalized the atmosphere even more—for a while at least. Although the law required publishers to submit printed material to their local police for review, policemen proved to be lax at their duties. With its passage, the only constraint on the printed word was the so-called "three-fold limiting clause," which, according to K. A. Papmehl, prohibited "the printing of anything prejudicial to the Christian religion, the government, or common decency."[22] The consequences for Russian culture were far-reaching. As Isabel de Madariaga has written, "Now, at last, the government recognized that intellectual and literary life had acquired its own momentum, it could stand on its own feet and look after itself."[23] Yet rather than adapt to these freer conditions, the Society continued to suppress discussion of "political" topics lest it risk losing Catherine's protection.

There was no better time for the Society to show some nerve than the late 1780s. Between 1786 and 1788, Russia faced its worst agricultural crisis in decades as crop failure struck the empire's grain-surplus regions, causing famine and triggering drastic inflation in St. Petersburg and Moscow.[24] A two-front war with the Ottoman Empire and Sweden added to the devastation. Yet in the face of it all, only one article in the *Trudy* acknowledged the crisis. Signed by an "anonymous well-wisher" and published in 1790, it presented an ambitious plan for putting an end to St. Petersburg's dependency on grain imports from the south and making cereal agriculture in the region completely self-sufficient. Its centerpiece was a capital-intensive project to drain huge stretches of northern swampland over a 50-year period using prisoners and hired workers as a labor force.[25] As had long been the custom for *Trudy* contributors, the author divorced the technical dimensions of agriculture from their social and political framework. There was barely any mention of serfdom or the government's inability to fix the chronic problems of poverty and hunger. Instead, the proposal ended with an appeal for funding from the Empress, who only needed to say the word in order to transform "all that slime, muck, and swamp" into "eternally paved roads, gardens, meadows, and pastures."[26]

The Society's inability to make itself relevant to the Russian public did not go unnoticed by contemporary writers. In an unpublished essay, also written during the 1786–88 famine, the court historian Mikhail Shcherbatov launched a pointed attack on Russia's most venerable free association:

> At a time when the Economic Society through its essays has labored all these years to encourage estate management, at a time when all of our labors should be directed towards farming, [agriculture] has completely failed. Instead, just like our unenlightened ancestors, who knew not a word of estate management and did not read any scholarly essays, our stacks of grain are rotting, and we with all our enlightenment and all our incentives do not have seeds in plentiful years.[27]

Since the Society had failed in its charge, Shcherbatov urged establishing a "State College of Agriculture and Estate Management" to correct the deficiencies of the rural economy. Modeling it after Petrine colleges, he placed it under the Senate's authority and made it subject to the General Regulation. Shcherbatov also assigned to it all the responsibilities that the Free Economic Society had assumed for itself but failed to carry out: detailed land surveys and inventories; the introduction of new crops; news of modern forest maintenance techniques; the establishment of experimental villages and model farms; and the resettlement of Russian peasants on the virgin lands of the

frontier. He even copied the Society's main method for promoting enlightenment—medals and awards in recognition of exemplary estate management.[28]

The publisher Novikov offered his own veiled criticism. As the driving
force behind Russia's satirical journals of the 1760s and 1770s—most of
which folded after only a few months—he had certainly learned from his
mistakes in the Russian book market. In 1779 Novikov relocated his business operations to Moscow, a highly symbolic move denoting his intention
to build a reading public independent of the official culture of the capital.[29]
One of his first decisions as a bookseller there was to decline the Society's
request to offer the *Trudy*.[30] Anticipating that it would not sell very well,
he instead chose to market reading material that was topical, interesting,
eclectic, and not too challenging. Novikov's strategy paid off. Within a few
years, his flagship publication, *Moscow News*, had increased its circulation
to 4,000 subscribers, making it the most successful journal in Russia up to its
time.[31] Significantly, *Moscow News* offered Bolotov's *Economic Magazine*
as a regular supplement. The former *Trudy* correspondent had also learned a
few things about the proclivities of his readers. In the preface to volume one,
he promised them an eye-catching array of "orderly and disorderly" experiments, short essays, correspondence, and question-and-answer sessions. To
the reader who found little to his liking, Bolotov offered the gentle reminder:
"I write not only for you, but for the many."[32]

The Society tried to follow Bolotov's example by issuing its own economic
weekly in the mid-1780s, a time when *Trudy* publication had slowed to once
a year and public interest in the organization had all but evaporated. Proposed
by President Ivan Andreevich Osterman, one of Catherine's most trusted
diplomats and also a great patron of the Society, it was called, appropriately
enough, *Economic Weekly*. The assembly did not like Osterman's idea and
evidently tried to talk him out of it. Publishing and selling leftover copies
of the *Trudy* was difficult enough; doing the same for a weekly newspaper
would be almost impossible.[33] In the end, Osterman had his way. The six-
page weekly appeared for the first time in April 1786 with a large pressrun of
2,400 copies. Funded by Catherine and filled with the same kind of articles
and experiments that appeared in the *Trudy*, it lasted for only two years before
folding in 1788, the final year of Osterman's presidency.

*****

Amidst all the bad news and negative criticism, there were a few glimmers
of hope. In March 1779, one year after the long-delayed publication of the
Trudy's thirtieth volume and shortly before its reappearance under a slightly
revised title, a letter arrived at the assembly hall from a certain Norov, the
economic director of Sloboda Ukraine, who detailed his efforts to distribute

the journal in his province. Norov had dispatched chancellery workers across Sloboda Ukraine to comb its estates and villages for subscribers. Even more unusual, he had them conduct a poll of the most popular articles in the 30 volume set and appended the data to his letter.[34] Norov did not explain why he did this, but perhaps he anticipated that certain topics covered in the *Trudy* were inapplicable to the region's specific topographical, geographical, and social characteristics and would have little appeal to its residents.

Norov's register presents a total of 337 items requested from the towns and hinterlands of four districts: Ostrogozhsk, Izium, Sumy, and Kharkov.[35] Nearly two-thirds of the items (210) come from the Ostrogozhsk section, which lists each *Trudy* item that was requested, volume-by-volume. For instance:

> Volume One:
> Five copies [of the following articles]: On soil qualities; On locating springs and wells in arid locations; On Siberian peas.
> Four copies [of the following articles]: Method for tempering iron; Economic questions on rural housekeeping and agriculture.
> One copy [of the following articles]: On planting trees; On the construction of living quarters for commoners; On the use of metal containers.[36]

From this we know what some Ostrogozhsk residents selected from the first volume of the *Trudy*; we also know what they did not select, and, by inference, the topics in which they probably had little or no interest. For a glance into more idiosyncratic reading tastes, we can turn to the selections from Izium, Sumy, and Kharkov. These three districts trailed significantly behind Ostrogozhsk in their number of requests: Kharkov (88), Sumy (20), and Izium (16). Yet they do reveal a socially heterogeneous spectrum of ordinary readers: five captains, six lieutenants, two Cossack atamans, and a motley variety of other titles (second major, *sotnik*, titular counselor, *ratmeister*, hussar, deacon, and registrar).[37] It bears emphasizing that two Kharkov readers account for more than half of all items from the three regions: Captain Ivan Merkulov (48) and Benigna Petrovna Debrinskaia (22). Nothing is known about their educational backgrounds, but their wide-ranging interests suggest that perhaps they had some connections to the Kharkov Collegium.[38] Merkulov's list in particular displays discriminating tastes and a certain interest in the writings of Rychkov, Oleshev, and Bolotov—the three writers most responsible for propagating the image of the enlightened seigneur.[39]

For all its uniqueness and specificity, the small numbers of readers in the register still make it a problematic source for two reasons. First, 40 people in a remote corner of Ukraine obviously do not represent the Russian Empire. Yet it should also be stressed that they showed an overwhelming preference for the sort of practical reading matter one would expect to find on the book-shelves of the provincial gentry. In fact, they almost unanimously rejected the highbrow theoretical essays and detailed managerial treatises in demand by St. Petersburg's service culture. Second, we do not know if provincial nobles like Merkulov and Debrinskaia ever read their selections. The Society's correspondence records over the following two decades make no reference to any of the names in the register. In all likelihood, the *Trudy* was more like a "free gift" for isolated rural folk whose narrow horizons crippled their ability to join, let alone be cognizant of, a broader reading public. Nearly all sixteen items in the Izium section, for instance, were devoted to animal husbandry and apiculture.[40] Like peasants whose collectivist traditions often discouraged risky innovations, readers there tended to filter out the message of scientific agriculture.

In analyzing Norov's register, we must bear in mind that the *Trudy* was written mainly for a Great Russian audience, lords with middling to large estates in the central regions where the three-field system, serfdom, and the peasant commune predominated. Most of the managerial and technical improvements advocated by the Society sought to correct the deficiencies stemming from these three institutions. As Table 5.1 indicates, most of its offerings addressed what Bolotov called the "fundamental elements" of agriculture: cereals, forest preservation, general household maintenance, farm tools, health and medicine, livestock (including medical treatment, disease prevention, and fodder), apiculture, land use, distilling, fertilizer, fibers, farm buildings, and potatoes. The relevance of these subjects for Russian agriculture requires little comment. Suffice it to say that, despite the empire's extensive regional variation, most of the articles in this category focused on the interlocking components of the rural economy in the central industrial and black-earth regions. In contrast, the 47 economic experiments and marginalia grouped in the miscellaneous category had little connection to the fundamental elements of traditional agriculture. Most of these short pieces concentrate on minerals, industrial crops like cotton, silk, and tobacco, and light industries such as fishing, leatherworking, and dye production. Nearly half came from the pen of Rychkov.

Many items also addressed theoretical and descriptive themes that were national in scope. These editorials, economic descriptions, and managerial treatises totaled 43 items (19 percent). As we have already seen, many of these pieces were commissioned by the Society's patrons through high-profile essay contests on the "peasant question"; others were opinion pieces submitted by provincial writers on similar issues. Undoubtedly the most substantive items in this category were the 23 topographical descriptions written in response to Klingshtedt's economic questionnaire of 1765. The descrip-

Table 5.1.   Topical Breakdown of *Trudy* Items (1765-75)

Topic	Number of items	% (items)	Pages	% (pages)
Fundamental elements				
Cereals	21	9.5	386	6.2
Livestock maintenance	12	5.3	381	6.2
General household maintenance	11	4.8	182	3
Farm tools	10	4.4	137	2.2
Apiculture	10	4.4	498	8.1
Forestry	10	4.4	354	5.7
Health and medicine	9	4	259	4.2
Land use	8	3.5	445	7.2
Distilling	8	3.5	139	2.2
Fertilizer	8	3.5	308	5
Potatoes	4	1.8	72	1.2
Fiber crops	2	0.9	59	0.9
Farm buildings	2	0.9	16	0.2
Subtotal	**115**	**50.9**	**3236**	**52.3**
Theory/description				
Topographical surveys	23	10.2	815	13.3
Editorials	11	4.8	282	4.7
Estate and household management	9	4	993	16.2
Subtotal	**43**	**19**	**2090**	**34.2**
Miscellaneous				
Economic experiments, marginalia	47	21.3	781	12.7
Announcements, speeches, letters	20	8.8	52	0.8
Subtotal	**67**	**30.1**	**833**	**13.5**
Total	**225**	**100**	**6159**	**100**

Source: *Trudy Vol'nago Ekonomicheskago Obshchestva*, 1-30 (St. Petersburg, 1765-75).

tions appeared in the *Trudy* over the course of the next eight years, offering a wealth of economic and social data for numerous locales. Of course, it is highly unlikely that even the most civic-minded provincial readers knew of the Society's ambitious projects and essay contests. Active participation in Russia's service culture was a privilege reserved for the wealthy and well-connected or a gift of good fortune for men like Rychkov and Bolotov who possessed the ambition, energy, and talent to make their voices heard.

As luck would have it, the *Trudy* published topographical surveys for the five districts of Sloboda Ukraine on the eve of the implementation of the Statute on the Provinces. These sources confirm that the agriculture and estate life of the region developed under vastly different conditions than those in the Russian heartland. Located southeast of the Hetmanate and to the south and west of the Belgorod defensive line, Sloboda Ukraine first emerged in the mid-seventeenth century as a cluster of Cossack regiments: Sumy, Ostro-gozhsk, Izium, Akhtyrka, and Kharkov. Before the completion of the Izium defenses in 1683, the region lacked clearly defined southern frontiers, result-ing in occasional Tatar raids from the southern steppes. The Izium defensive line effectively ended the Tatar threat.[41] Under Peter I, Sloboda Ukraine began to draw closer to Russia. With the completion of the provincial reform in 1782, four of the regimental towns served as district centers for the newly formed Kharkov guberniia: Kharkov, Sumy, Akhtyrka, and Izium; Ostro-gozhsk, the fifth regimental town, was transferred to neighboring Voronezh guberniia.[42]

Like the Hetmanate, Sloboda Ukraine's cultural and social complexity stemmed from Cossack traditions and the perils of life on an unruly frontier. As a border region, it attracted a steady influx of Ukrainian peasants and Cos-sacks fleeing religious and social violence in Poland. In exchange for military service, the five Cossack regiments enjoyed a limited degree of autonomous administration under the authority of the Belgorod *voevoda*, although the lati-tude allowed to them paled in comparison to the autonomy accorded the Cos-sacks of the Hetmanate.[43] The Cossacks there developed an unusual system of free homesteading which produced a patchwork of estates of varying sizes.[44] Along with these distinctive administrative and land tenure arrangements came distilling and trade monopolies for the Cossacks. In the eighteenth century these important privileges facilitated the region's transformation into a leading center of alcohol production and a mecca for fairs and bazaars, the vast majority of which were strictly local in scope, but which nevertheless gave the region a lively mercantile character.[45]

Due to Sloboda Ukraine's early union with Muscovy, its integration into the empire in the eighteenth century aroused little controversy or protest.[46] As the frontier moved further south and the military threat from the Tatars receded, its population rapidly rose as peasants from the more densely popu-lated center colonized the region's fertile black soil.[47] These developments are indicative of the decline of frontier culture and the simultaneous emer-gence of what Denis J. B. Shaw has called a "civil-oriented society" marked by a growing presence of Great Russian magnates, and a "new economic spirit" evident in increased trade and alcohol production.[48] The development of the region also put an end to the local peasantry's traditional freedom of movement, symbolized by the 1763 law requiring peasants to receive permits from their lords before departing their estates. Although intended to raise revenues and enhance the region's agricultural performance, many correctly saw it as the first step in the legal institution of serfdom. Over the course of the 1760s and 1770s, large landowners took advantage of the decree by using strong-arm methods to bind peasants to estates. The Introduction of the Statute on the Provinces between 1779 and 1782 provided the opportunity for the introduction of the poll tax, which vividly signified the region's final absorption into the Russian Empire.[49]

Yet Sloboda Ukraine still retained certain characteristics that distinguished it from much of European Russia. Unlike the central industrial region, its fertility ensured that it would remain a major grain and livestock producer. Four out of five of the regional respondents to the Society's questionnaire of the 1760s noted standard rye yields of 10:1, significantly higher than the scanty harvests of the non-black-earth and central black-earth regions.[50] Toward the closing years of Catherine's reign the inhabitants had also begun to experiment successfully with wheat, which by this time constituted 12 percent of the region's annual harvest—an impressive advance over wheat production in the central areas where the harvest for that crop stagnated between two and six percent of the annual yield.[51] Similarly, its expansive meadows and grasslands encouraged animal husbandry on a scale unfeasible in the more settled parts of European Russia.[52] In contrast to the more settled provinces of the center, the peasants of Sloboda Ukraine benefited from larger landholdings and fewer barshchina days despite the unremitting influx of settlers and the central government's efforts to restrict the peasantry's traditional freedom of movement. According to the fifth revision census in 1795, an average peasant landholding in Ostrogozhsk measured from 20 to 30 desiatiny, an unusually large allotment, especially when contrasted with the meager peasant holdings in Russia.[53] In addition, the peasants of the region typically performed two days of barshchina for their lords, one day less than the average number of barshchina days in the central industrial and agricultural regions.[54] Just as the generous land allotments certainly eased the peasantry's lot, so did the relaxation of labor dues free them up for other activities. The responses to the Society's questionnaire repeatedly denounce the numerous holidays and trade fairs, the cheap vodka and *vareniki* bursting with cheese, all-night parties, and the peasant's ceaseless quest for "freedom."[55]

A number of factors thus account for the region's distinct economic identity: the natural fertility of the soil; generous land and cattle holdings; the peasantry's relative freedom of movement; an unusually large number of bazaars and trading fairs; and a remarkably fluid social structure. Equally important was its belated and unbalanced integration into the emerging "all-Russian" market. Much of this was due to the region's lack of navigable waterways. While the more northerly portions of the black-earth zone became grain suppliers for the central industrial region through the waterways of the Volga basin, Sloboda Ukraine and the neighboring Hetmanate found themselves deprived of accessible outlets for exporting their grain. The annexation of the Crimea in 1783 and the subsequent opening of the Black Sea to Russian exports did not improve the situation, for most of the grain supplied to southern ports came from New Russia.[56] These circumstances left Sloboda Ukraine with only cattle to export, a fact amply demonstrated by the responses to the Society's questionnaire. All five *Trudy* correspondents matter-of-factly reported that most landowners raised livestock for sale on the national market and reaped lucrative profits from it. Vodka, the region's other major product, was sold and consumed in local pubs.[57] Aside from its cattle, Sloboda Ukraine had relatively little to offer. As the empire's markets grew more unified and displayed signs of regional specialization, Sloboda Ukraine started to lag behind, a victim of its own abundance and geographical misfortunes.[58]

Such was the situation in 1779 when the Society received Norov's register. Table 5.2 provides a topical breakdown of these items according to the same classification scheme used for Table 5.1. One discrepancy immediately rises to the surface: the register indicates virtually no local interest in any of the Society's famous competitions. Indeed, with the exception of five orders for economic descriptions from their own province (which amounted to only 1.5 percent of all requests), all other Society initiatives for tapping domestic and international public opinion stimulated no response. Instead, readers were naturally concerned with economic and agricultural matters specific to their region, and the *Trudy* clearly satisfied some of their demands. Animal husbandry was one sector of the regional economy profitable enough to respond to rationalizing improvements, and readers showed interest in stud farms, hay and grass production, and the treatment of livestock disease. Fedot Udolov, one of the Society's most prolific correspondents in these years, authored a popular piece on establishing horse farms (eight requests) presented in a simple question-answer format. A sample of the questions reflects his pragmatic approach: "Where can horse farms be set up?" "What rules should be observed for the horse farm economy?" "How to pick the best stallions and mares for mating?" Perhaps more significant was Udolov's recommendation to establish horse farms in regions like Sloboda Ukraine, where fodder and forage were plentiful.[59] Some readers even expressed curiosity in the methods perfected by the "English pomeshchiki" for clover production, a sign, perhaps, that some of them applied these scientific advances on their own estates.[60]

Similar tendencies are evident in the impressive number of orders for articles on treating cattle disease. The Society had largely ignored the subject until 1770 when it sponsored a major competition to find an effective remedy for cattle plague and the next year devoted a large portion of the *Trudy* to

Table 5.2. Topical Breakdown of *Trudy* Items Requested by Readers in
Sloboda Ukraine

Topic	Number of Items	Percentage
Fundamental elements		
Cereals	41	12.2
Forestry	24	7.1
Livestock maintenance	66	19.6
General household maintenance	30	8.9
Farm tools	15	4.5
Health and medicine	12	3.6
Apiculture	26	7.7
Land use	16	4.7
Distilling	41	12.2
Fertilizer	6	1.7
Potatoes	0	0
Fiber crops	6	1.7
Farm buildings	1	0.3
Subtotal	**284**	**84.2**
Theory/description		
Topographical surveys	5	1.5
Editorials	10	3
Labor/estate/household management	0	0
Subtotal	**15**	**4.5**
Miscellaneous		
Economic experiments, marginalia, etc.	38	11.3
Announcements, speeches, letters	0	0
Subtotal	**38**	**11.3**
Total	**337**	**100**

Source: RGIA, f. 91, op. 1, d. 399, ll. 23-30.

instructions, editorials, and a questionnaire.[61] In the meantime it received several articles from the provinces. One was from Pastor Eisen, who described a useful medicinal grass for curing jugular illness in swine. The other was a remedy for sheep pox from Aleksei Rudnev of Kashira, who recommended feeding peas soaked in wine to infected sheep and sprinkling alcohol on their snouts and scabs.[62] Both of these pieces proved to be quite popular with *Trudy* readers, receiving eight and ten orders, respectively. Like nearly all the items selected by Norov's readers, they are notable not just for their almanac-style brevity but also for their revelatory quality. In publicizing his treatment, Rudnev was voluntarily giving away his family secret to the Society's readership, no small sacrifice in the fiercely competitive world of petty landowners.

After cattle breeding, distilling was the most profitable enterprise in the region. With only limited access to the great markets and trading centers of the empire, liquor sales served as the primary means for nobles to increase personal income. One of the Society's earliest essay competitions had focused on alcohol production, an initiative to which Norov's readers responded with startling enthusiasm—ten of them actually ordered the announcement.[63] Aside from this, by far the most popular alcohol-related items were Johann Model's technical manual for traditional distilling and Rychkov's brief description of grass roots suitable for flavoring vodka (ten and six requests, respectively). As a prefatory note, Rychkov assured his readers that expertise in the natural sciences was not essential for distilling, only a healthy curiosity and experimental spirit.[64] Model took a slightly different approach. Playing up to his audience's practical sensibilities and profit motives, he provided step-by-step instructions covering the entire distilling process, appending explanations of the natural distilling process in language comprehensible to the layperson.[65]

This common-sense approach surfaced in readers' choices for items focusing on cereal cultures and forest maintenance, separate branches of the economy that converged in the distilling industry. As with all other requests, the results for these categories suggest that Norov's readers regarded the journal primarily as a farmer's almanac. The most widely read article on grain (six requests) was Pastor Grasman's remedy for wheat blight. Briefly describing a few of his experiments, Grasman updated an ancient and simple method first described by Pliny: soaking wheat seeds in a mixture of crushed limestone and water.[66] A similar practicality is evident in Oleshev's analysis of the rye failure of 1766, a piece that garnered five requests. Like Grasman, Oleshev focused on problem solving, arguing that crop failures stemmed from landowners' indifference to technical details like field drainage, careful plowing, and attentive planting.[67] If the register indicated any taste for enlightening rhetoric, it usually came in the form of grandfatherly wisdom, such as Model's advice in an article on grain storage to "[think] during good times about bad times, and during good harvests about crop failures," or the same author's heartfelt praise for the humble farmer in another piece on seed preparation: "The wise intention of Providence consisted in the fact that man would reap the rewards of diligence and labor and would be led to that fulfillment which nature alone cannot produce."[68]

The *Trudy*'s offerings on forest maintenance likewise elicited a favorable response, primarily because they directly addressed widespread concerns over the region's diminishing timber supplies. Although its forests were not completely denuded, the situation by the 1760s had begun to arouse some anxiety in Society correspondents. According to the economic questionnaires, four districts (Kharkov, Sumy, Ostrogozhsk, Akhtyrka) reported an alarming decline in wood reserves, and the Ostrogozhsk correspondent singled out the wasteful burning practices of distilleries as the primary cause.

The correspondent from Sumy even warned of "extreme shortages" in 10 years "if a better economy is not established."[69] The Society published a number of practical instructions on the subject, among which several pieces by the court gardener Ekleben and Bolotov (five and eight pieces, respectively) impressed some readers in the region.[70] Another item that proved somewhat popular was Bolotov's primer on forest management (five requests, all from Ostrogozhsk). Like the answers to the questionnaire, Bolotov attributed shortages and rising wood prices to the absence of rational techniques. Instead of planning and estimating their annual wood consumption, nobles and peasants cut trees upon momentary demand without exploiting forest reserves to their full potential. Bolotov's solution lay in establishing order: dividing reserves into twenty equal portions; rotating them over a twenty-year period; keeping careful watch over reserves to prevent theft and waste; and using timber more efficiently.[71]

Livestock, grain, hay, trees, and vodka: a small sample of readers displayed some awareness of how they fit into the empire's agrarian economy and what they might do to improve it. At the same time, the register revealed the incompatibility of elite and popular reading choices. Even on a subject as uncontroversial as animal husbandry, the two groups had diverging agendas. Whereas readers in Sloboda Ukraine focused on cattle breeding, Society leaders emphasized the challenges of increasing fertilizer production for the central industrial and agricultural regions.[72] As early as 1767 the Society had published an excerpt from one of Johann Heinrich von Justi's books on the subject,[73] after which articles on manure production, artificial fertilizer, and alternative field-rotation systems proliferated on the pages of the *Trudy*.[74] None of these pieces resonated with Norov's readers. As for its heavily publicized competition for instructions on cattle disease, only two requested the winning submission. Written by Dr. Andrei Bacheracht, chief physician of the Russian fleet and member of the Medical College, it had more in common with scholarly treatises than the revealed secrets of Bolotov, Eisen, and Rudnev.[75] It was also written for nobles in possession of vast numbers of serfs and cattle.[76] Beginning with a meticulously thorough description of the symptoms of cattle plague, it provided equally detailed autopsy reports of infected livestock and explanations of the plague's various causes before divulging measures for prevention and treatment. Most nobles in Sloboda Ukraine lacked the means to afford such a luxury, let alone take the costly and labor-intensive steps for preventing cattle plague before it struck. The register indicates that they perceived such epidemics as a fact of life, capable of being mitigated, but never eliminated altogether.

The extensive selections of Merkulov and Debrinskaia indicate that at least a few readers in the region regarded the journal as something more than a home-improvement manual.[77] For Merkulov especially, the *Trudy* served as a window on the traditional farming customs of Great Russia described and catalogued by Bolotov, Rychkov, and Oleshev. For these three, Russian agriculture required full commitment from a class of resident landowners who personally managed their properties. As we have already seen, the respondents to the Society's questionnaire regarded Sloboda Ukraine as a hodgepodge of abundant harvests, extravagant waste, and potentially untold wealth. Not until the gradual implementation of serfdom under Catherine II did the region's landowners begin to realize its vast economic potential.[78] While this undoubtedly weakened the last vestiges of Sloboda Ukraine's traditional freedoms, it also strengthened the appeal of self-sufficient estates, benevolent landowners, and hardworking peasants—in a word, the justification of serfdom that had been developing on the pages of the *Trudy* since its first appearance. The *Trudy*'s provincial correspondents understood that serfdom required some positive underpinnings if it were to survive for very long. Yet as the register also makes clear, there was virtually no space in the provincial reader's mental landscape for either the Enlightenment of Western Europe or even of Catherine II's court. As W. R. Augustine observed in his important study of instructions submitted to the Legislation Commission of 1767, Russia's provincial gentry regarded the Westernizing state and its service elite with a mix of apprehension and dependence. Estranged from the world of state service yet insecure, if not superfluous, in their roles as landowners, the gentry remained "devoid of . . . the spirit of Enlightenment."[79] The only viable option for their ambitions lay in the realm of traditional agriculture and estate management.

When we consider the Free Economic Society's provincial readers, it is hard to find much evidence pointing to the existence of a unified Russian public in the eighteenth century. At this point, Russia's reading public was a small and highly exclusive social category that remained entrenched in the two capitals and sank only superficial roots in the countryside. On occasion a Merkulov, Debrinskaia, or Bolotov might differentiate him- or herself from the mass of illiterates or pedestrian readers, but such a distinction, as Douglas Smith has written, "marked one as unique and separate from the majority. The print sphere made literate individuals more cognizant of each other by linking them in a network of shared communication."[80] In fact, Norov's register presents a truly stratified and hierarchical readership, not unlike the "command structure" which John LeDonne has observed in the empire's ruling class as a whole: "enlightened" service nobles and aristocrats at the apex, consuming a policy-oriented literature; modest provincial gentry in the middle like Bolotov, Rychkov, Merkulov, and Debrinskaia, for whom enlightenment meant rational housekeeping, orderly agriculture, and innovations when necessary;

and the masses of nameless country gentry at the base, whose reading preferences were decidedly utilitarian and unspeculative.[81]

This conclusion confirms Gary Marker's earlier findings on elite and
popular reading patterns in the eighteenth century. In general, elite readers
shared what Marker calls a "ready-made universalism" which they imbibed
in school and from their travels abroad. By contrast, popular readers tended
to prefer "practical publications that played a role in everyday life and more
topical literary or informational books that functioned as leisure reading."[82]
The distinction between elite intellectual preferences and the utilitarian inclinations of popular readers fits the well-known image of a society torn asunder
by a Westernized nobility and a stagnant majority wallowing in "tradition."
Marker's dividing line suggests that by the end of the eighteenth century
Russia's public sphere had developed two distinct readerships with steadily
diverging cultural orientations. The first was an audience whose representatives were often admitted into the Society and who voiced their demand for
an economic literature through the vehicle of the public essay contest. The
Trudy's second readership, by contrast, was composed of practical-minded
provincial landowners. Although they had few connections with the capital
and its service culture, they at least possessed the sort of hands-on knowledge
of the rural economy that most aristocrats did not. Given the choice between
an editorial proposing limited property rights for peasants and a primer on
cattle maintenance, they invariably opted for the latter because at least it
promised results that were tangible and immediately beneficial to lords and
peasants. Just when the most Westernized elements in Russian society were
beginning to question the efficacy and morality of serfdom, middling landowners had come to identify the country estate and orderly agriculture with
the servile regime.

*****

If connecting with provincial nobles posed a problem for the Society,
reaching peasants was virtually impossible. To the ruling elite, peasants were
ignorant, lazy, superstitious, crude, vengeful, dirty, and drunken creatures;
serfdom alone held these vices in check.[83] As Johann Georgii wrote in 1783,
peasants always chose "the shortest path" to achieve their subsistence goals,
and, "with the exception of drunkenness, show little inclination for the luxuri-
ous life." "The villager usually sees only the present," he continued, and for
this reason it was the "duty of the supreme power" to show him not just how
to survive, but to improve his lot.[84] When the Society published a new economic survey in 1791, only one short paragraph in all of 60 pages dealt with
the peasantry: "Describe the amusements, dexterity, morals, ambition, way of
life, wellbeing, lack of reason, insensitivity, lack of knowledge, superstition,

ignorance, poverty, and filthiness of Russian and other villagers. Causes of and means for their correction."[85]

To be sure, many nobles saw themselves as their peasants' benefactors, but this was obviously not the same as seeing them as human beings. On the rare occasion they mention peasants in their private correspondence, they depict them as beasts of burden whose fate was to till the land, tend to the cattle, and serve their masters. They displayed sympathy for their serfs only when the latter were victimized by "grubby" pomeshchiki or ravaged by epidemics and famines.[86] The *Trudy* served up scenarios like these as regular fare because they were high dramas which always cast the lord in a heroic role. When peasants were commended publicly, it was for their manual labor and not their intellectual abilities. At its twenty-fifth anniversary celebration in 1790, for instance, the assembly announced a set of competitions with cash prizes of 10 rubles in order to inspire peasants to "work hard, correct agriculture, and be distinguished from others." The list of tasks included planting trees and potatoes, spinning and weaving cloth, draining swamps, and fertilizing fields with limestone. Peasants were required to present written evidence of their improvements from their masters and two noble neighbors—an almost unachievable standard given the low educational level of Russia's provincial nobility.[87]

One Society member who went against the grain and tried to raise peasants to the level of scientific farmers was Ivan Mikhailovich Komov. Born into the family of a village priest in 1750, Komov was sent to the capital in 1767 with a group of seminarians to study at the Academy of Sciences University. The following year he accompanied the academician and future Society member Samuel Gmelin on the latter's exploration of the Caspian Sea region, an ill-fated mission that resulted in its capture by Caucasian tribesmen and its leader's death in captivity in 1774. Despite the expedition's unhappy outcome, Komov managed to profit from it. In a 1770 dispatch to the Academy, Gmelin described him as "one of the very best students," an appraisal which proved useful to Komov upon his return to the capital in June 1775.[88] As soon as he arrived back he was ordered by the government to pack his bags for Britain. The person behind this turn of events was Father Andrei Afonas'evich Samborskii, who worked in England almost uninterruptedly from 1765 to 1783 in a variety of capacities: as chaplain, chaperone for Russian students, unofficial cultural attaché, and, to quote Anthony Cross, "errand boy" for London's colony of Russian aristocrats.[89] Samborskii particularly admired English farming, whose productivity after 1750 had begun to outstrip agricultural output on the continent. His tireless advocacy of English agriculture earned him Society membership in 1779. In a letter of June 1775 Samborskii requested that Catherine send a group of Russians "who have already acquired some knowledge in science and foreign languages" to England in order to "be initiated into all aspects of agriculture," including soil science, farming tools, animal husbandry, and fertilizer.[90] Komov was a natural choice, and in 1776 he and five others left for England. They remained there for eight years. Samborskii's patronage enabled Komov to immerse himself in the world of English culture, science, and farming—including lectures at Oxford University, a walking tour of parts of the country, and induction into the Bath Society for the Encouragement of Agriculture, Arts, Manufactures, and Commerce. Samborskii also introduced him to Arthur Young (admitted into the Society as an honorary member in 1779), the most renowned and prolific agricultural writer of the eighteenth century and a major influence on Komov's own writings.[91]

When Komov returned to Russia in 1785 he was voted unanimously into the Free Economic Society, appearing only once at the assembly before being whisked away yet again, this time to Moscow to serve as the province's director of domestic science (*domovodstvo*).[92] Until his death in 1792, Komov was known as the farming tsar of the old capital, publicizing the achievements of English agriculture to his native country and adapting its methods to Russia's farming traditions and extreme northern climate. Assisting him was his most useful and powerful patron yet—Prince Alexander Alekseevich Viazemskii, General Procurator of the Senate and Society member since 1765. It was to him that Komov dedicated his masterpiece, *On Agriculture* (*O zemledelii*), described by one historian as the "encyclopedia of eighteenth-century Russian agriculture."[93] An advocate of the new agronomy himself, Viazemskii provided Komov with a piece of his own land for use as a model farm and agricultural school.[94] Significantly, Komov directed his practical work mainly toward peasants. At first he delivered lectures at the University of Moscow, but quickly learned that peasants would respond more favorably to experiments on his model farm. We know relatively little about this side of his career, only that the governor-general and vice-governor of Moscow praised his knowledge of agriculture and especially the "orderly supervision" of his peasant apprentices.[95] We do know, however, that he reaped hardly any monetary compensation for his efforts. Although he managed to break into the ranks of the hereditary nobility with the rank of College Assessor, Komov remained the eternal student in material circumstances and spirit. As he wrote shortly before his death: "Poor I was born, poor I live, and poor I shall die despite all my economies."[96]

Soviet historians referred to Komov and writers like him as "raznochintsy intellectuals"—commoners of various backgrounds who the absolutist state educated and then employed in low-status jobs. Although in the pay of nobles and royalty, most of them never forgot their origins, and their literary work as a result reflected the "progressive" aspirations of their class.[97] So goes the argument at any rate. Yet Komov knew how to speak the language of the elite—his writings are seasoned with the same rhetorical bows to reason, enlightened sociability, and rustic virtue that infused the *Trudy*'s discourse. Like other provincial correspondents, he succumbed to the agromania so popular during the eighteenth century. "Just as a man can survive without arms and legs," he wrote in the preface to *On Agriculture*, "so can the state [survive] without industry and commerce; but without agriculture, like without a head, one cannot live." He also accepted the Cincinnatus myth, identifying the country life with purity and simplicity and disparaging city life for breeding luxury, parasitism, avarice, and a "thirst for all things foreign." Whereas merchants and craftsmen alone profited from their occupations, all orders of society benefited from agriculture: "[The] poor worker (*rabotnik*) receives more pay for his labor, the rich pomeshchik receives more obrok for his land, while the sovereign and state receive more revenues and arms."[98] Beyond praising agriculture as the basis of civilization, Komov linked Russia's economic progress to its cultural Westernization since Peter the Great. As a result of the Free Economic Society's efforts, Russians and Europeans pooled their knowledge, publicized their discoveries, and, so he maintained, profited immensely. Peasants, on the other hand, seemed forever stuck in the past. For them, the cardinal rule of agriculture was "[to plow, harrow, and sow as their forefathers did." "From this comes that immoveable stubbornness which they attach to old customs, no matter how stupid they are," Komov concluded, "so that they have neither the strength nor reason to force anything new, although it would be incomparably more useful than the old."[99]

Above all else, Komov sought to elevate farming to a science whose practices could help transform the northern wastelands of Russia into fertile soil: "We have such a surplus [of land] that most of it lies empty. Nothing will improve it until people understand how to do it . . . it is better to get a lot from a little than a little from a lot."[100] Many other Society writers before him had tried and failed to locate this Holy Grail. As we have seen, in the 1760s Fedot Udolov perceived the problem in terms of labor management, advising lords to tighten the reins on peasant communal institutions in order to raise productivity. In the following decade writers began floating more technical solutions. Bolotov recommended enhancing soil fertility by drastically increasing fallow and grazing land, an eccentric solution, which, had he ever instituted it, would have made him even more of a laughingstock to his neighbors than he already was. Several years later, Pastor Grasman urged landowners to establish his sophisticated eleven-field system in the open lands to the south, a project which made sense in theory but defied common sense in practice. Now in the 1780s Komov similarly proposed snatching Russian agriculture from the hands of its "hungry, stupid, and dirty" practitioners and raising it to a level suitable for "reasonable and noble people."[101]

He envisioned the gradual introduction of two new field rotation systems to achieve his dream (see Figures 5.3 and 5.4). The first was designed for Russia's barren northern regions where inhabitants were scarce, land plentiful, and infertility rampant; the second was intended for the central regions where the land was inadequate to support the population. During the first year of its implementation, customary routines would undergo no major disruptions: all peasants had to do was to divide each field in half, creating six new fields for experimentation. One-third of the arable land would still be sown with winter grain, while the remaining two-thirds would be designated for a mixture of fallow, spring crops, artificial grasses, and potatoes. Over the course of the next five years, peasants would steadily accustom themselves to the vital features of the new English agriculture: the use of nitrate-rich root crops such as potatoes and clover to replenish the soil's fertility, and, in a swipe at Bolotov's seven-field system, the elimination of all fallow land.[102] He predicted that by the end of the cycle the combination of clover, potatoes, and additional manure would put an end to the scarcity that kept Russian peasants on the brink of perpetual ruin. More than this, the example of a small, yet fertile, piece of land would have a catalytic effect, as plowmen adapted the six-field rotation and similar innovations to the enormous variety of soils and climates in the empire.[103]

Like most of the Society's projects in the eighteenth century, it is difficult to determine the impact of Komov's landmark book. It certainly improved upon Samborskii's *Description of Practical English Agriculture*, a pamphlet which relied heavily on Arthur Young's writings but made no effort to apply them to Russian conditions.[104] According to Komov's Soviet biographer, *On Agriculture* sold out within a year of its publication, resulting in a second edition and making it arguably the most widely circulated handbook on farming of its time in Russia.[105] By the early nineteenth century, the English farming methods he and Samborskii had popularized in Russia received an additional shot of publicity from Modest Petrovich Bakunin (uncle of the future anarchist) and Dmitrii Markovich Poltoratskii, two other Society members with significantly higher profiles and a good deal more influence than their late colleague.[106] Yet these men made no attempt to teach peasants the new methods, and Bakunin snubbed the author of *On Agriculture* when he claimed that Russia lacked any economic writers worth mentioning. He explicitly urged his noble readers to institute English techniques exclusively on their own demesnes, in effect abandoning peasants to permanent stagnation under the three-field rotation.[107] The cultural schism between lord and peasant instituted by Peter I now began to assume concrete expression in land use and landscape, a development which Komov could neither have anticipated nor tolerated.

Table 5.3. Komov's Six-field Rotation for Northern Russia

	1789	1790	1791	1792	1793	1794
Field one	Spring grain/grass	Grass	Winter grain	Root crops	Spring grain/grass	Grass
Field two	Spring grain/no grass	Root crops	Spring grain/grass	Grass	Grass	Winter grain
Field three	Root crops	Spring grain/grass	Grass	Winter grain	Spring grain/grass	Grass
Field four	Fallow	Winter grain	Spring grain/no grass	Root crops	Grass	Winter grain
Field five	Winter grain	Spring grain/grass	Grass	Grass	Winter grain crops	Root crops
Field six	Winter grain	Spring grain/no grass	Winter grain	Spring grain/grass	Grass	Spring grain

Table 5.4. Komov's Six-field Rotation for Central Russia

	1789	1790	1791	1792	1793	1794
Field one	Spring grain/grass	Grass	Winter grain	Root crops	Spring grain/grass	Grass
Field two	Spring grain/no grass	Root crops	Spring grain/grass	Grass	Winter grain	Root crops
Field three	Root crops	Spring grain/grass	Grass	Winter grain	Root crops	Spring grain/grass
Field four	Fallow	Winter grain	Spring grain/grass	Grass	Winter grain	Root crops
Field five	Winter grain	Spring grain/grass	Grass	Winter grain	Root crops	Spring grain/grass
Field six	Winter grain	Spring grain/no grass	Root crops	Spring grain/grass	Grass	Winter grain

Source: I. Komov, *O zemledelii*, 215.

Despite such blatantly aristocratic biases, Bakunin and his friends still managed to arouse the wrath of conservative critics who claimed that English farming methods were ill suited to the needs of Russian agriculture. Count Fedor Vasil'evich Rostopchin, later to become a hero as the mayor of Moscow during the Napoleonic wars, went so far as to deride the English plow in favor of the traditional wooden *sokha*, proving that even farm tools could become the objects of furious controversy in times of national crisis.[108] Rostopchin also won renown as one of the most reactionary defenders of serfdom in the early nineteenth century. As Alexander Martin has noted, he claimed to speak for the masses of Russian nobles who rejected any and all enlightened reforms as an assault upon their interests and way of life.[109] Rostopchin's vindication of the sokha and serfdom call to mind the sentiments expressed long before by the Free Economic Society's provincial correspondents, who believed that the enormity of available land in the southern reaches of the empire was all the safety valve that Russian agriculture required. The inexorable expansion of serfdom, the commune, and the three fields into virgin lands of the empire rendered foreign innovations—be they plows, potatoes, or natural law theory—redundant, unprofitable, and corrosive.

*****

More than natural law theory and English agronomy, it was the rise of sentimentalist literature in the 1780s and 1790s that undermined the negative perceptions of Russian peasants held by so many Russian nobles. Alexander Radishchev's *A Journey from St. Petersburg to Moscow* (1790) helped launch the trend, but not before stirring up a huge controversy first. Modeled after the English novelist Laurence Sterne's *Sentimental Journey*, Radishchev's magnum opus consisted of a series of sentimentalist vignettes set on the highway connecting the two capitals. As the narrator burrows deeper into the heartland, he meets a pageant of stylized characters, mostly drawn from the peasantry, provincial gentry, and clergy, whose stories of exploitation, misery, and corruption unveil the tyranny lurking behind Russia's enlightened façade. The *Journey* shattered the paradigm that had framed so much of the Free Economic Society's discourse since the 1760s: the belief that peasants needed to demonstrate excellence at their "natural occupation" before earning emancipation in the distant future. Instead, Radishchev urged the public to forget about the "good intentions which we have not been able to carry out."[110] Thus, in the village of Khotilov, his traveler uncovers a bundle of "projects for the future" collecting dust in the post office. One project praises the government for trying to limit "slavery," but points out that the nobility had foiled its efforts.[111] When the traveler later arrives in Vyshnii Volochok, he hears of a nobleman who had retired early from service with the intention of making a living through modern agriculture. The lord does virtually everything that the *Trudy* and its correspondents have recommended. He transfers his serfs from obrok to barshchina; he institutes a disciplined and orderly labor regime; he undermines the power of the commune by equalizing peasant landholdings; and he removes all the village misfits, forcing them to eat *shchi* (cabbage soup) in the manor house "according to the Lacedaemonian custom." The results are impressive:

> Where the crops were a failure elsewhere, his grain showed a fourfold return, when others had a good crop, his grain had a tenfold return or better. In a short time he added to his two hundred souls another two hundred victims of his greed, and, proceeding with them just as with the first, he increased his holdings year after year, thus multiplying the number of those groaning in his fields. Now he counts them by the thousand and is praised as a famous agriculturalist.[112]

As is well known, Radishchev's exposé of Russia's enlightened establishment earned him swift and severe retribution. Within weeks of the book's appearance the remaining copies were confiscated and destroyed, while the police searched furiously for its anonymous author. Radishchev was soon arrested and imprisoned in the Peter and Paul Fortress; the following month he was sentenced to death, a punishment which Catherine later commuted to Siberian exile. His fate vividly symbolized the terrible risks of speaking one's mind on an issue as sensitive as the peasant question. In the wake of the controversy, writers learned how to romanticize peasants without getting arrested for it. Two years after the *Journey*, Nicholai Karamzin published the short story *Poor Liza*, which famously declared that "peasants, too, can love" and launched a whole genre of popular peasant romances devoid of political commentary and criticism. The sentimentalist bug infected even the Free Economic Society. In his first appearance before the assembly in 1792, Fedor Iosifovich Tumanskii reminded his colleagues of the debt they owed the common "villager" (*selianin*) for all the luxuries they enjoyed in their lives: clothing, embroidery, and fine tables overloaded with food and wine.[113] Tumanskii had moved in the same literary circles as Radishchev in the late 1780s, and the latter's influence is evident.[114] The following year the *Trudy* announced some recent innovations of Russian peasants. It was the first time that the journal had ever depicted them as rational actors in their own right. Written by Dr. Matthew Guthrie, an Englishman in Russian service, it exhorted the academics and aristocrats in the Society "to learn from peasants who have utilized certain rural crafts passed down by word of mouth from father to son for many centuries; here you will find that the natural zeal of man, backed up by longstanding practice, has led to the same innovations that scholarly investigations have."[115]

This new positive image of the peasant received greater publicity in 1793 when the Society awarded honorary membership to the German physician Hans Kaspar Hirzel, the renowned author of *The Rural Socrates*, a tribute to the Swiss peasant Jacob Gujer (1716–85), also known as Kleinjogg, or Little

Jake. First published in 1761 and translated into French and English soon after, the book earned Hirzel membership in dozens of economic associations and made its title character a household name for philosophes and enlightened monarchs alike. To the philosophes, Gujer presented living proof of the goodness, rationality, and perfectibility of humanity. To kings and nobles, he personified hard work, persistence, and deference to his social betters. Once, when Prince Ludwig Eugen of Württemburg paid him a visit, Gujer reportedly told his royal guest that "we are both good if each of us does what he should. You lords and princes must order us peasants what to do, for you have the time to decide what is best for the state and it is for us peasants to obey you and work with diligence and loyalty."[116] *The Rural Socrates* appeared in Russian translation in 1789. In its preface, the translator V. V. Novikov (no relation to the publisher) hoped that Russian peasants would emulate Gujer's example, but admitted in the same breath that "it would be in vain—they don't read books." Instead, he appealed to the only audience available to him: "How honorable it would be for our fatherland if all our noblemen were transformed into Kleinjoggs and their peasants into their children!"[117]

Hirzel attributed Gujer's remarkable achievements to an unusual combination of thrift, diligence, and technical savvy—all characteristics of a Protestant upbringing. Although Gujer lacked book learning and eloquence, he possessed a natural intelligence and curiosity that motivated him to break with peasant economic custom. Understanding the critical importance of animal husbandry for cereal cultures, he concentrated his efforts on the production of manure, accumulating a huge compost pile, using fodder from his own fields, and experimenting with alternative fertilizers like turf and marl. "Kleinjogg never suffers prejudice of any kind to lead him to the rejection of new experiments," Hirzel marveled.[118] After repeated tests, he devised his own fertilizer made from animal dung, gravel, and sand, which "has converted the worst land imaginable into excellent corn fields." While not working in his fields, he applied his energy and talents to his gardens, woods, and meadows, assembling all branches of his economy into a finely tuned machine whose individual parts worked together in perfect harmony.[119] There was no great secret to Gujer's success, just an enormous capacity for work, the ability to reason, and faith in the established authorities. Above all, he firmly believed that peasants should forget about Providence and begin to assert control over their own lives. Hirzel called it "a thorough reformation of manners." Within the confines of his home, Gujer put a stop to "the intrusion of all false and irregular desires," forbidding the consumption of alcohol and meat and refusing to observe superfluous holidays and public festivities that disrupted the work routine. The only pleasure he permitted his family was the security of a bountiful harvest.[120]

Inspired in part by Gujer's example, the Society in 1796 launched its own project to transform the Russian peasantry into intelligent and virtuous farmers who excelled at their natural occupation and quietly accepted servitude as their lot in life. Sponsored by Platon Aleksandrovich Zubov, the last of Catherine's favorites, the contest promised a gold medal for the best "people's book" (*narodnaia kniga*) written "in the language of the common people" and filled with "examples, stories, and conversations" concerning "various things, which, although not new, are still unknown to the Russian peasantry." "Such a people's book," the announcement continued, "written in plain language and with a common-sense understanding of the needs, morals, customs, and prejudices of the Russian peasant, would not fail to have little by little a widespread beneficial effect, and especially if noblemen would make it pleasing to the villager and promote its practical application."[121]

The final result of Zubov's competition was a three-volume tome published in 1798 and 1799 entitled *The Village Mirror or All-Purpose People's Book* (*Derevenskoe zerkalo ili Obshchenarodnaia kniga*).[122] Its epigram promised the blessings of a pastoral utopia to all readers if only they took the moral of the story to heart: "Not only to be read but fulfilled."[123] The improbable tale unfolds in a village called Spasibo (literally "Thank You") whose retired lord, a good-hearted serviceman named Veleslav ("Magnanimous"), plans to travel abroad for three years to study scientific farming. To manage the estate in his absence, he hires Pravdinin ("Mr. Right"), a petty officer from Moscow whose virtue and knowledge of agriculture make him an outstanding choice for the job: "He wanted to reform completely the souls of his peasants so that instead of recalcitrant, lazy, and depraved people, he would turn them into diligent, good, and honest villagers obedient to the authorities and management; he wanted to correct agriculture and to introduce all the useful discoveries in rural economics like those instituted in various parts of the Russian state and in foreign lands."[124] Pravdinin's tutorials far surpass the "complete course of agriculture" that Jakob Sievers had envisioned when he first urged Catherine to create the Society in the 1760s. In addition to farming and animal husbandry, he instructs peasants in moral philosophy, personal hygiene, time management, childrearing, and household maintenance. All his efforts are rewarded when Veleslav finally returns home to see his fields filled with grain, his meadows covered in grass and clover, his herds large and healthy, and his peasants working harder than ever before. Before the entire village Veleslav commends his steward for his improvements and compensates him with a nearby estate, which Pravdinin appropriately names Nagrada ("Reward").[125]

The hero of *The Village Mirror* personifies the miracle-working qualities that the Society had always wanted to see in stewards. Pravdinin adapts the core message of scientific agriculture to the social and cultural conditions of the Russian village. Rather than bark out orders, he tries to teach peasants through stories of commoners whose triumphs and failures reflect their own virtues and vices. First there is Dosuzhev, a poor *odnodvorets* (homesteader) who travels all the way to Switzerland where Jacob Gujer (thinly disguised as a peasant named Erich) cheerfully shares with him his philosophy as well as a few house-keeping tips. Back in Russia, he records his own maxims in a notebook: "If you want cattle to produce more fertilizer, give them more fodder." "That which is most necessary, begin first." "The lazy desire, but do not receive." Dosuzhev's reforms trigger a chain reaction of improvements across his district as others apply his methods and praise him as Russia's own Kleinjogg.[126] Then there is Vaniukha, a well-meaning peasant with a weakness for vodka. After numerous reproaches from the village priest, he manages to stay away from the tavern for three weeks, only to relapse into his old ways when his friends pressure him to partake in a libation at a local wedding. The consequences are devastating: he loses his land and cattle; his wife and children are distributed to other families in the village; he dies alone and no one remembers him.[127] And finally there is Stepanida, the ugly village girl who nobody wanted to marry except for Luk'ian, who detects in her all the qualities of a good housekeeper. Their life together proves to be happy and peaceful: "Intelligent people know how to get used to an unpleasant face if the person behind it is good." By contrast, her beautiful sister Nadezha falls for a fop from St. Petersburg who poses as a baron. They eventually wed and have children, but because she lacks adequate housekeeping skills, their marriage ends in disaster—he leaves her and then marries another woman while still betrothed to Nadezha. When his bigomy finally comes to light, he flees to the Ottoman Empire. Alone and penniless, Nadezha relinquishes her children to Stepanida and dies of the plague.[128]

While not spinning his didactic tales, Pravdinin engages the village through discussion circles, or *kruzhki*, which enable them to cultivate their natural reason. After one such conversation, a woman steps forward to thank him "for teaching our muzhiki about women's matters." Visibly moved by her gratitude, Pravdinin promises to stop by her hut to sample her cooking and share his *pirogii* recipe with her. "Ah my dear," she responds approvingly, "you know all about village life (*derevenskoe zhit'e i byt'e*) through and through."[129] On another occasion he tries to convince the crowd of the advantages of enclosing the fallow field and sowing clover on it: permanent stabling of livestock, increased manure production, bigger harvests. They all reject his proposal except for one man—a certain Soshnikov who "in fact knew that Pravdinin had spoken the truth." Acting on Pravdinin's advice, he begins growing clover on some of his own land and before long the whole village follows his example. "They say that the inhabitants of Spasibo are thinking about abolishing the fallow," the author concludes, "and in order to do this are selecting the best people and sending them to see how it is done by an honorable nobleman in Tula."[130]

In its "discovery" of Russian peasant virtues, *The Village Mirror* reveals the same impulses at work in the sentimentalist literature of the day. Pravdinin holds the country life and the hard-working, intelligent, and thrifty peasant in the highest esteem. Yet none of this implies equality between the classes—if anything, *The Village Mirror* seeks to strengthen and perpetuate the hierarchies that structured so much of Russian life under serfdom. Like the great patrons of the Free Economic Society, Veleslav represents a fuzzy enlightenment of good intentions. Seeking to improve the lot of his serfs, at the beginning of the tale he organizes labor competitions for them that are virtually identical to the ones sponsored by the Society earlier in the decade.[131] Pravdinin, for his part, blithely accepts Veleslav's benign uselessness as part of the natural order of things. In any case, managing an estate is more suitable for someone of his own status—a retired junior officer who wants nothing more than "to serve a good lord and direct his economic affairs."[132] Like the regular members of the Free Economic Society, his is a practical enlightenment that gets results—provided there is someone to listen to him. Enter the peasants of Spasibo. Most of them, it seems, have the natural ability to become rational agriculturalists—Pravdinin is there to make them aware of this fact. He wants them to conduct their own experiments, put new methods to the test, and even go back to the old ways if the new ones fail. Still, there are limits to their reason. They require constant reminders that they are bondsmen born to serve God and their "boyars."[133] In one particularly revealing passage, Pravdinin leaves the village for a fortnight to see if the peasants can manage on their own. Predictably, disaster ensues—they spend all their days in the tavern, stop listening to their elders, and refuse to perform barshchina. The entire order unravels in a few short weeks. "You promised to follow my orders!" Pravdinin cries out to them upon his return. "Unhappy peasants, you forgot God, your debt to the sovereign, to your pomeshchik, and to me."[134] Never again will the village be abandoned to the "willfulness" (*svoevol'stvo*) of his peasants.

The peasant question had come full circle. Ever since the Society's prize essay competition of 1766–68, champions of forced labor in Russia had employed negative arguments against their opponents, prophesizing the catastrophic collapse of agriculture and perhaps even civilization itself if peasants were given freedom and property. Now they had a more powerful discursive weapon in their arsenal—the idea of "enlightenment." All told, the book attracted 213 subscribers, most from the middle and higher ranks of the service nobility, men of wealth and education who may have taken its title literally and wanted to see a bit of themselves in Veleslav and Pravdinin.[135] *The Village Mirror* taught them that the pursuit of enlightenment was accessible for everyone—great aristocrats, noblemen in the country, and even the humblest of commoners—provided it did not threaten the social order. The Society's last great project of the eighteenth century offered serf owners of all stations a coherent worldview, one that combined morality, agronomy, and reason into a justification of serfdom.

NOTES

1. *Ezhemesiachnyia sochineniia* (January 1755): 4. See also *Sobranie lushchikh sochinenii* 1 (1762): 2–3.

2. K. V. Sivkov, "Voprosy sel'skogo khoziaistva v russkikh zhurnalakh poslednei treti XVIII v.," 560.

3. See Robert Darnton, *The Kiss of Lamourette: Reflections in Cultural History* (New York: Norton, 1990), 112.

4. A. Iu. Samarin, *Chitatel' v Rossii vo vtoroi polovine XVIII veka (po spiskam podpischikov)* (Moscow: Izdatel'stvo MGUP, 2000), 135, 201. In 1786, for example, the Society sold a total of 859 books, averaging 71 items per month. Most of these were sold from its Nevskii Prospect headquarters. See RGIA, f. 91, op. 1, d. 29, l. 9ob.

5. On A. K. Nartov's work for the Russian Conference at the Academy of Sciences, see Marker, *Publishing*, 56.

6. Christian Pecken, *Domashni lechebnik, ili prostyi sposob lecheniia* (St. Petersburg: Akademiia nauk, 1765). For additional information on the book's publication and circulation see *Svodnyi katalog russkoi knigi XVIII veka, 1725–1800* (Moscow, Gosudarstvennoi biblioteki imeni V. I. Lenina, 1966), volume 2, 393.

7. John Brown, "The Publication and Distribution of the *Trudy* of the Free Economic Society, 1765–1796," *Russian Review* 36 (1977): 342–43.

8. S. Ogorodnikov, *Aleksandr Ivanovich Fomin (po neizdannym dokumentam)* (Archangel: Guberuskaia tipografiia, 1910), 4, 5–7. Examining the Russian book market for the late eighteenth century, Gary Marker has found similar patterns of utilitarian and light reading preferences on a national scale. See *Publishing*, 188–93, 201–9.

9. RGIA, f. 91, op. 1, d. 5, l. 26, l. 57.

10. RGIA, f. 91, op. 1, d. 7, l. 48, l. 53; d. 13, l. 30; d. 14, l. 1.

11. RGADA, f. 17, op. 1, d. 72, ll. 1-2.

12. RGIA, f. 91, op. 1, d. 15, l. 12.

13. RGIA, f. 91, op. 1, d. 399, ll. 97–123.

14. Brown, "Publication and Distribution of the *Trudy*," 342.

15. RGIA, f. 91, op. 1, d. 17, ll. 17–18.

16. Brown, "Publication and Distribution of the *Trudy*," 346.

17. Ol'ga Aleksandrovna Tsapina, "Voina za Prosveshchenie? Moskovskii universitet i dukhovnaia tsenzura v kontse 50-kh-nachale 70-kh gg. VXIII v.," in *Eighteenth-Century Russia: Society, Culture, Economy* eds., Roger Bartlett and Gabriela Lehmann-Carli (Berlin: LIT-Verlag, 2007), 159.

18. *Ezhemesiachnyia sochineniia* (January 1755): 6.

19. "Ustav Vol'nago Ekonomicheskago Obshchestva s populneniiami k prezhnemu, utverzhdennyi obshchim soglasiem chlenov Fevralia 24 dnia, 1770 godu," *Trudy* 17 (1771): 207.

20. Jones, *Nikolay Novikov*, 38.

21. Wirtschafter, *Russian Enlightenment Theater*, 87–88.

22. K. A. Papmehl, *Freedom of Expression in Eighteenth-Century Russia* (The Hague: Nijhoff, 1971), 29, 90.

23. Madariaga, *Russia in the Age of Catherine the Great*, 537.

24. Kahan, *The Plow*, 13.

25. "O Sanktpeterburgskoi zhitnitse," *Trudy* 40 (1790): 58, 63–64, 67–83.

26. Ibid., 119.

27. "Razsuzhdenie o nyneshnem v 1878 [sic] godu pochti povsemestnom golod v Rossii, o sposobakh onomu pomoch' i vpred predupredit' podobnoe neshchastie," in *Sochineniia kniazia M.M. Shcherbatova* ed. I. P. Khrushchov (St. Petersburg: Izdatel'stvo kniaz'ia B.S. Shcherbatova, 1896), 634–35.

28. Ibid., 668–82.

29. Papmehl, 81.

30. See the assembly's correspondence with Mikhail Kheraskov from April to September 1779 in RGIA, f. 91, op. 1, d. 19, l. 32.

31. Jones, *Nikolai Novikov*, 152–54.

32. "Vstuplenie," *Ekonomicheskii magazin* 1 (1780): 5–7.

33. RGIA, f. 91, op. 1, d. 25, ll. 68-68ob, d. 27, l. 44ob.

34. RGIA, f. 91, op. 1, d. 399, l. 22.

35. These units reflect the region's political boundaries prior to the implementation of Catherine II's Statute on the Provinces in May 1779. The only major town missing from Norov's register is Akhtyrka, situated on the Vorskla River approximately one hundred miles west of Belgorod.

36. RGIA, f. 91, op. 1, d. 399, l. 23.

37. By contrast, out of the 104 men admitted into the Society in its first decade (excluding seven honorary foreign members), only nine held relatively low-ranking positions: two captains, two lieutenants, one titular counselor, one ensign, two ober-bergmeisters, and one ober-secretary. See the register appended to *Prodolzhenie Trudov Vol'nago Ekonomicheskago Obshchestva* 1 (1779): no pagination.

38. On the Kharkov Collegium, see David Saunders, *The Ukrainian Impact on Russian Culture, 1750–1850* (Edmonton: Canadian Institute of Ukrainian Studies, 1985), 49–50.

39. Merkulov's choices suggest the same kind of deliberation that P. I. Khoteev has detected in the private libraries of two other southern landowners, Jacob Andreevich Markovich of Left-Bank Ukraine and Ivan Petrovich Annenkov of Kursk, the latter who purchased the first volume of the *Trudy*. Like Merkulov and Debrinskaia, they also had to use every opportunity to acquire quality secular literature. See *Kniga v Rossii v seredine XVIII v.: Chastnye knizhnye sobranii* (Leningrad: Nauka, 1989), 26–34. Although it is impossible to determine if such deliberation was representative of the provincial gentry as a whole, it is clear that Merkulov and others like him were not content to purchase French novels "by the pound," to quote Richard Pipes, *Russia under the Old Regime* (New York: Scribners, 1974), 255.

40. RGIA, f. 91, op. 1, d. 39, ll. 25–26.

41. G. A. Sanin, "Iuzhnaia granitsa Rossii vo 2-i polovine XVII-1-i polovine XVIII vv.," *Russian History/Histoire Russe* 19 (1992): 439–41; Denis J. B. Shaw, "Southern Frontiers of Muscovy, 1550–1700," in *Studies in Russian Historical Geography*, volume 1, eds. J. H. Bater and R. A. French (London: Academic Press, 1983), 130–31.

42. Kabuzan, *Narodonaselenie Rossii v XVIII-pervoi polovine XIX v.*, 186–87.

43. Zenon Kohut, *Russian Centralism and Ukrainian Autonomy: Imperial Absorption of the Hetmanate, 1760s–1830s* (Cambridge, MA: Harvard University Press, 1988), 16–17, 24–31.

44. Shaw, "Southern Frontiers of Muscovy," 130–31; Blum, *Lord and Peasant in Russia*, 417; Carol Belkin Stevens, *Soldiers on the Steppe: Army Reform and Social Change in Early Modern Russia* (DeKalb, IL: Northern Illinois University Press, 1995), 30–36; Denis J. B. Shaw, "Urbanism and economic development in a pre-industrial context: the case of southern Russia," *Journal of Historical Geography* 3 (1977): 113–15; Judith Pallot and Denis J. B. Shaw, *Landscape and Settlement in Romanov Russia, 1613–1917* (Oxford: Oxford University Press, 1990), 24–25, 37.

45. Shaw, "Urbanism and economic development," 115. By the late eighteenth century, Ostrogozhsk still remained a major hub of the distilling industry, importing grain from Orel and Kursk for the production of spirits. See Pallot and Shaw, 77; and R. E. F. Smith and David Christian, *Bread and Salt: A Social and Economic History of Food and Drink in Russia* (Cambridge: Cambridge University Press, 1984), 204-5. According to B. N. Mironov's calculations, 31.2 percent of all mercantile transactions in the empire in the 1780s took place in southwest Russia, Ukraine, and New Russia. The central industrial and agricultural regions, by comparison, accounted for only 18.8 percent and 22.2 percent, respectively. Although some of the products bought and sold in Ukraine were destined for the central and northern areas, the vast majority of them stayed in the region. See *Vnutrennyi rynok Rossii vo vtoroi polovine XVIII-pervoi polovine XIX v.* (Leningrad: Nauka, 1981), 236–37.

46. Saunders, 27. Debates in the Legislative Commission of 1767–68 over Sloboda Ukraine's absorption into the empire are briefly covered in Kohut, 173–75.

47. According to V. M. Kabuzan's figures, between 1719 and 1782 the population of Sloboda Ukraine (Kharkov guberniia after 1782) nearly doubled from 206,447 to 375,573. Like most other districts on the edge of the heartland, the region also experienced a steady growth in the number of privately owned peasants (from 85,442 in 1719 to 170,912 in 1782) and in the proportion of serfs to the population of the region at large (from 41.39 percent in 1719 to 45.51 percent in 1782). See *Izmeniia v razmeshchenii Rossii v XVIII-pervoi polovine XIX v.* (Moscow: Nauka, 1971), 67, 79, 87, 103. On the massive population transfers in eighteenth-century Russia, see Kahan, 16.

48. Shaw, "Urbanism and economic development," 118. See also John LeDonne, "The Frontier in Modern Russian History," *Russian History/Histoire Russe* 19 (1992): 151. On the establishment of large estates in southern Russia and Ukraine in the 1760s by powerful Russian families such as the Vorontsovs, Trubetskois, and Buturlins, see Rubinshtein, *Sel'skoe khoziaistvo Rossii*, 53, 59–61, 67.

49. Madariaga, *Russia in the Age of Catherine the Great*, 67–74, 310–14; idem, "Catherine II and the Serfs," 36–37; Blum, *Lord and Peasant in Russia*, 417–78. For a useful case study of enserfment on the estates of one Cossack family throughout Left-Bank Ukraine see I. A. Gurzhii, "K voprosu o kharaktera pomeshchichego khoziaistva na levoberezhnoi Ukraine vo vtoroi polovine XVIII v." *Istoricheskie zapiski* 34 (1950): 334–5.

50. See, in *Trudy* 8 (1768): "Prodolzhenie otvetov, na predlozhennye v pervoi chasti Vol'nago Ekonomicheskago Obshchestva voprosy, o nyneshnem sostoianii v

raznykhguberniiakh i provintsiiakh zemledeliia i domostroitel'stva, po Slobodskoi Ukrainskoi provintsii" (76), "Toizhe Slobodskoi gubernii po Iziumskoi provintsii" (101–2), "Po Akhtyrskoi provintsii" (134), and "Po Ostrogozhskoi provintsii" (160–61). The only province of Sloboda Ukraine reporting relatively low yields was Sumy, which typically had a ratio of 1:5, in times of crop failure dropping to 1:2 ("Po Sumskoi provintsii," 187–88). Compare these figures with the output/seed ratios for rye and wheat from the central industrial and agricultural regions from the 1760s in Kahan, 50.

51. For a comparison of the proportion of field crops sown in the Russian Empire in the 1780s and 1790s see Rubinshtein, *Sel'skoe khoziaistvo Rossii*, 338–39.

52. Landowners of every magnitude throughout Sloboda Ukraine managed to operate a stud farm despite their ignorance of selective breeding methods and nonchalance towards basic maintenance. See *Trudy* 8 (1768): 78, 91–92, 103–4, 120, 152, 189, 209. Only the Ostrogozhsk correspondent stressed that stud farms in his province were generally of poor quality (ibid., 177–78). For information on similarly impressive livestock economies in the Hetmanate see Gurzhi, 337.

53. V. I. Semevskii, *Krest'iane v tsarstvovanie Imperatritsy Ekateriny II*, volume 1, 30. See also peasant landholding figures for Tambov peasants in Steven Hoch, *Serfdom and Social Control: Petrovskoe, A Village in Tambov* (Chicago: University of Chicago Press, 1986), 23–28. Much of this land was not arable permanently incorporated into the three-field system. Most plowland was cultivated using *perelog* or field-grass husbandry. The average size of a single peasant's arable holdings was thus probably around five desiatiny, supplemented by extensive fallow and grassland for supporting livestock. See Pallot and Shaw, 69–71; L. V. Milov, "O roli perelozhnykh zemel v russkom zemledelii vtoroi poloviny XVIII v.," *Ezhegodnik po agrarnoi istorii vostochnoi Evropy* 4 (Riga: Akademiia nauk SSSR, 1963): 279–88; Rubinshtein, *Sel'skoe khoziaistvo Rossii*, 209. Without specifying the agricultural systems, correspondents from Kharkov and Sumy simply claimed that farmers "used" all the available land in their respective provinces. In contrast, writers from Ostrogozhsk, Akhtyrka, and Izium noted that a great deal of land went to waste due to "idleness" and "traditional privileges" of the local peasantry, possible a disparaging reference to the perelog system. See *Trudy* 8 (1768): 84, 112, 147, 168–69, 197.

54. Semevskii, *Krest'iane v tsarstvovanie Imperatritsy Ekateriny II*, volume 1, 96–98.

55. *Trudy* 8 (1768): 98–100, 130–33, 158–59, 186, 218–20. On Ukraine's distinctive distilling methods and pub-oriented drinking culture see Smith and Christian, 223.

56. B. B. Kafengauz, *Ocherki vnutrennego rynka Rossii pervoi poloviny XVIII v.* (Moscow: Nauka, 1958), 289, 294; Kahan, 51–52; Robert Jones, "Ukrainian Grain and the Russian Market in the Late Eighteenth and Early Nineteenth Centuries," in I. S. Koropeckyj, ed., *Ukrainian Economic History: Interpretative Essays* (Cambridge, MA: Harvard University Press, 1991), 221–21; Pallot and Shaw, 208–9.

57. *Trudy* 8 (1768): 79, 90, 105–6, 118, 138–39, 164, 206; Smith and Christian, 221–23.

58. A native of the Hetmanate, Prince Oleksandr Bezborodko summarized the dilemma of estate management in Ukraine in a letter of 1797: "What will you get out

of your oast-house? A real Little Russian property. You buy the grain and distill the drink, you buy grain again and so on. Organizational cycles which never throw out cash; you can't live or set yourself up on cycles" (quoted in Saunders, 73).

59. F. Udolov, "Prakticheskiia primechaniia o soderzhanii konskikh zavodov, s prisoedinennymi konym nekotorymi k ekonomii sluzhashchimi sovetami, osnovannymi na iskusstve," *Trudy* 6 (1767): 156–226.

60. Klingshtedt, "O privedenii v lushchee sostoianie senokosov, o raznykh rodakh trav upotrebliaemykh v drugikh gosudarstvakh k seianiiu lugov, o potrebnom zemledelii dlia vozrashcheniia semian, i o upotreblenii onykh trav," *Trudy* 3 (1766): 53–78.

61. "Kratkoe nastavlenie, kakim obrazom postupat' v sluchae zarazy mezhdu rogatym skotom, a kak onoi pol'zovat'," *Trudy* 17 (1771): 1–71.

62. Eisen, "Nastavlenie k predokhraniiu i lecheniiu svinei ot bolezni sostoiashchei v opukholi shei," *Trudy* 24 (1773): 185–87; A. Rudnev, "O sposobi izbavliat' ovets ot ospy, i o lechenii sei bolezni," *Trudy* 15 (1770): 76–79.

63. Klingshtedt, "Predstavlenie VEO ot sochlena onago, vitse-prezidenta-fon Klingshteta," *Trudy* 2 (1766): 267–76.

64. Rychkov, "O travianykh koreshkakh i semianakh prigodnykh k vinnoi sidke," *Trudy* 9 (1768): 75–82.

65. Model, "Mnenie i primechaniia o vinokurenii," *Trudy* 3 (1766): 190–233.

66. G. Grasman, "O golovne vo pshenitse," *Trudy* 20 (1772): 111–16. Another article that appears twice in the register by St. Petersburg governor Stepan Ushakov likewise recommended a variation on Pliny's method. See "Delo sovershenno ispytannoe v plodorodii ozimago khleba," *Trudy* 23 (1773): 17–20.

67. A. Oleshev, "O neurozhae rzhi, a osiblivo v 1766 goda," *Trudy* 5 (1767): 36–38.

68. J. Model, "Mnenie o zberezhenii khleba," *Trudy* 4 (1766): 177; idem, "Fizicheskiia i khimicheskiia razsuzhdeniia o natural'nom udobrenii semian, i o umnozhenii chrez to khleborodiia," *Trudy* 2 (1766): 69.

69. *Trudy* 8 (1768): 86–87, 148, 171–72, 200–201.

70. Ekleben, "O Sibirskom gorokhovom dereve, i o velikoi ego pol'ze," *Trudy* 1 (1765): 60–73; Bolotov, "O novom rode sazhdeniia derev," *Trudy* 29 (1775): 233–63.

71. Bolotov, "O rublenii, popravlenii, i zavedenii lesov," *Trudy* 4 (1766): 68–80, 84–92.

72. Its first piece on this subject was a brief extract from a Swedish essay on stall construction and basic maintenance of manure, translated by Nartov: "Sposob k unavozheniiu k popravleniiu pashni," *Trudy* 2 (1766): 57–62.

73. Justi, "Primechaniia o pravil'nom uravnenii khlebopashestva s skotorodstvom," *Trudy* 6 (1767): 113–22.

74. In addition to Bolotov's two installments on the seven-field system and Grasman's various proposals for introducing the new English agriculture, consult also Staehlin, "Vypis' sochinenaia statskim sovetnikom von Stahlinym iz nemetskoi knizhki prislannoi v Vol'noe Ekonomicheskoe Obshchestvo, pod imeniem 'nastavleniia o gipse,'" *Trudy* 10 (1768): 97–114; Bolotov, "O udobrenii zemel'," *Trudy* 15 (1770): 1–65; Nartov, "O loshadinom navoze," *Trudy* 19 (1771): 132–54; Regensburger, "O prigotovlennii navoza," *Trudy* 18 (1771): 169–209; Nartov, "O udobrenii pashen iskustvom. O izvesti, materialakh onoi, i o sposobe kak onuiu zhech'," *Trudy* 19 (1771):

115–31; Bolotov, "O upotreblenii v pol'zu skotskago navoza v stepnykh i takikh mestakh, gde zemli onym unavozhivat' obyknoveniia net," *Trudy* 23 (1773): 138–61; and Rozenkampf, "O prichinakh neurozhaia khleba v Liflandii, *Trudy* 26 (1774): 92–97.

75. A. Bacheracht, "O padezhe rogatago skota," *Trudy* 21 (1772): 1–64.

76. Ibid., 62–63.

77. RGIA, f. 91, op. 1, d. 399, ll. 27–29. The topical breakdown for Merkulov's selections runs as follows: cereals (8); livestock maintenance (8); apiculture (7); distilling (6); miscellaneous (6); general household maintenance (4); farm tools (3); editorials (2); health and medicine (2); land use (1); and forest preservation (1). Debrinskaia's selections, although smaller, point to similarly wide-ranging interests: livestock maintenance (6); general household maintenance (5); cereals (4); apiculture (2); land use (2); farm tools (1); distilling (1); and health and medicine (1).

78. See the responses to the Society's economic questionnaire from Izium, Akhtyrka, and Ostrogozhsk in *Trudy* 8 (1768): 109, 112, 142–43, 170–71.

79. Augustine, 387.

80. Smith, *Working the Rough Stone*, 47–52, 58–63.

81. LeDonne, *Absolutism and Ruling Class*, 15–21.

82. Marker, *Publishing*, 201–2.

83. Michael Confino, "Le paysan russe jugé par la noblesse au XVIIIe siècle," *Revue des études Slaves*, 38 (1961): 51–63.

84. I. Georgii, "Koronovannyi otvet na zadannuiu Vol'nym Ekonomicheskim Obshchestvom v 1780 godu zadachu o pobichnykh krest'ianskikh rabotakh," *Trudy* 33 (1783): 103–4, 106.

85. "Nachertanie ko vsegdashnei zadache i nagrazhdeniiu tekh sochinitelei, koi khoziaistvennyia opisaniia chastnykh Rossiiskikh namestnichestve soobshchat' emu budut," *Trudy* 43 (1791): 298.

86. Marasinova, *Psikhologiia elity rossiiskogo dvorianstvo*, 204, 207–8, 214.

87. RGIA, f. 91, op. 1, d. 35, ll. 191–96. After two years, the assembly had made only two awards. See RGIA, f. 91, op. 1, d. 38, ll. 22ob–25ob; d. 41, l. 314.

88. V. P. Gur'ianov, *I.M. Komov: Ego zhizn' i deiatel'nost'* (Moscow: Izdatel'stvo moskovskogo obshchestva ispytatelei prirody, 1953), 32, 36.

89. A. G. Cross, *By the Banks of the Thames: Russians in Eighteenth-Century Britain* (Newtonville, MA: Oriental Research Partners, 1980), 41.

90. Ibid., 62.

91. Ibid., 68–69; Gur'ianov, 51.

92. RGIA, f. 91, op. 1, d. 27, l. 56.

93. I. Komov, *O zemledelii* (Moscow: Tipografiia Ponomareva, 1788); I. F. Kopyl, "Iz istorii russkoi agronomii XVIII v. (I. M. Komov o zemledelii)," in *Iz istoricheskogo opyta sel'skogo khoziaistva SSSR*, sbornik VII (1969): 98.

94. Gur'ianov, 65.

95. Ibid., 62–64.

96. Quoted in Cross, *By the Banks of the Thames*, 70.

97. Shtrange, *Demokraticheskaia intelligentsia v Rossii*; Gur'ianov (11, 57) also uses this term to describe Komov and his generation.

98. Komov, *O zemledelii*, 1, 4, 12–13.

99. Ibid., 24–25.

100. Ibid., 212–13.

101. Ibid., 25–26.

102. Ibid., 210.

103. Ibid., 216.

104. A. A. Samborskii, *Opisanie prakticheskago anglinskago zemledeliia* (Moscow, 1781).

105. Gur'ianov, 73–74.

106. Cross, *By the Banks of the Thames*, 88–90.

107. Modest Bakunin, *Pravila rukovodstvuiushchiia k novumu razdelu i obrabotyvaniiu polei s pokazaniem nuzhnykh sel'skikh zavedenii* (St. Petersburg: Akademiia nauk, 1800), 7, 8, 13, 16.

108. Confino, *Domaines et seigneurs*, 282–87.

109. Alexander Martin, *Romantics, Reformers, Reactionaries: Russian Conservative Thought and Politics in the Reign of Alexander I* (DeKalb, IL: Northern Illinois University Press, 1997), 104–5.

110. A. N. Radishchev, *A Journey from St. Petersburg to Moscow*, ed., Roderick Page and translated by Leo Weiner (Cambridge, MA: Harvard University Press, 1958), 154.

111. Ibid., 151.

112. Ibid., 159.

113. "Rech' nadvornago sovetnika Feodora Iosifovicha Tumanskago pri priniatii ego v chleny Ekonomicheskago Obshchestva," *Trudy* 46 (1792): 129–30.

114. G. P. Makogonenko, *Radishchev i ego vremia* (Moscow: Gosudarstvennoe izdatel'stvo khudosh. literatury, 1956), 344–51.

115. Gutrii, "Nekotoryia izobreteniia Rossiiskikh krest'ian," *Trudy* 48 (1793): 262.

116. Quoted in Blum, *The End of the Old Order in Rural Europe*, 295.

117. I. K. Girtsel, *Sel'skoi Sokrat, ili opisanie ekonomicheskikh i nravstvennykh pravil zhizni filosofa-zemledel'tsa*, (Moscow: Izdatel'stvo moskovskago universiteta, 1789), 13, 15.

118. *Rural oeconomy: or Essays on the Practical Parts of Husbandry to Which is added The Rural Socrates: Being Memoirs of a Country Philosopher*, translated by Arthur Young from the French (London: Printed for T. Beckett, 1773), 264–76.

119. Ibid., 296, 298, 304–5.

120. Ibid., 316, 328–32.

121. RGIA, f. 91, op. 1, d. 53, ll. 111-13; Khodnev, 390–91.

122. The identity of the anonymous author remains a matter of some dispute. In an article first published in 1991, L. V. Milov argued that it was Andrei Bolotov, a claim he continued to repeat in *Veliorusskii pakhar'*. Milov points out a number of interesting parallels between Bolotov's works and *The Village Mirror*: a strong emphasis on balancing cereals, grass farming, and animal husbandry; a pronounced interest in medicine and electricity; a critical attitude towards hunting; plentiful references to Tula province; and lots of bad, didactic poetry. Apart from these few sketchy similarities in content and style, however, Milov produces no convincing evidence

linking the book's actual provenance to Bolotov. See L. V. Milov, "A.T. Bolotov—avtor krest'ianskoi entsiklopedii," *Voprosy istorii* 7–8 (1991): 14–19, 20–22. Milov also ignores the fact that the prize went to Vasilii Mikhailovich Severgin, an adjunct at the Academy of Sciences and Society correspondent since 1791. On Severgin, see Khodnev, 391.

123. *Derevenskoe zerkalo ili Obshchenarodnaia kniga*, three volumes (St. Petersburg: Pri Gubernskom Pravlenii, 1798–1799).

124. Ibid., volume one, 17–18.

125. Ibid., volume three, 204, 210–20, 280.

126. Ibid., volume one, 68–76, 82, 93.

127. Ibid., volume two, 134–38.

128. Ibid., 239–42, 243–44, 248, 250–51.

129. Ibid., 16–20.

130. Ibid., volume one, 129, 139–40, 144–45, 151.

131. Ibid., 20–23.

132. Ibid., 32.

133. Ibid., volume three, 205.

134. Ibid., volume two, 255.

135. Samarin, 66.

Conclusion

A monarchical government presupposes, as has been said, distinctions, ranks, and even a nobility based on birth . . . This form of government may be said to resemble the system of the universe itself, in which there is a force that constantly pushes all bodies away from the center, and a power of gravitation that attracts these bodies to it. Honor sets all the parts of the body politic in motion, and by its very action connects them; thus every individual moves towards the public good, while he has been thinking only of promoting his own interests.

—Montesquieu, from *The Spirit of the Laws*

The history of the Free Economic Society under Catherine the Great highlights three essential characteristics of Imperial Russian public culture. First, its close alignment with the court and the state ensured its quasi-governmental status. The Society's purpose was to assist in the completion of Russia's Europeanization begun by Peter the Great, a service for which its members were rewarded with praise before the public and the gratitude of the monarch. Here it was following the lead of Catherine II, whose own reforms similarly aimed to infuse her ruling class with the spirit of honor which Montesquieu had insisted informed the spirit of all true monarchies. Of course, the Society also claimed to be driven by "patriotism," a quality which Montesquieu assigned to ancient republics and the spirit of equality shared by their citizens. We should not be misled by the Society's rhetoric. The customs that it put into practice reinforced the primacy of the Russian state, the rank and status distinctions of its own members, and the privileges of the nobility in general. None of this was unique to Russia—economic associations across Europe all billed themselves as junior partners of their Crowns. In this regard the Society took the same path as its counterparts in the West. By cooperating with the state, patiently building and sustaining ties to its patrons, and catering to their needs when the occasion demanded, it produced the survival tools employed by hundreds of other public associations after 1800.[1] It was a game that required patience, perseverance, and the acceptance of limitations. Dependent on the whim and good will of the ruling elite, Andrei Nartov and his friends maintained the Society's identity and autonomy by volunteering their services to the established authorities and requesting nothing in return except for the means to continue doing their work and, naturally, a little bit of the credit.

While Catherine's charter provided the parameters and protection for the Society's public sphere, it was left to the assembly to determine how to use that space. Here the course of action was fraught with ambiguity. As Iurii Lotman once wrote, the eighteenth-century nobility consisted of private individuals driven by interests specific to their privileged order—promotion of family names, the enrichment of their estates, and the cultivation of personal honor. At the same time, these people moved within the world of "Russian bureaucratism," a sphere defined by state service, "regulation mania," and the ubiquitous *chinovniki* (bureaucrats) of St. Petersburg. For Lotman, Russia's cultural achievements were almost exclusively the product of the former sphere, whose inhabitants sought to forge a space and way of life free of the regulations and hierarchy that permeated officialdom. By contrast, officialdom "left no traces in the country's spiritual life, producing no culture, no ethics, not even an ideology."[2] The tensions between these two spheres were quite subtle and usually expressed in the nobleman's need for meaningful personal relationships with like-minded individuals, as opposed to the more "pragmatic contacts" made in service.[3]

The Society's attempts to forge a public forum reveal similarly contradictory impulses and underscore its inherent fragility. Although a significant portion of notable members were attracted by the organization's claims to patriotism and usefulness, there is little evidence to support the impression that the Society, simply by virtue of its non-governmental status, favored a new climate of "sociability." When new members joined their colleagues in the assembly, instead of equality, camaraderie, and public service, they encountered the same habits of deference and hierarchy that they experienced on a regular basis in the military service and civil administration. As David Ransel has argued, the Petrine principles of rationality which inspired both Russia's bureaucracy and public culture failed to defuse "the traditional patrimonial system based on personal delegation of authority."[4] Consequently, joining the Society came to signify a type of "fictitious service" not unlike that of the knightly orders that proliferated in Russia in the eighteenth century. Even the provincial correspondents who were far removed from St. Petersburg regarded membership as a means of personal advancement. For Bolotov it offered a springboard to literary fame; for Rychkov it promised a return to state service; and for dozens more it served to distinguish themselves and earn praise from their notable colleagues in the capital.

Second, through the *Trudy* the Free Economic Society publicized a new social type in Russian culture, the rational seigneur dedicated to improving agriculture and ameliorating the condition of his peasants. Far from merely publishing technical manuals, it aspired to galvanize nobles to useful action on their estates as an acceptable substitute for conventional state service. This aspect of the Society's mission did not come without its complications and unintended consequences. While state service offered the nobleman a chance for worldly success, life in the provinces promised little but frustration borne out of the futility of trying to inspire serfs to work harder at their "natural occupation." The writings of Rychkov, Bolotov, Oleshev, Wol'f and many others reflect a creeping despondency and in some cases disillusionment with their choice to fashion themselves into rural enlighteners.

Yet in retrospect the Society was probably just fidgeting from the "teething troubles" endemic to so many of Catherine's reform initiatives.[5] Recent scholarship suggests that as the Statute on the Provinces steadily took root, so did the discourse of the enlightened seigneur which the *Trudy* had propagated. As John Randolph has illustrated, when the young Aleksandr Mikhailovich Bakunin retired to Tver province in 1792, he intended to transform his family estate of Priamukhino into "a laboratory for the creation—and not merely the representation—of virtuous social norms." The impetus came from Nikolai Aleksandrovich Lvov, a Free Economic Society member whose writings had inspired many nobles to transplant the values and practices of Russia's public culture into their private homes in the country.[6] Interestingly, Bakunin's projects for improvement included a blueprint for the "enlightenment" of Priamukhino's serfs which recapitulated the evolution of the peasant question on the pages of the *Trudy* in almost every detail: a prefatory condemnation of "slavery" on moral and economic grounds; a "social contract" between lord and serf that granted the latter a hereditary leasehold in exchange for a fixed rent; numerous incentives for peasants to maintain single-family households; and mandatory improvements like swamp drainage, sowing potatoes, and the construction of stone living quarters.[7]

Although Bakunin's plan for protective tutelage was never implemented, its author's famous home offered a model for others to follow in succeeding years. By the reign of Nicholas I (1825–55), Tver province boasted a network of improving lords who similarly had retired early from service to devote themselves to farming. Many belonged to the Moscow Agricultural Society, which aimed to apply scientific agronomy to Russian conditions through practice and experimentation.[8] Representative of the new trend were D. P. Shelekhov and V. A. Preobrazhenskii, two staunch opponents of the three-field system and the "old way" of agriculture who worked tirelessly to introduce Western techniques within the framework of the traditional manorial regime. Like Bakunin, they believed that the landed nobility should serve the common good by living on their estates and teaching their peasants scientific farming techniques.[9] Such attachments to the country estate acquired nostalgic overtones. Michael Hughes and Susan Smith-Peter have shown that Slavophilic writers perceived no contradiction between their idealized villages, uncontaminated by the vices of the city, and the application of Western agriculture. As the Slavophile A. Chikhachev wrote in his local Vladimir newspaper in the 1850s, it was the gentry's paternal responsibility to promote the happiness and welfare of their peasant "children" by disseminating rational farming methods.[10] All these ideas had appeared in the *Trudy* in one form or another since the 1760s. On the eve of the emancipation of the serfs they had become commonplace assumptions for educated nobles.

Which raises the third and final point. Confronted with the peasant question from the moment of its establishment, the Society constructed a two-tiered defense of serfdom that reflected, in broad strokes, the dualism of its membership and the Russian nobility itself. The magnates in the Society saw the issue from their commanding perches in St. Petersburg, a function of lifelong service, absenteeism, and their enormous holdings in land and serfs. All the plans which earned their endorsement—Beardé's plea for gradual emancipation, the instructions for estate managers, Grasman's project on land allotments, *The Village Mirror*—sought to increase the landowner's power at the expense of the village commune with a flurry of regulatory measures, all in the name of reforming the morals of their peasants and winning them over to rational farming. In his study of "enlightened seigneurialism," Edgar Melton has argued that this theoretical approach to estate management made little impact because it was "based on more or less abstract norms of conduct."[11] Since few of these projects ever made it past the speculative stage, they instead provided serfdom with the gloss of enlightenment—not unlike what Peter the Great had done for Russia as a whole. The rank-and-file Society members approached the peasant question from quite a different perspective. For these men it remained an "economic" issue best solved by the pomeshchik who set an example for his peasants and neighbors merely through his physical presence on the estate. When Erik Laksman called upon the gentry to internalize the habits of the scientific farmer at a young age, he displayed some insight into their dilemma: given the inherently slow pace of agricultural progress, landowners would have to submit to the laborious yet rewarding routines of science. Yet higher productivity and increased profits also required the gentry's long-term personal commitment to their estates and the country life in general, a risk few Russian nobles were willing to take in the eighteenth century. Moreover, as the provincial correspondents insisted, the servility of the manorial regime and the subsistence economies of the peasantry imposed severe limitations upon their managerial projects in practice. Their experience on the front lines taught them what their aristocratic colleagues understood in the abstract—that enlightenment belonged to the nobility alone.

The historian Peter Kolchin has contended that the many social divisions within the Free Economic Society "rendered them incapable of developing a coherent argument" in favor of forced labor. Serf owners never constructed an ideological defense of serfdom because, as he argues, its abolition did not spell the end of life as they knew it, only the loss of a financial investment. "Russian noblemen, who formed a dependent group of state servitors with few ties to their peasants, their communities, or each other," he concludes, "put forth a worldview without force or finesse, one that expressed little more than their desire to preserve as many of their privileges as possible." Unlike southern planters of the United States, who fashioned an abstract ideology of slavery anchored in racial differences, sectional loyalties, and the distinctive culture of plantation life, Russian serf owners lacked the need and even the desire for elaborating an equally enduring ideology. The absence of a truly independent public sphere in Russia further discouraged the development of a defense of serfdom because so long as an open debate over the peasant question was prohibited, serf owners had little to discuss in print aside from the technicalities of agriculture.[12] On one level, the Society's handling of the peasant question clearly supports Kolchin's argument. Its decision to suppress the debate on all "political questions" meant that public discourse would rarely progress beyond the most narrowly class-bound and self-serving justifications for serfdom. On the other hand, the idea of noble enlightenment that evolved on the pages of the *Trudy* transcended the narrow confines of Petrine utilitarianism to include the utopian goal of the moral and economic regeneration of rural Russia. What had hitherto found discursive expression either as the Christian patriarch of the *Domostroi* or an educated squire modeled after the ancients, the *Trudy* converted into a replica of Russia's reforming monarchs, combining Peter I's restless activism and passion for order with Catherine's sense of legality and humanity.

The Free Economic Society called this enlightenment. It was a far cry from the contemporaneous European movement of the same name which used reason as a weapon to abolish serfdom, not perpetuate it indefinitely. Indeed, the discourse of the enlightened seigneur offered a civilizing mission not unlike the "white man's burden" taken up by Europeans in the nineteenth century. Like the imperialists in Africa and Asia, the nobles of the Free Economic Society—absentee, residential, and all points in-between—justified their power over their serfs by claiming to raise them to a higher level of civilization just as Peter I had done to their ancestors generations earlier. And like the anti-heroes of Kipling's poem, the certainty of their ultimate failure ensured the continuation of serfdom and all its attendant vices—until the final day of reckoning in February 1861.

*****

Certainly the Free Economic Society's greatest accomplishment was its longevity. Lasting until 1915, it became a permanent feature of Imperial Russia's public landscape and a monument to the persistence of its supporters. Membership steadily climbed—by 1862 it boasted more than 1,200 members. As in the eighteenth century, most of them were concentrated in St. Petersburg and participated mainly in a ceremonial capacity. In 1859 the Society began distinguishing between "active" and "honorary" members, thus formalizing a division of labor which had existed for almost a century. Within a few years it even instituted a dual presidency—one for directing meetings, the other for maintaining contacts with the court.[13] In the meantime, the Society continued recruiting prominent academics, intellectuals, and scientists: the chemist D. I. Mendeleev; the historians K. D. Kavelin and V.I. Semevskii; the sociologist M. M; P. N. Miliukov, leader of the liberal Cadet Party; and the "legal" Marxists M. I. Tugan-Baranovskii and P. B. Struve, to name only a few. It also continued to issue the *Trudy* with only one major interruption in publication from 1821 to 1841. For a while in the 1850s, the *Trudy* even achieved popularity due in large part to some aggressive advertising by its entrepreneurial editor, V. P. Burnashev, who increased its circulation to 4,500. To quote Joan Klobe Pratt, for the first time ever "the journal drew more articles than the editor could print." The *Trudy*'s success did not last for long—Burnashev turned out to be more interested in business than enlightenment, and the assembly dismissed him from his post in 1857.[14] For the remainder of its existence the *Trudy*'s editors and writers struggled to find the elusive balance between the tastes of its potential audience and its own scientific proclivities.

Much of the credit for the Society's viability goes to Admiral Nikolai Semenovich Mordvinov, a leading official under Alexander I (1801–25) and Society member since 1778. As president from 1823 to 1840, he increased the Society's endowment from about 100,000 rubles (60,000 of which he donated himself) to 230,000 rubles. This helped to ensure its financial solvency and lay to rest its chronic fears of bankruptcy and ruin.[15] Mordvinov also initiated a thorough restructuring of the organization which reflected his economic vision and priorities. A political economist and patriot, he wanted the Society to redouble its practical work so as to harness Russia's resources more efficiently and enable it to compete better with the rising industrial powers of Western Europe.[16] According to the new Charter of 1824, the assembly elected a president who in turn appointed chairmen of six "departments," each one specializing in practical fields such as agronomy, rural management, education, handicrafts and trade, health care, and forestry. Under Mordvinov's leadership, the new arrangement enabled the Society to focus on improving living conditions for Russia's rural population and promoting economic development. Instead of publishing the *Trudy*, it dedicated its time and resources to establishing agricultural schools for peasants (much as Ivan Komov had done) and coordinating inoculation campaigns against smallpox.[17] Serfdom and the heavy hand of the autocracy limited the Society's effectiveness in these endeavors. Nevertheless, its efforts to branch out into the countryside and involve rank-and-file landowners in practical work bore fruit. By the end of Nicholas I's reign (1825–55), the Society had established a reliable network of its own correspondents across the Empire.

Alexander II's ascension to the throne in 1855 and the ensuing Great Reforms compelled the Free Economic Society to create a new charter once again. The Charter of 1859 retained the same basic structure as before, trimming the six departments down to three and placing them under the authority of the assembly. Specializing respectively in agriculture, manufacturing, and the "auxiliary sciences," the tripartite division lasted until the early twentieth century despite a revision to the charter in 1872. The Third Department of Auxiliary Sciences soon became the Society's nerve center. Its Committee on Political Economy held public debates on the sort of controversial issues that the Society used to sidestep: tax policy, the sale of state lands, the future of the peasant commune, and industrialization. These discussions became so lively that the Ministry of Interior, alarmed by such bold displays of autonomy, intervened to suppress them.[18] The Third Department's collaboration with the rising "third element" of educated professionals met with somewhat less resistance from state authorities, at least for a while. Working closely with the physicians attached to the *zemstvos*, the new institutions of local government created in 1864, the Medical Committee of the Third Department set up a network of smallpox vaccination clinics, which, after 1905, came to form a vital part of the public health system in rural Russia.[19] Similarly, beginning in the 1880s its Committee on Literacy partnered with the Ministry of Education and local governments to distribute books and journals across the empire. As with the campaign against smallpox, it drew on the support of the "third element," above all thousands of schoolteachers linked with the zemstvos and the district (*volost'*) schools.

In retrospect, the protean nature of the Free Economic Society enabled it to adjust smoothly to Russia's post-serf order. Here it showed much in common with the non-governmental organizations of our own day. Had the autocracy shown the same adaptability, then both might have survived the revolutionary convulsions of the early twentieth century. Yet rather than ride the rising wave of societal initiative generated by the Great Reforms, the government moved to muzzle and eventually suppress it. In 1859, the Society became attached to the Ministry of State Domains, putting an end to its autonomous legal status. When the Society later tried to coordinate all the agricultural associations in Russia in joint ventures, the state prohibited the project on the grounds that it constituted independent political activity.[20] None of this deterred the Society from pursuing its practical work—as noted above, it scored remarkable successes in its vaccination and book-distribution campaigns. However, Russia's industrialization drive after 1891 and the devastating famine of 1891–92 set the government and the Society on a collision course. In 1899, an imperial decree mandated that the Society revise its charter to exclude so-called "outsiders," namely the statisticians, teachers, and medical professionals linked with the zemstvo movement.[21] Rather than comply as it had done so many times before, the assembly voted overwhelmingly against closing its ranks to the "third element." Trapped in a legal limbo, the Society met more infrequently after 1900. Although it continued to publish beekeeping, soil science, and pedagogical literature, the *Trudy* ceased publication after 1901. For a fleeting moment during the 1905 Revolution the Society commanded national attention when the newly formed St. Petersburg Soviet convened in its assembly hall. That was its swan song. Hardwired since the eighteenth century to cooperate with the monarchy, the Free Economic Society had no business overthrowing it. It closed its doors in 1915, two years before the final collapse of the old order which had created and nurtured it for 150 years.

NOTES

1. Joseph Bradley, "Pictures at an Exhibition: Science, Patriotism, and Civil Society in Imperial Russia," *Slavic Review* 67 (2008): 938–39.
2. Iurii Lotman, *Besedy o russkoi kul'ture: Byt i traditsii russkogo dvorianstva* (St. Petersburg: Iskusstvo SPB, 1994), 26–37, 41.
3. E. N. Marasinova, "Mentalitet rossiiskogo dvorianstva poslednei treti XVIII veka (po materialam epistoliarnykh istichnikov)," *Canadian-American Slavic Studies* 36 (2002): 264–69; idem, "Obraz imperator v soznanii elity rossiiskogo dvorianstva poslednei treti XVIII veka (po materialam epistoliarnykh istichnikov)," in *Tsar i tsarstvo v russkom obshchestvennom soznanii*, ed. A. A. Gorskii, (Moscow: Institut rossisskoi istorii RAN, 1999), 152.
4. David L. Ransel, "Character and Style of Patron-Client Relations in Russia," in Antoni Maczak and Elisabeth Mueller-Leuckner, eds., *Klientelsysteme im Europa der Frühen Neuzeit* (Munich: R. Oldenbourg, 1988), 214.

5. Madariaga, *Russia in the Age of Catherine the Great*, 362.

6. John Randolph, *The House in the Garden: The Bakunin Family and the Romance of Russian Idealism* (Ithaca, NY: Cornell University Press, 2007), 51, 61–62.

7. Ibid., 74–77, 80.

8. Kozlov, 268–71.

9. Mary W. Cavender, *Nests of the Gentry: Family, Estate, and Local Loyalties in Provincial Russia* (Newark: University of Delaware Press, 2007), 121–25, 130–35, 140–42.

10. Michael Hughes, "'Independent Gentlemen': the Social Position of the Moscow Slavophiles and its Impact on their Political Thought," *Slavonic and East European Review* 71 (1993), 74–79; Susan Smith-Peter, *The Russian Provincial Newspaper and Its Public, 1788-1864* (Pittsburgh, PA: Center for Russian and East European Studies, 2008), 29–32.

11. Melton, 705.

12. Kolchin, 169, 175–77, 182.

13. Pratt, "The Russian Free Economic Society, 1765–1915," 122, 128, 138.

14. Ibid., 96, 99.

15. Ibid., 65.

16. Susan P. McCaffray, "What Should Russia Be? Patriotism and Political Economy in the Thought of N.S. Mordvinov," *Slavic Review* 59 (Fall 2000): 581–82.

17. Joan Klobe Pratt, "The Free Economic Society and the Battle against Smallpox: A 'Public Sphere' in Action," *Russian Review* 61 (October 2002): 563–64.

18. Pratt, "The Russian Free Economic Society, 1765–1915," 152–53.

19. Pratt, "The Free Economic Society and the Battle against Smallpox," 573–75.

20. Pratt, "The Russian Free Economic Society, 1765–1915," 119, 170, 233.

21. Ibid., 277–78.

Bibliography

PRIMARY SOURCES

1. Archival materials:

Arkhiv Rossiiskoi Akademii Nauk, St. Petersburg:
    fond 27, opis' 3 (G.F. Müller)
    fond 141, opis' 1 (P.I. Rychkov)
Rossiiskii Gosudarstvennyi Arkhiv Drevnei Aktov, Moscow:
    fond 10, opis' 2 (Kabinet Ekateriny)
    fond 17, opis' 1 (Nauka, literatura, iskusstvo)
Rossiiskaia Natsional'naia Biblioteka, St. Petersburg:
    fond 89 (Bolotovy)
Rossiiskii Gosudarstvennyi Istoricheskii Arkhiv, St. Petersburg:
    fond 91 (Vol'noe ekonomicheskoe obshchestvo)

2. Contemporary periodicals:

Ekonomicheskii magazin. Moscow, 1780–89.
Ezhemesiachniia sochineniia. St. Petersburg, 1755–64.
Novoe prodolzhenie Trudov Vol'nago Ekonomicheskago Obshchestva, volumes 1–2.
    St. Petersburg, 1795–97
Prodolzhenie Trudov Vol'nago Ekonomicheskago Obshchestva, volumes 1–19. St.
    Petersburg, 1779–94.
Sobranie luchshikh sochinenii. Moscow, 1762.
Trudy Vol'nago Ekonomicheskago Obshchestva, volumes 1–30. St. Petersburg,
    1765–75.

3. Published materials:

Aksakov, S. T. *The Family Chronicle*, translated by M. C. Beverly. New York: Dutton, 1961.

Alopeus, Samuel. *Kratkoe opisanie marmornykh i drugikh kamennykh lomok, gor, i kamennykh porod nakhodiashchikhsia v Rossiiskoi Karelii.* St. Petersburg: Akademiia nauk, 1787.

Bakunin, M. *Pravila rukovodstvuiushchiia k novumu razdelu i obrabotyvaniiu polei s pokazaniem nuzhnykh sel'skikh zavedenii.* St. Petersburg: Akademiia nauk, 1800.

Beliavskii, M. T., ed. "Novye dokumenty ob obsuzhdenii krest'ianskogo voprosa v 1766–1768 gg." *Arkheograficheskii ezhegodnik za 1958* (1960): 387–430.

Beliavskii, M. T. and L. A. Loone, eds. "Dokumenty ob obsuzhdenii krest'ianskogo voprosa v Vol'nom ekonomicheskom obshchestva." *Arkheograficheskii ezhegodnik za 1960* (1962): 345–66.

Bilarskii, P. S., ed. *Materialy dlia biografii Lomonosova.* St. Petersburg: Akademiia nauk, 1865.

Bolotov, A. T. *Zapiski Andreia Timofeevicha Bolotova, 1737–1796*, two volumes. Tula: Priokskoe knizhnoe izdatel'stvo, 1988.

Budilovich, A., ed. *Lomonosov kak pisatel': sbornik materialov dlia razsmotreniia avtorskoi deitel'nosti Lomonosova.* St. Petersburg: Akademiia nauk, 1871.

Derevenskoe zertsalo ili Obshchenarodnaia kniga, three volumes. St. Petersburg: Prigubernskom pravlenii, 1798–99.

Fitzlyon, Kiril, trans. *The Memoirs of Princess Dashkova: Russia in the Time of Catherine the Great.* Durham, NC: Duke University Press, 1995.

Fomin, Alexandr. *Opisanie Belago moria s ego beregami i ostravami voobshche.* St. Petersburg: Akademiia nauk, 1797.

Girtsel, I.K. *Sel'skoi Sokrat, ili opisanie ekonomicheskikh i nravstvennykh pravil zhizni filosofa-zemledel'tsa.* Moscow: Izdatel'stvo moskovskogo universiteta, 1789.

Glinka, Fedor. "1–i kadetskii korpus volyn' i dal'neishiia snosheniia moi s Miloradovichem." *Moskvitianin* 1 (1846).

Gmelin, S. G. *Puteshestvie po Rossii dlia izsledovaniia trekh tsarstv estestva*, three volumes. St. Petersburg: Akademiia nauk, 1771–85.

"Instruktsiia prikashchiku Muromskoi votchiny sela Kacharova, dannaia grafom Petrom Borisovechem Sheremetevym." *Universitetskaia izvestiia* (Kiev), 44, 7 (July 1904): 79–95; 45, 8 (August 1905): 96–103.

Khrushchov, I. P., ed. *Sochineniia kniazia M.M. Shcherbatova.* St. Petersburg: Izdatel'stvo kniaz'ia B.S. Shcherbatova, 1896.

Komov, I. *O zemledelii.* Moscow: Tipografiia Ponomareva, 1788.

Labzina, Anna Evdokimovna. *Days of a Russian Noblewoman: The Memories of Anna Labzina, 1758–1821.* Translated and edited by Gary Marker and Rachel May. DeKalb, IL: Northern Illinois University Press, 2001.

Lepekhin, I. I. *Dnevnye zapiski puteshestviia po raznym provintsiiam Rossiiskogo gosudarstvo*, volume one. St. Petersburg: Akademiia nauk, 1768–69.

Levshin, V., *Vseobshchee i polnoe domovodstvo*, four parts in two volumes. Moscow, 1795.

Lomonosov, Mikhail. *Dlia pol'zy obshchestva*. Moscow: Sovetskaia Rossiia, 1990.

Montesquieu. *Selected Political Writings*. Edited and translated by Melvin Richter. Indianapolis, IN: Hackett, 1990.

Nartov, A. A. *Rasskazy o Petre Velikom (po avtorskoi rukopisi)*. St. Petersburg: Istoricheskaia illiustratsiia, 2001.

Novikov, Nikolai. *Opyt istoricheskago slovaria o rossiiskikh pisateliakh*. St. Petersburg,1772.

Oleshev, Aleksei. *Vozhd' k istinnomu blagorazumniiu i k sovershennomu shchastiiu*. St. Petersburg, 1780.

"*Osada Orenburga (Letopis' Rychkova)*." In A. S. Pushkin, *Polnoe sobranie sochinenii v -shesti tomakh*, volume 4 (Moscow-Leningrad: Akademiia nauk, 1936).

Pallas, P. S. *Puteshestvie po raznym provintsiiam Rossiiskoi imperii*, three volumes. St. Petersburg: Akademiia nauk, 1773–78.

Pecken, C. *Domashni lechebnik, ili prostyi sposob lecheniia*. St. Petersburg: Akademiia nauk, 1765.

Pol'noe sobranie zakonov Rossiiskoi Imperii, 45 volumes. St. Petersburg: Tipografiia 2 otdeleniia sobstvennoi E.I.V. kantseliarii, 1830.

Pouncy, Carolyn, trans. and ed. *The Domostroi: Rules for Russian Households in the Time of Ivan the Terrible*. Ithaca, NY: Cornell University Press, 1994.

"Proekt D.S.S. i chlena dvortsovoi kontsiliarii Ivana Elagina ob opredelenii v neot"emlemoe vladenie dvortsovym krest'ianam zemlii i o razdache kazennykh dereven, za izvestnuiu platu, na vremennoe i opredelennoe vladenie vol'nym soderzhateliam." *Sbornik kniaza Obolenskago* 12 (Moscow, 1859): 5–80.

Radishchev, A. *A Journey from St. Petersburg to Moscow*. Edited by Roderick Page and translated by Leo Weiner. Cambridge, MA: Harvard University Press, 1958.

Reddaway, W. F., ed. *Documents of Catherine the Great: The Correspondence with Voltaire and the Instruction of 1767, in the English Text of 1768*. Cambridge: Cambridge University Press, 1931.

Rural Oeconomy: or Essays on the Practical Parts of Husbandry to Which is added The *Rural Socrates: Being Memoirs of a Country Philosopher*, translated by Arthur Young from the French. London: Printed for T. Beckett, 1773.

Rychkov, P. I. *Opyt kazanskoi istorii drevnikh i srednikh vremian*. St. Petersburg: Akademiia nauk, 1767.

———. *Topograficheskiia Orenburgskaia, to est': obstoiatel'noe opisanie orenburgskoi gubernii*. St. Petersburg: Imp. Akademiia nauk, 1762.

Samborskii, A. *Opisanie prakticheskago aglinskago zemledeliia*. Moscow, 1781.

Shcherbatov, M. M. *Neizdannye sochinenii*. Moscow: OGIZ, 1935.

———. *On the Corruption of Morals in Russia*. Edited and translated by A. Lentin. Cambridge: Cambridge University Press, 1969.

Shchipanov, I. Ia., ed., *Izbrannye proizvedeniia russkikh myslitelei vtoroi poloviny XVIII veka*, two volumes. Moscow: Izdatel'stvo moskovskogo universiteta, 1952.

Smilianskaia, E. B., ed. *Dvorianskoe gnezdo serediny XVIII veka: Timofei Tekut'ev i ego Instruktsiia o domashnikh poriadkakh*. Moscow: Nauka, 1998.

Tatishchev, V. N. *Dukhovnaia*. St. Petersburg, 1773.

————. "Kratkiia ekonomicheskiia do derevni slediushchiia zapiski." *Vremennik Imperatorskogo Moskovskago Obshchestva istoriia drevnostei rossiskikh* 1–2 (1852): 12–32.

"Uchrezhdenie Gr. P.A. Rumiantsvev." in "Materialy dlia istoriia votchinnago upravlenii v Rossii." *Universitetskaia izvestiia* (Kiev) 43, 12 (December 1903): 1–32; 44, 6 (June 1904): 33–64; 44, 7 (July 1904): 65–75.

Veselova, A. IU. "Iz naslediia A.T. Bolotova 'O pol'ze, proiskhodiashchei ot chteniia knig," *XVIII vek* 21(1999): 358–61.

Volynskii, A. I. "Instruktsiia dvoretskomu Ivanu Nemchinovu o upravlenii domu i dereven (1724 goda)." *Mosvitianin*, 1–4 (1854): 11–43.

"Zapiski Petra Ivanovicha Rychkova." *Russkii arkhiv* 3 (1905): 289–340.

SECONDARY SOURCES

Akademiia nauk SSSR: Personal'nyi sostav. Moscow, 1974.

Alefirenko, P. K. "Russkaia obshchestvennaia mysl' pervoi poloviny XVIII stoletiia o sel'skom khoziastve." *Materialy po istorii zemledeliia SSSR* sbornik 1 (1952): 511–52.

Aleksandrov, V. A. *Sel'skaia obshchina v Rossii (XVII-nachalo XIX v)*. Moscow: Nauka, 1976.

Alekseev, V. N. "Graf R.I. Vorontsov," *Voprosy istorii* 4 (2009): 144–48.

Allan, D. G. C. "The Society of Arts and Government, 1754–1800: Public Encouragement of Arts, Manufacturers and Commerce in Eighteenth-Century England." *Eighteenth-Century Studies* 7 (1974): 434–52.

Alexander, John. *Bubonic Plague in Early Modern Russia: Public Health and Urban Disaster*. Baltimore, MD: Johns Hopkins University Press, 1980.

————. *Catherine the Great: Life and Legend*. New York: Oxford University Press, 1989.

Anisimov, Evgenii. *The Reforms of Peter the Great: Progress through Coercion in Russia*. Translated by John T. Alexander. Armonk, NY: M.E. Sharpe, 1993.

Augustine, W. R. "Notes toward a Portrait of the Eighteenth-Century Russian Nobility." *Canadian Slavic Studies* 4 (1970): 373–425.

Aurova, N. N. "Idei prosveshcheniia v 1–m kadetskom korpuse (konets XVIII-pervaia chetvert' XIX v.)." *Vestnik Moskovskogo Universiteta* series 8 (1996): 34–43.

Baehr, Stephen. *The Paradise Myth in Eighteenth-Century Russia: Utopian Patterns in Early Secular Literature and Culture*. Stanford, CA: Stanford University Press, 1991.

Bak, I.S. "A. I. Polenov (Filosofskie, obshchestvenno-politicheskie i ekonomicheskie vzgliady)." *Istoricheskie zapiski* 28 (1949): 182–202.

————. *Antifeodal'nye ekonomicheskie ucheniia v Rossii vtoroi poloviny XVIII v.*. Moscow: Nauka, 1958.

————. "Dmitrii Aleksandrovich Golitsyn." *Istoricheskie zapiski* 26 (1948): 258–72.

————. "Ekonomicheskie vozzreniia P.I. Rychkova." *Istoricheskie zapiski* 16 (1945): 126–38.

Barran, Thomas. *Russia Reads Rousseau*. Evanston, IL: Northwestern University Press, 2002.

Barsukov, A. R. "Zhizneopisanie Kniazia Gr. Gr. Orlova." *Russkii Arkhiv* 2 (1871): 1–146.

Bartlett, Roger P. "Catherine II's Draft Charter to the State Peasantry." *Canadian-American Slavic Studies* 23 (1989): 36–57.

———. "Defences of Serfdom in Eighteenth-Century Russia." In *A Window on Russia*, edited by Maria di Salvo and Lindsey Hughes. Rome: La Fenice, 1996.

———. "The Free Economic Economic Society: The Foundation Years and the Prize Competition of 1766 on Peasant Property." in *Russland zur Zeit Katharinas II: Absolutismus—Aufklärung—Pragmatismus*, edited by Eckhard Hübner, Jan Kusber, and Peter Nitsche. Cologne: Bohlav, 1998.

———. "German Popular Enlightenment in the Russian Empire: Peter Ernst Wilde and Catherine II." *Slavonic and East European Review* 84 (2006): 256–78.

———. *Human Capital: The Settlement of Foreigners in Russia, 1762–1804*. Cambridge: Cambridge University Press, 1979.

———. "J.J. Sievers and the Russian Peasantry under Catherine II." *Jahrbücher für Geschichte Osteuropas* 32 (1984): 16–33.

———. "Russia's First Abolitionist: The Political Philosophy of J.G. Eisen." *Jahrbücher für Geschichte Osteuropas* 39 (1991): 161–76.

Beliavskii, M. T. "Frantsuztskie prosvetiteli i konkurs o sobstvennosti krepostnykh krest'ian v Rossii." *Vestnik Moskovskogo Universiteta*, series 9 (1960): 26–51.

———. *Krest'ianskii vopros v Rossii nakanune vosstaniia E.I. Pugacheva*. Moscow: Izdatel'stvo moskovskogo universiteta, 1965.

———. *Lomonosov i osnovanie Moskovskogo universiteta*. Moscow: Izdatel'stvo moskovskogo universiteta, 1955.

———. "Prosvetiteli na konkursa o sobstvennosti krest'ian v Rossii." *Vestnik Moskovskogo Universiteta* series 9 (1961): 58–76.

———. "Vopros o krepostnom prave i polozhenie krest'ian v 'nakaze' Ekateriny II." *Vestnik Moskovskogo Universiteta* series 9 (1963): 44–63.

Berdyshev, A. P. *Andrei Timofeevich Bolotov—vydaiushchiisiia deiatel' nauki i kul'tury, 1738–1833*. Moscow: Nauka, 1988.

———. *A.T. Bolotov: Pervyi russkii agronom*. Moscow: Akademiia nauk, 1948.

Black, J. L. *Citizens for the Fatherland: Education, Educators, and Pedagogical Ideals in Eighteenth-Century Russia*. Boulder, CO: East European Quarterly, 1979.

———. *G.-F. Müller and the Imperial Russian Academy*. Kingston: McGill-Queen's University Press, 1986.

Blanchard, Ralph. "A Proposal for Social Reform in the Reign of Catherine II: Aleksei Polenov's Response to the Free Economic Society Competition of 1766–68." PhD diss., State University of New York, Binghamton, 1972.

Blum, Jerome. *The End of the Old Order in Rural Europe*. Princeton, NJ: Princeton University Press, 1978.

———. *Lord and Peasant in Russia from the Ninth to the Nineteenth Century*. Princeton, NJ: Princeton University Press, 1961.

———. *Noble Landowners and Agriculture in Austria, 1815–1848*. Baltimore, MD: Johns Hopkins University Press, 1948.

Bradley, Joseph. "Pictures at an Exhibition: Science, Patriotism, and Civil Society in Imperial Russia." *Slavic Review* 67 (2008): 934–66.

———. "Subjects into Citizens: Societies, Civil Society, and Autocracy in Tsarist Russia." *American Historical Review* 107 (2002): 1094–1123.

Brokhaus, F. A., and I. A. Efron, eds., *Entsiklopedicheskii slovar'*, 41 volumes. St. Petersburg, 1890–1904.

Brown, J. H. "The Free Economic Society and the Nobility, 1765–96: Some Observations." *Canadian-American Slavic Studies* 14 (1980): 427–31.

———. "A Provincial Landowner: A.T. Bolotov (1738–1833)." PhD diss., Princeton University, 1977.

———. "The Publication and Distribution of the *Trudy* of the Free Economic Society, 1765–1796." *Russian Review* 36 (1977): 341–50.

Cavender, Mary W. *Nests of the Gentry: Family, Estate, and Local Loyalties in Provincial Russia*. Newark, DE: University of Delaware Press, 2007.

Chartier, Roger, *The Order of Books: Readers, Authors, and Libraries in Europe between the Fourteenth and Eighteenth Centuries*, translated by Lydia G. Cochrane. Stanford, CA: Stanford University Press, 1994.

Chechulin, N. D. *Russkoe provintsial'noe obshchestvo vo vtoroi polovine XVIII veke*. St. Petersburg: Tipografiia V.S. Balasheva, 1889.

Clark, Peter. *British Clubs and Societies, 1580–1800: The Origins of an Associational World*. Oxford: Oxford University Press, 2000.

Confino, Michael. *Domaines et Seigneurs en Russie vers la fin du XVIII siècle*. Paris: Institut d'études slaves d'Université de Paris, 1963.

———. "Le paysan russe jugé par la noblesse au XVIIIe siècle." *Revue des Études Slaves* 38 (1961): 51–63.

———. "Les enquêtes économiques de la 'Société libre d'économie de Saint-Pétersbourg' (1765–1820)." *Revue Historique* 227 (1962): 155–80.

———. "La politique de tutelle des seigneurs russes envers leurs paysans vers la fin du XVIIIe siècle." *Revue des Études Slaves* 37 (1969): 39–69.

———. "On Intellectuals and Intellectual Traditions in Eighteenth- and Nineteenth-Century Russia." *Daedalus* 101 (1972): 117–50.

———. "Seigneurs et intendants en Russie aux XVIIIe-XIXe siècles." *Revue des Études Slaves* 41 (1962): 61–91.

———. *Systèmes agraires et progrès agricole: L'assolement triennial en Russie aux XVIIIe-XIXe siècles*. Paris: Mouton, 1971.

Cracraft, James. *The Petrine Revolution in Russian Culture*. Cambridge, MA: Harvard University Press, 2004.

Cross, Anthony. *By the Banks of the Neva: Chapters from the Lives and Careers of the British in Eighteenth-Century Russia*. Cambridge: Cambridge University Press, 1997.

———. *By the Banks of the Thames: Russians in Eighteenth-Century Britain*. Newtonville, MA: Oriental Research Partners, 1980.

Czap, Peter. "The Perennial Multiple Family Household, Mishino, Russia, 1782–1858." *Journal of Family History* 7 (1982): 5–26.

Daniel, Wallace. "Conflict between Economic Vision and Economic Reality: The Case of M.M. Shcherbatov." *Slavonic and East European Review* 67 (1989): 42–67.

———. *Grigorii Teplov: A Statesman at the Court of Catherine the Great*. Newtonville, MA: Oriental Research Partners, 1991.

Darnton, Robert. *The Kiss of Lamourette: Reflections in Cultural History*. New York: Norton, 1990.

Druzhinin, N. M. "Prosveshchennyi absoliutizm v Rossii." In *Absoliutizm v Rossii, XVII-VIII vv.*, eds. N. M. Druzhinin, N. I. Pavlenko, and L. V. Cherepnin. Moscow: Nauka, 1964.

Dukes, Paul. *Catherine the Great and the Russian Nobility*. London: Cambridge University Press, 1967.

———. "The Russian Enlightenment." In *The Enlightenment in National Context*, edited by R. Porter and M. Teich. Cambridge: Cambridge University Press, 1981.

Efremov, A. V. *Petr Ivanovich Rychkov: istorik i pisatel*. Kazan: Tatarskoe knizhnoe izdatel'stvo, 1995.

Elias, Norbert. *The Court Society*. Translated by Edmund Jephcott. New York: Pantheon, 1983.

Faizova, I. V. *"Manifest o vol'nosti" i sluzhba dvorianstva v XVIII stoletii*. Moscow: Nauka, 1999.

Farrow, Lee. *Between Crown and Clan: The Struggle to Define Noble Property Rights in Imperial Russia*. Newark: University of Delaware Press, 2004.

Foster, G. M. "Peasant Society and the Image of the Limited Good." *American Anthropologist* 67 (1965): 293–315.

Gay, Peter. *The Enlightenment: An Interpretation*, two volumes. New York: Norton, 1967, 1969.

Givens, Robert. "Servitors or Seigneurs: The Nobility and the Eighteenth-Century Russian State." PhD diss., University of California, Berkeley, 1975.

Gize, M. E. "Andrei Andreevich Nartov (biograficheskii ocherk)." *Kraevedcheskie zapiski: Issledovaniia i materialy* 4 (1996): 6–36.

Glagoleva, Ol'ga. "A.T. Bolotov kak chitatel'." In *Rukopisnaia i pechatnaia kniga v Rossii: problemy sozdaniia i rasprostraneniia*, edited by A. A. Zaitseva, M. V. Kukushkina, and V. A. Somov. Leningrad: BAN, 1988.

———. "A.T. Bolotov—uchenyi, pisatel', entsiklopedist." *Voprosy istorii* 11 (1988): 3–16.

———. "Imaginary World: Reading in the Lives of Russian Provincial Noblewomen, 1750–1825." In *Women and Gender in 18th-century Russia*, edited by Wendy Rosslyn. Burlington, VT: Ashgate, 2003.

———. *Russkaia provintsial'naia starina: ocherki kul'tury i byta Tul'skoi gubernii XVIII-pervoi poloviny XIX vv.*. Tula: Ritm, 1993.

Gleason, Walter. *Moral Idealists, Bureaucracy, and Catherine the Great*. New Brunswick, NJ: Rutgers University Press, 1981.

Gordon, A. V. "Rossiiskoe prosveshchenie: znachenie natsional'nykh arkhetipov vlasti."In *Evropeiskoe prosveshchenie i tsivilizatsiia Rossii*, edited by S. Ia. Karp and S. A. Mezin. Moscow: Nauka, 2004. 116–28.

Grekov, B. D. "Opyt issledovaniia khoziaistvennykh anket XVIII veka." In *Izbrannye trudy*, volume 3. Moscow: Nauka, 1960.

Griffiths, David. "Catherine II: The Republican Empress." *Jahrbücher für Geschichte Osteuropas* 21 (1973): 323–44.

———. "Catherine's Charters: A Question of Motivation." *Canadian-American Slavic Studies* 23 (1989): 58–82.

———. "In Search of Enlightenment: Recent Soviet Interpretations of Eighteenth-Century Russian Intellectual History." *Canadian-American Slavic Studies* 16 (1982): 317–56.

Gur'ianov, V. P. *I.M. Komov: Ego zhizn' i deiatel'nost'*. Moscow: Izdatel'stvo moskovskogo obshchestva ispytatelei prirody, 1953.

Gurzhii, I. A. "K voprosu o kharaktera pomeshchichego khoziaistva na levoberezhnoi Ukraine vo vtoroi polovine XVIII v." *Istoricheskie zapiski* 34 (1950): 333–38.

Habermas, J. *The Structural Transformation of the Bourgeois Public Sphere*, translated by T. Burger and F. Lawrence. Cambridge, MA: MIT Press, 1989.

Hahn, Roger. *The Anatomy of a Scientific Institution: The Paris Academy of Sciences, 1666–1803*. Berkeley: University of California Press, 1971.

Hoch, Steven. *Serfdom and Social Control: Petrovskoe, A Village in Tambov*. Chicago: University of Chicago Press, 1986.

Home, R. W. "Science as a Career in Eighteenth-Century Russia: The Case of F.U.T. Aepinus." *Slavonic and East European Review* 51 (1973): 75–94.

Hosking, Geoffrey. "Patronage and the Russian State. *Slavonic and East European Review* 78 (2000): 301–20.

Hughes, Lindsey. *Russia in the Age of Peter the Great*. New Haven: Yale University Press, 1998.

Hughes, Michael. "'Independent Gentlemen': the Social Position of the Moscow Slavophiles and its Impact on their Political Thought." *Slavonic and East European Review* 71 (1993): 66–88.

Im Hof, Ulrich. *The Enlightenment*. Oxford: Oxford University Press, 1994.

Jones, Robert. *The Emancipation of the Russian Nobility, 1762–1785*. Princeton, NJ: Princeton University Press, 1973.

———. *Provincial Development in Russia: Catherine II and Jacob Sievers*. New Brunswick, NJ: Rutgers University Press, 1984.

———. "Ukrainian Grain and the Russian Market in the Late Eighteenth and Early Nineteenth Centuries," in *Ukrainian Economic History: Interpretative Essays*, edited by I. S. Koropeckyj. Cambridge, MA: Harvard University Press, 1991.

Jones, W. Gareth. *Nikolay Novikov: Enlightener of Russia*. Cambridge: Cambridge University Press, 1984.

Justin, Emile. *Les Sociétés Royales d'Agriculture au XVIII siècle (1757–1793)*. Saint-Lo: 15 Rue de la Marne, 1935.

Kabuzan, V. M. *Izmeniia v razmeshchenii naseleniia Rossii v XVIII-pervoi polovine XIX v.*. Moscow: Nauka, 1971.

————. *Narodonaselenie Rossii v XVIII-pervoi polovine XIX v. (po materialam revizii)*. Moscow: Nauka, 1963.

Kahan, Arcadius. *The Plow, the Hammer, and the Knout: An Economic History of Eighteenth-Century Russia*. Chicago: University of Chicago Press, 1985.

Kamenskii, A. B. *Ot Petra I do Pavla I: Reformy v Rossii XVIII veka*. Moscow: RGGU, 1999.

————. "Znachenie reform Ekateriny II v russkoi istorii." In *A Window on Russia*, di Salvo and Hugfas.

Karataev, N.K. *Ocherki po istorii ekonomicheskikh nauk v Rossii XVIII veka*. Moscow: Nauka, 1960.

Kaufengauz, B. B. *Ocherki vnutrennego rynka Rossii pervoi poloviny XVIII v.*. Moscow: Nauka, 1958.

Khodarkovsky, Michael. *Russia's Steppe Frontier: The Making of a Colonial Empire, 1500–1800*. Chicago: University of Chicago Press, 2002.

Khodnev, A. I. *Istoriia Imperatorskago Vol'nago Ekonomicheskago Obshchestva s 1765 do 1865*. St. Petersburg, 1865.

Khoteev, P. I. *Kniga v Rossii v seredine XVIII v.: Chastnye knizhnye sobranii*. Leningrad: Nauka, 1989.

Kingston-Mann, Esther. *In Search of the True West: Culture, Economics and the Problems of Russian Development*. Princeton, NJ: Princeton University Press, 1999.

Kohut, Zenon. *Russian Centralism and Ukrainian Autonomy: Imperial Absorption of the Hetmanate*. Cambridge, MA: Harvard University Press, 1987.

Kolchin, Peter. *Unfree Labor: American Slavery and Russian Serfdom*. Cambridge, MA: Harvard University Press, 1987.

Kopyl', I.F. "Iz istorii russkoi agronomii XVIII v. (I.M. Komov o zemledelii)," in *Iz istoricheskogo opyta sel'skogo khoziaistva SSSR*, sbornik VII (1969): 84–98.

Kozlov, Sergei. *Agrarnyi traditsii i novatsii v doreformennoi Rossii (tsentral'nonechernozemnyi gubernii)*. Moscow: ROSSPEN, 2002.

Krieger, Leonard. *An Essay on the Theory of Enlightened Despotism*. Chicago: University of Chicago Press, 1975.

Kugler, Michael. "Provincial Intellectuals: Identity, Patriotism, and Enlightened Peripheries." *The Eighteenth Century* 37 (1996): 156–73.

Lappo-Danilevskii, A. S. "Ekateriny II i krest'ianskii vopros." In *Velikaia reforma: Russkoe obshchestvo i krest'ianskii vopros v proshlom i nastoiashchem*, volume one, edited by A. K. Dzhivelegov. Moscow: Izdatel'stvo I.D. Sytina, 1911.

La Vopa, Anthony. "Conceiving a Public: Ideas and Society in Eighteenth-Century Europe." *Journal of Modern History* 64 (1992): 79–116.

Leckey, Colum. "Andrei Bolotov: Portrait of an Enlightened Seigneur." In *Russian and Soviet History: From the Time of Troubles to the Collapse of the Soviet Union*, edited by S. Usitalo and W.B. Whisenhunt. Lanham, MD: Rowman & Littlefield, 2008.

————. "Patronage and Public Culture in the Russian Free Economic Society, 1765–96." *Slavic Review* 62 (2005): 355–79.

————. "Provincial Readers and Agrarian Reform, 1760s–70s: The Case of Sloboda Ukraine." *Russian Review* 61 (2002): 535–59.

LeDonne, John. *Absolutism and Ruling Class: The Formation of the Russian Political Order.* New York: Oxford University Press, 1991.

———. *Ruling Russia: Politics and Administration in the Age of Absolutism.* Princeton, NJ: Princeton University Press, 1984.

Leonard, Carol. *Reform and Regicide: The Reign of Peter III of Russia.* Bloomington, IN: Indiana University Press, 1993.

Liashchenko, P. I. *Istoriia narodnogo khoziaistva SSSR,* volume one. Moscow: Gosudarstvennoe izdatel'stvo politicheskoi literatury, 1947.

———. "Krepostnoe sel'skoe khoziaistvo Rossii v XVIII veke." *Istoricheskie zapiski* 15 (1945): 97–127.

Lotman, Iu. *Besedy o russkoi kul'ture: byt' i traditsii russkogo dvorianstva.* St. Petersburg: Iskusstvo-SPB, 1994.

———. "The Poetics of Everyday Behavior in Eighteenth-Century Russian Culture." in *The Semiotics of Russian Cultural History,* edited by Alexander D. Nakhimovsky and Alice Stone Nakhimovsky. Ithaca, NY: Cornell University Press, 1985.

Lounsbery, Anne. "'No, this is not the provinces!' Provincialism, Authenticity, and Russianness in Gogol's Day." *Russian Review* 64 (2005): 259–80.

Lowood, Henry. *Patriotism, Profit, and the Promotion of Science in the German Enlightenment: The Economic and Scientific Societies, 1760–1815.* New York: Garland, 1991.

Madariaga, Isabel de. "Catherine II and the Serfs: A Reconsideration of Some Problems." *Slavonic and East European Review* 52 (1974): 34–62.

———, "Catherine the Great." In *Enlightened Absolutism,* edited by H. M. Scott. Ann Arbor, MI: University of Michigan Press, 1990.

———. *Russia in the Age of Catherine the Great.* New Haven, CT: Yale University Press, 1981.

Mah, Harold. "Phantasies of the Public Sphere: Rethinking the Habermas of Historians." *Journal of Modern History* 72 (2000): 153–82.

Makogonenko, G. P. *Radishchev i ego vremia.* Moscow: Gosudarstvenno izdatel'stvo khudosh. literatury, 1956.

Malia, Martin. *Russia under Western Eyes: From the Bronze Horseman to the Lenin Mausoleum.* Cambridge, MA: Harvard University Press, 1999.

Marasinova, E. N. "Mentalitet rossiiskogo dvorianstva poslednei treti XVIII veka (po materialam epistoliarnykh istochnikov)." *Canadian-American Slavic Studies* 36 (2002). 251–75.

———. "Obraz imperator v soznanii elity rossiiskogo dvorianstva poslednei treti XVIII veka (po materialam epistoliarnykh istochnikov)." in *Tsar i tsarstvo v russkom obshchestvennom soznanii,* edited by A. A. Gorskii. Moscow, 1999.

———. *Psikhologiia elity rossiiskogo dvorianstva poslednei treti XVIII veka (po materialam perepiski).* Moscow: ROSSPEN, 1999.

Marker, Gary. "The Creation of Journals and the Profession of Letters in the Eighteenth Century." In *Literary Journals in Imperial Russia,* edited by Deborah A. Martinson. Cambridge: Cambridge University Press, 1997.

———. *Publishing, Printing, and the Origins of Intellectual Life in Russia, 1700–1800.* Princeton, NJ: Princeton University Press, 1985.

Marrese, Michelle Lamarche. *A Woman's Kingdom: Noblewomen and the Control of Property in Russia, 1700–1861*. Ithaca, NY: Cornell University Press, 2002.

Martin, Alexander. *Romantics, Reformers, Reactionaries: Russian Conservative Thought and Politics in the Reign of Alexander I*. DeKalb, IL: Northern Illinois University Press, 1997.

Matvievskii, P. E., and A. V. Efremov. *Petr Ivanovich Rychkov, 1712–1777*. Moscow: Nauka, 1991.

Mavrodin, V. V., *Klassovaia bor'ba i obshchestvenno-politicheskaia mysl' v Rossii v XVIII veke (1773–1790–e gg.)*. Leningrad, 1975.

McCaffray, Susan P. "Confronting Serfdom in the Age of Revolution: Projects for Serf Reform in the Time of Alexander I." *Russian Review* 64 (2005): 1–21.

———, "What Should Russia Be? Patriotism and Political Economy in the Thought of N. S. Mordvinov." *Slavic Review* 59 (2000): 572–96.

McClellan, James. *Science Reorganized: Scientific Societies in the Eighteenth Century*. New York: Columbia University Press, 1985.

McConnell, Allen: *A Russian Philosophe: Alexander Radishchev, 1749–1802*. The Hague, 1964.

Medushevskii, A. N. *Proekty agrarnykh reform v Rossii (XVIII-nacahlo XXI veka)*. Moscow: Nauka, 2005.

Melton, Edgar. "Enlightened Seigneurialism and Its Dilemmas in Serf Russia, 1750–1830." *Journal of Modern History* 62 (1990): 675–708.

Melton, James Van Horn. *The Rise of the Public in Enlightenment Europe*. Cambridge: Cambridge University Press, 2001.

Miliukov, Pavel. *Ocherki po istorii russkoi kul'tury*, three volumes. Paris: Sovremennyia zapiski, 1930.

Mil'kov, F. N. *P.I. Rychkov: Zhizn' i geograficheskie trudy*. Moscow: Gosudarstvennoe izdatel'stvo geograficheskoi literatury, 1953.

Milov, L. V. "A.T. Bolotov—avtor krest'ianskoi entsiklopedii." *Voprosy istorii* 7–8 (1991): 13–25.

———. "O proizvoditel'nosti truda v zemledelii Rossii v seredine XVIII v. (po materialam monastyrskoi barshchiny)." *Istoricheskie zapiski* 85 (1970): 207–67.

———. "O roli perelozhnykh zemel' v russkom zemledelii vtoroi poloviny XVIII v." *Ezhegodnik po agrarnoi istorii vostochnoi evropy* 4 (Riga: Akademiia nauk SSSR, 1963).

———. *Velikorusskii pakhar' i osobennosti rossiiskogo istoricheskogo protsessa*, second edition. Moscow: Nauka, 2006.

Mironov, B. N. "Sel'skoe khoziaistvo v 60–kh godakh XVIII veka (po dannym Senatskoi ankety 1767 goda)." In *Materialy po istorii sel'skogo khoziaistva SSSR*, sbornik one. Moscow: Nauka, 1980.

———. "Vliianie revoliutsii tsen' v Rossii XVIII veka na ee ekonomicheskoe i sotsial'no-politicheskoe razvitie." *Istoriia SSSR* 1 (1991): 86–101.

———. *Vnutrennyi rynok Rossii vo vtoroi polovine XVIII-pervoi polovine XIX v.*. Leningrad: Nauka, 1981.

Montmarquet, James. *The Idea of Agrarianism: From Hunter-Gatherer to Agrarian Radical in Western Culture*. Moscow, ID: University of Idaho Press, 1989.

Moon, David. *The Russian Peasantry: The World the Peasants Made.* London: Longman, 1999.

Munck, Thomas. *The Enlightenment: A Comparative Social History, 1721–1794.* London: Hodder Arnold, 2000.

Munro, George E. *The Most Intentional City: St. Petersburg in the Reign of Catherine the Great.* Madison, NJ: Fairleigh Dickinson University Press, 2008.

Nersesova, E. A. "Ekonomicheskoe sostoianie kostromskoi provintsii Moskovskoi gubernii po khoziaistvennym anketam 1760–kh godov." *Istoricheskie zapiski* 40 (1952): 154–85.

Newlin, Thomas. "The Return of the Russian Odysseus: Pastoral Dreams and Rude Awakenings." *Russian Review* 55 (1996): 448–74.

———. "Rural Ruses: Illusion and Anxiety on the Russian Estate, 1775–1815." *Slavic Review* 57 (1998): 295–319.

———. *The Voice in the Garden: Andrei Bolotov and the Anxieties of Russian Pastoral.* Evanston, IL: Northwestern University Press, 2001.

Ogarkov, V. V. *Vorontsovy, ikh zhizn' i obshchestvennaia deiatel'nost.* St. Petersburg: Tipografiia 'obshchestvennaia pol'za', 1892.

Ogorodnikov, S. *Aleksandr Ivanovich Fomin (po neizdannym dokumentam).* Archangel: Guberuskaia tipografiia, 1910.

Okenfuss, Max J. *The Rise and Fall of Latin Humanism in Early Modern Russia: Pagan Authors, Ukrainians, and the Resiliency of Muscovy.* Leiden: Brill, 1995.

Omel'chenko, Oleg. *"Zakonnaia monarkhiia" Yekateriny II: Prosveshchennyi absoliutizm v Rossii.* Moscow: O.A. Omel'chenko, 1993.

Oreshkin, V.V. "Problemy chastnoi krest'ianskoi sobstvennosti na zemliu v krepostnoi Rossii XVIII v." *Voprosy ekonomiki* 1 (1992): 144–53.

———. *Vol'noe ekonomicheskoe obshchestvo v Rossii, 1765–1917.* Moscow: Nauka, 1963.

Pallot, Judith and Denis J.B. Shaw. *Landscape and Settlement in Romanov Russia, 1613–1917.* Oxford: Oxford University Press, 1990.

Papmehl, K., *Freedom of Expression in Eighteenth-Century Russia.* The Hague: Nijhoff, 1971.

Pekarskii, P. I. *Snosheniia P.I. Rychkova s Akademieiu nauk v XVIII stoletii.* St. Petersburg: Akademiia nauk, 1866.

———. *Zhizn' i literaturnaia perepiska Petra Ivanovicha Rychkova.* St. Petersburg: Akademiia nauk, 1867.

Pipes, Richard, *Russia under the Old Regime.* New York: Scribners, 1974.

N. Iu. Plavinskaia, "Kak perevodili Montesk'e v Rossii?" In *Evropeiskoe prosveshchenie i tsivilizatsiia Rossii*, edited by Karp and Mezin. 281–86

Poe, Marshall T. *"A People Born to Slavery": Russia in Early Modern European Ethnography, 1476–1748.* Ithaca, NY: Cornell University Press, 2000.

Pratt, Joan Klobe. "The Free Economic Society and the Battle against Smallpox: A 'Public Sphere' in Action." *Russian Review* 61 (2002): 560–78.

———, "The Russian Free Economic Society, 1765–1915." PhD diss., University of Missouri, 1983.

Prescott, James Arthur. "The Russian Free Economic Society: Foundation Years." *Agricultural History* 51 (1977): 503–12.

Prisenko, G. P. *Prosvetitel' V.A. Levshin.* Tula, 1990.

Raeff, Marc. *Origins of the Russian Intelligentsia: The Eighteenth-Century Nobility.* New York: Harcourt Brace, 1966.

———. *Political Ideas and Institutions in Imperial Russia.* Boulder, CO: Westview, 1994.

———. *The Well-Ordered Police State: Social and Institutional Change through Law in the Germanies and Russia.* New Haven, CT: Yale University Press, 1983.

Rak, V. D. "Perevodchik V. A. Priklonskii (materiali k istorii tverskogo 'kul'turnogo Gnezda' v 1770–1780–e gody," *XVIII vek* 13 (1981): 244–61.

Randolph, John. *The House in the Garden: The Bakunin Family and the Romance of Russian Idealism.* Ithaca, NY: Cornell University Press, 2007.

Ransel, David. "Character and Style of Patron-Client Relations in Russia." In *Klientelsysteme im Europa der Frühen Neuzeit,* edited by Antoni Maczak and Elisabeth Mueller-Leuckner. Munich: R. Oldenbourg, 1988.

———. *The Politics of Catherinian Russia: The Panin Party.* New Haven, CT: Yale University Press, 1975.

Riasanovsky, Nicholas. *A Parting of Ways: Government and the Educated Public in Russia, 1801–1855.* Oxford: Oxford University Press, 1976.

Rice, James L. "The Bolotov Papers and Andrei Timofeevich Bolotov, Himself." *Russian Review* 35 (1976): 125–54.

Robertson, John. *The Case for the Enlightenment: Scotland and Naples, 1680–1760.* Cambridge: Cambridge University Press, 2005.

Romanovich-Slavatinskii, A. *Dvorianstvo v Rossii s nachala XVIII veka do otmeny krepostnogo prava.* St. Petersburg: Tipografiia ministerstva vnutrennykh del, 1870.

Roosevelt, Priscilla. *Life on the Russian Country Estate: A Social and Cultural History.* New Haven, CT: Yale University Press, 1995.

Rubinshtein, N.L. *Sel'skoe khoziaistvo Rossii vo vtoroi polovine XVIII v.* Moscow: Gosudarstvennoe izdatel'stvo politicheskoi literatury, 1957.

——— "Ulozhennaia komissiia 1754–1766 gg. i ee proekt novogo ulozheniia 'O sostoianii poddanykh voobshche'." *Istoricheskie zapiski* 38 (1951): 208–51.

Russkii biograficheskii slovar', 25 volumes. St. Petersburg-Petrograd: Izdanie Imperatorskago Russkago Istoricheskago Obshchestva, 1896–1918.

Samarin, A. Iu. *Chitatel' v Rossii vo vtoroi polovine XVIII veka (po spiskam podpischikov).* Moscow: Izdatel'stvo MGUP, 2000.

Sanin, G. A. "Iuzhnaia granitsa Rossii vo 2–i polovine XVII–1–i polovine XVIII vv." *Russian History/Histoire Russe* 19 (1992): 433–57.

Saunders, David. *The Ukrainian Impact on Russian Culture, 1750–1850.* Edmunton: Canadian Institute of Ukrainian Studies, 1985.

Schmidt, Sigur. "Obshchestvennoe samosoznanie noblesse russe v XVI-pervoi treti XIX v.," *Cahiers du Monde Russe et Soviétique,* XXXIV, 1–2 (1993), 11–31.

Semevskii, V. I. *Krest'iane v tsarstvovanie Imperatritsy Ekateriny II,* two volumes. St. Petersburg: Tipografiia M.M. Stasiulevicha, 1901–3.

———. *Krest'ianskii vopros v Rossii v XVIII i pervoi polovine XIX veka*, two volumes. St. Petersburg: Tipografiia tovarishchestva 'obshchestvennaia pol'za', 1888.

Sevast'ianova, A. A. *Russkaia provintsial'naia istoriografiia vtoroi poloviny XVIII veka*. Moscow: Arkheograficheskaia komissia Rossiiskoi akademiia nauk, 1998.

Shafer, R. J. *The Economic Societies in the Spanish World (1763–1821)*. Syracuse, NY: Syracuse University Press, 1958.

Shaw, Denis J. B. "Southern Frontiers of Muscovy, 1550–1700." In *Studies in Russian Historical Geography*, volume 1, edited by J. H. Bater and R. A. French. London: Academic Press, 1983.

———. "Urbanism and economic development in a pre-industrial context: the case of southern Russia." *Journal of Historical Geography* 3 (1977): 107–22.

Shchepetov, K. N. *Krepostnoe pravo v votchinakh Sheremetevykh*. Moscow: Izdatel'stvo dvortsa muzeia, 1947.

Shtrange, M. M. *Demokraticheskaia intelligentsia v Rossii v XVIII veke*. Moscow: Nauka, 1965.

Shovlin, John. *The Political Economy of Virtue: Luxury, Patriotism, and the Origins of the French Revolution*. Ithaca, NY: Cornell University Press, 2006.

Sivkov, K. V. "Nakazy upraviteliam XVIII v. kak istochnik dlia istorii sel'skogo khoziaistva v Rossii." In *Akademiku Borisu Dmitrievnu Grekovu ko dniu semidesiatiletiia. Sbornik statei*, edited by V. P. Volgin. Moscow: Akademiia nauk, 1952.

———. "Voprosy sel'skago khoziaistva v russkikh zhurnalakh poslednei treti XVIII v." *Materialy po istorii zemledeliia SSSR*, sbornik 1 (1952): 553–613.

Smith, Douglas. *Working the Rough Stone: Freemasonry and Society in Eighteenth-Century Russia*. DeKalb, IL: Northern Illinois University Press, 1999.

Smith, R. E. F., and David Christian. *Bread and Salt: A Social and Economic History of Food and Drink in Russia*. Cambridge: Cambridge University Press, 1984.

Smith-Peter, Susan, "How to Write a Region: Local and Regional Historiography." *Kritika* 5 (2004): 527–42.

———. *The Russian Provincial Newspaper and Its Public, 1788–1864*. Pittsburgh, PA: Center for Russian and East European Studies, 2008.

Somov, V. A. "Dva otveta Vol'tera na Peterburgskom konkurse o krest'ianskoi Sobstvennosti." In *Evropeiskoe prosveshchenie i tsivilizatsiia Rossii*, edited by Karp and Mezin. 150–165

Stevens, Carol Belkin. *Soldiers on the Steppe: Army Reform and Social Change in Early Modern Russia*. DeKalb, IL: Northern Illinois University Press, 1995.

Stites, Richard. *Serfdom, Society, and the Arts in Imperial Russia: The Pleasure and the Power*. New Haven, CT: Yale University Press, 2005.

Sunderland, Willard. *Taming the Wild Field: Colonization and Empire on the Russian Steppe*. Ithaca, NY: Cornell University Press, 2004.

Svodnyi catalog russkoi knigi XVIII veka, 1725–1800, five volumes. Moscow, 1962–67.

Troitskii, S.M. *Rossiia v XVIII veke*. Moscow: Nauka, 1982.

Tsapina, Ol'ga Aleksandrovna. "Voina za Prosveshchenie? Moskovskii universitet i dukhovnaia tsenzura v kontse 50–kh-nachale 70–kh gg." In *Eighteenth-Century Russia: Society, Culture, Economy*, edited by Roger Bartlett and Gabriela Lehmann-Carli. Munster: LIT-Verlag, 2007.

Usitalo, Steven, "Russia's 'First' Scientist: The (Self-) Fashioning of Mikhail Lomonosov," in *Russian and Soviet History: From the Time of Troubles to the Collapse of the Soviet Union*, edited by Usitalo and Whisenhunt.

Viskovatov, Alexander. *Kratkaia istoriia pervago kadetskago korpusa*. St. Petersburg: Voennaia tipografiia glavnago shtaba,1832.

Vucinich, Alexander. *Science in Russian Culture: A History to 1860*. Stanford, CA: Stanford University Press, 1963.

Whittaker, Cynthia H. *Russian Monarchy: Eighteenth-Century Rulers and Writers in Political Dialogue*. DeKalb, IL: Northern Illinois University Press, 2003.

Wirtschafter, Elise K. *The Play of Ideas in Russian Enlightenment Theater*. DeKalb, IL: Northern Illinois University Press, 2003.

———. *Russia's Age of Serfdom, 1649–1861*. Malden, MA: Blackwell, 2008.

———. *Social Identity in Imperial Russia*. DeKalb, IL: Northern Illinois University Press, 1997.

Wittmann, Reinhard. "Was there a Reading Revolution at the End of the Eighteenth Century?" *A History of Reading in the West*, translated by Lydia G. Cochrane, edited by Guglielmo Cavallo and Roger Chartier. Amherst, MA: University of Massachusetts Press, 1999.

Wolff, Larry. *Inventing Eastern Europe: The Map of Civilization on the Mind of the Enlightenment*. Stanford, CA: Stanford University Press, 1994.

Wortman, Richard. *Scenarios of Power: Myth and Ceremony in Russian Monarchy*, volume one. Princeton, NJ: Princeton University Press, 1995.

Zagorskii, F. N. *Andrei Konstantinovich Nartov, 1693–1756*. Leningrad, 1969.

Zhivov, V. M. "Gosudarstvennyi mif v epokhu prosveshchenniia i ego razrushenie v Rossii kontsa XVIII veka." In *Iz istorii russkoi kul'tury, volume 4 (XVII-nachalo XIX veka)*, edited by A. D. Koshelev. Moscow, 1996.

———. *Language and Culture in Eighteenth-Century Russia*, translated by Marcus Levitt. Boston: Academic Studies Press, 2009.

———. "'Vsiakaia vsiachina' i sozdanie Ekateriniskogo politicheskogo diskursa." In *Eighteenth-Century Russia: Society, Culture, Economy*, edited by Bartlett and Lehmann-Carli.

Index

Academy of Sciences (St. Petersburg), 20, 91, 112–13, 123, 142
Agafi, Dmitrii, 106
agrarianism: defined, 4–5
    praised in discourse of Free Economic Society, 110, 111–12, 124–25, 130, 132, 160, 167–70
    praised in Russian periodicals of 1750s and 1760s, 35–37
agricultural revolution, 45
agriculture: annual work routines, 53
    crops, 48, 52; crop failures, 48, 49
    "decay" of, 46, 53, 55.
    field-grass husbandry, 52
    output/seed ratios, 49, 51
    slash-and-burn (*podstoi*), 50
    three-field system, 48, 49–50, 52, 56, 129, 181–82. *See also* Sloboda Ukraine; Russia
Aksakov, S.T., 118
Alexander I, 62
Alopeus, Samuel, 108
Angal't, Fedor, 25, 87, 90–91
animal husbandry, 48, 49, 51, 52, 108, 132n15. *See also* Sloboda Ukraine
Anisimov, E., 8
Army Cadet Corps, 45, 90–91
Augustine, W.R., 156

Bacheracht, Andrei, 155
Bagrov, S.M., 118–19
Bakunin, A.M., 181
Bakunin, M.P., 161
Bartlett, Roger, 38, 74
barshchina, 47, 51. *See also* peasantry, serfdom
Bashkirs, 51
Basque Economic Society (Spain), 19
Beardé de l'Abbaye, 68–70, 73–75. *See also* peasant property competition (1766–68)
Beketov, N.A., 41n31, 105–06
Beliavskii, M.T., 68
Bezborodko, Oleksandr, 173–74n58
Bloch, Marc, 45
Bogoroditsk, 120, 122, 130
Bolotov, A.T., 138n122, 148, 155, 176–77n122, 180; as member of Free Economic Society, 28, 102, 105, 106, 130
    critique of three-field system, 129, 131, 160
    Ekonomicheskii magazine, 120, 122, 146
    life at Dvorianinovo, 121, 122, 123, 124, 130
    literary career of, 119–20

205

About the Auhor

Colum Leckey teaches history at Piedmont Virginia Community College in Charlottesville, Virginia.